Louis Kronenberger was born in Cincinnati in 1904. He was educated at public schools in that city and at the University of Cincinnati. Coming to New York in the middle 1920's, he joined the publishing firm of Boni & Liveright, where he stayed for seven years. During that period he became well known as a literary critic and essayist. After leaving Liveright he free-lanced for some time, contributing to the book review of the *New York Times*, the *Nation*, and the *New Republic*. In 1936 he was made an editor of *Fortune*. Two years later he became drama critic for *Time*, a post he continues to occupy. He has published two novels—*The Grand Manner* and *Grand Right and Left*—and a book on life in eighteenth-century England, *Kings and Desperate Men*, and has edited, among other books, the *Maxims of La Rochefoucauld*, *An Eighteenth-Century Miscellany*, *An Anthology of Light Verse*, *The Reader's Companion*, and *The Pleasure of Their Company*, an anthology of civilized writing. Recently he has been giving courses in both Columbia and Brandeis universities.

By

LOUIS KRONENBERGER

The Thread of Laughter 1952
CHAPTERS ON ENGLISH STAGE COMEDY
FROM JONSON TO MAUGHAM

The Pleasure of Their Company 1946
AN ANTHOLOGY
OF URBANE AND SOPHISTICATED WRITINGS
FROM THE CLASSICS TO THE MODERNS

Kings and Desperate Men 1942
LIFE IN EIGHTEENTH-CENTURY ENGLAND

THESE ARE *Borzoi Books*

PUBLISHED BY *Alfred A. Knopf* IN NEW YORK

THE THREAD OF LAUGHTER

Louis Kronenberger

THE THREAD

OF LAUGHTER

Chapters on

ENGLISH STAGE COMEDY

from

JONSON to MAUGHAM

NEW YORK: *ALFRED A. KNOPF*

1952

L. C. *catalog card number: 52–6421*

THIS IS A BORZOI BOOK,
PUBLISHED BY ALFRED A. KNOPF, INC.

FIRST EDITION

To Alice and Jack Plaut

Author's Note

THIS BOOK largely stems from something I long wanted to do, but a little from the way in which I did it. It is a reworking of courses given at Columbia and Brandeis universities, and though I hope it will interest the general reader—and have had him chiefly in mind—I would certainly not conceal its classroom origins: I would even like to think that the book itself may have classroom uses. I have reworked the original material a good deal, and have a good deal reduced it in size; but the plan of the book remains substantially the plan of the lectures.

This is, in other words, a survey rather than a synthesis; a kind of tour of English stage comedy during some three hundred years, with stops at all the major and a few of the minor points en route. It doesn't merely assess the playwrights, it specifically examines a number of the plays. Hence the book, if in no sense exhaustive, in no sense a "history," is everywhere concrete. If I have discussed—for one instance—just three plays by Shadwell, it is in the hope that the reader will in turn read those three for himself; had I (no more rewardingly) treated half a dozen, he might have been quite content to read *about* them, and come away with my opinions of Shadwell rather than first-hand ones of his own.

Although my procedure at times has resembled that of a mere

play reviewer, my purpose has yet been to treat critically a not unhomogeneous body of work. Much the most persistent and effective type of English stage comedy has been the comedy of manners—even though the two greatest playwrights of comedy, Ben Jonson and Bernard Shaw, have worked a quite different vein. As nobody since the 1920's has gone at English stage comedy with any blend of thoroughness and discernment, this book—whether or not it brings light to dark places—at least carries no coals to Newcastle. Nor in approach is it perhaps altogether conventional. English comedy being first and last concerned with worldlings, it has seemed important to look at the real life of which such comedy is predicated—to expound, as it were, the philosophy of worldliness. No one would write of mystical poets without adverting to the idea of God, or discuss modern living without reference to the machine age; no more, surely, can one survey the comedy of manners without treating of sexual dalliance or scandal. Hence what may quite often seem discursive is, in my own view, entirely pertinent.

I am indebted to Herbert Weinstock for a number of editorial suggestions, to Phyllis Sternau for a careful typing of the manuscript, and to Holly Bradford for help in compiling the index. For making possible the lectures out of which this book emerged I must thank Professors Oscar James Campbell and James L. Clifford of Columbia, President Abram L. Sachar of Brandeis, and Edward Kook. I owe a particular debt to Irving Howe for much discriminating and helpful criticism.

CONTENTS

(i x)

CONTENTS

(x)

THE THREAD OF LAUGHTER

CHAPTER I

Some Prefatory
Words on Comedy

COMEDY is not just a happy as opposed to an unhappy ending, but a way of surveying life so that happy endings must prevail. But it is not to be confused, on that account, with optimism, any more than a happy ending is to be confused with happiness. Comedy is much more reasonably associated with pessimism—with at any rate a belief in the smallness that survives as against the greatness that is scarred or destroyed. In mortal affairs it is tragedy, like forgiveness, that seems divine; and comedy, like error, that is human.

One might perhaps begin by talking about comedy in its philosophic sense, as an attitude toward life, rather than as a mere technical aspect of the theater. One might begin, in other words, by speaking of the comedy that unites such writers and writings as Lucian and Aristophanes, the *Decameron* and *Candide*, Congreve and Peacock and Sterne, *Pride and Prejudice* and *Le Bourgeois Gentilhomme*, rather than of the comedy that is the official label for such diverse plays as *Measure for Measure* and *The Man of Mode*, or *All's Well That Ends Well* and *The Importance of*

(3)

Being Earnest, or *The Misanthrope* and *Private Lives*. For obviously—despite immense differences—the same spirit animates an Aristophanes and a Jane Austen; whereas a vastly different spirit separates *Measure for Measure* from *The Importance of Being Earnest*. *Measure for Measure*, we feel, is not really comedy; and *The Misanthrope*, again, is something more than comedy. But coarse as Aristophanes can be and genteel as Jane Austen, broadly as Aristophanes can clown and exquisitely as Jane Austen can annihilate, the two have much the same vision of life, much the same eye for its absurdities. They have in full measure the comic point of view, as other writers have the tragic point of view. In the theater, comedy and tragedy are forms that can be used with some purity. Much Restoration comedy was indeed written with some purity. Today, when the theater is debased by the naturalistic drama, when the drama itself is three parts play to seven parts production, when the only comedy that most playwrights try for is standing-room comedy—today very little in the theater really expresses the comic sense of life. Far from probing, it seldom even honestly paints the surface. And the real trouble is not that the contemporary stage aims at artifice, but that it professes to aim at naturalness. It was one of the real virtues of the Restoration stage that it never sought—and never managed—to be "natural." It lied its head off about a good many of the appurtenances of life, but it managed to capture a surprising amount of the thing itself; and even its lies squared with the partial truth that life is a masquerade.

Comedy appeals to the laughter, which is in part at least the malice, in us; for comedy is concerned with human imperfection, with people's failure to measure up either to the world's or to their own conception of excellence. All tragedy is idealistic and says in effect, "The pity of it"—that owing to this fault of circumstance or that flaw of character, a man who is essentially good does evil, a man who is essentially great is toppled from the heights. But all comedy tends to be skeptical and says in effect, "The absurdity of it"—that in spite of his fine talk or noble resolutions, a man is the mere creature of pettiness and vanity and folly. Tragedy is always lamenting the Achilles tendon, the destructive flaw in man; but comedy, in a sense, is always looking for it. Not cheaply, out of malevolence or cynicism; but rather because even at his greatest, man offers some touch of the fatuous and small, just as a murderer, even at his cleverest, usually makes some fatal slip. In tragedy men aspire to more than they can achieve; in comedy, they pretend to more.

The difference, again, between the two is the very question of difference. A great tragic hero—an Oedipus or Lear—strikes us as tremendously far removed from common humanity. But comedy, stripping off the war-paint and the feathers, the college degrees or the military medals, shows how very like at bottom the hero is to everybody else. Tragedy cannot flourish without giving its characters a kind of aura of poetry, or idealism, or doom; comedy scarcely functions till the aura has been dispelled. And as it thrives on a revelation of the true rather than the trumped-up motive, as it is in one way sustained by imposture, so in another it is sustained by incongruity. Here is the celebrated philosopher cursing the universe because he has mislaid a book. Here are all those who, like King Canute, would bid the clock go backward or the waves stand still. Here is not only the cheat, but the victim who but for his own dishonest desires could never be cheated.

Comedy, in brief, is criticism. If through laughing at others we purge ourselves of certain spiteful and ungenerous instincts— as through tragedy we achieve a higher and more publicized catharsis—that is not quite the whole of it. Comedy need not be hostile to idealism; it need only show how far human beings fall short of the ideal. The higher comedy mounts, the airier and more brilliant its forms, the more are we aware of man's capacity for being foolish or self-deluded or complacent; in the very highest comedy, such as the finale of Mozart's *Marriage of Figaro*, we are in a very paradise of self-deceptions and misunderstandings and cross-purposes. At the heart of high comedy there is always a strain of melancholy, as round the edges there is all gaiety and ebullience and glitter; and Schiller was perhaps right in regarding high comedy as the greatest of all literary forms.

Comedy is criticism, then, because it exposes human beings

for what they are in contrast to what they profess to be. How much idealism, it asks, shall we find entirely free from self-love? How much beneficence is born of guilt, how much affection is produced by flattery? At its most severe, doubtless, comedy is not just skeptical but cynical; and asks many of the same questions, returning many of the same answers, as that prince—or at any rate duke—of cynics, La Rochefoucauld. "Pride," La Rochefoucauld remarked, "does not wish to owe, and vanity does not wish to pay." Or again: "To establish oneself in the world, one does all one can to seem established there." Of these and many similar maxims, a play or story might easily be written; from each much cold and worldly comedy, or harsh and worldly farce, might be contrived. But comedy need not be so harsh, and seldom is: though it can be harsher still, can be—as in Ben Jonson —gloating and sardonic. But always it is the enemy, not of virtue or idealism, but of hypocrisy and pretense; and what it does in literature is very much, I suppose, what experience does for most of us in life: it knocks the bloom off the peach, the gilt off the gingerbread.

But though the comic spirit is, in Meredith's phrase, "humanely malign," it is also kindly and even companionable, in the sense that it brings men together as fellow-fools and sinners, and is not only criticism but understanding. Comedy is always jarring us with the evidence that we are no better than other people, and always comforting us with the knowledge that most other people are no better than we are. It makes us more critical but it leaves us more tolerant; and to that extent it performs a very notable social function. Its whole character, indeed—quite aside from that point—is rather social than individual.

The social basis rests in the very subject-matter of comedy— in all that has to do with one's life as part of a group; with one's wish to charm or persuade or deceive or dazzle others. Thus no exhibitionist can exist in solitude, no hypocrite or poseur can work without an audience. There are indeed so many social situations that engender comedy that many of them are notably hackneyed. There are all kinds of classic family jokes—the mother-in-law joke preëminently; but equally the rich-uncle theme, or the country cousin, or the visiting relative who forgets to leave, or the one that proffers advice, or the one that prophesies disaster. Right in the home there is the precocious brat or the moping adolescent; there are countless varieties of comic servants; and there is finally the question, though it perhaps belongs in a different category, of who heads the family— the husband or the wife.

The idea of husband and wife more likely belongs with the social aspects of sex, with the War Between the Sexes as it is fought out in the drawing room. As a purely sexual conflict, this war would not be social; but by the same token it would not be comedy. The question whether man really makes the decisions —including the decision to marry—or is merely permitted to think he does, is, whatever the answer, thoroughly social in nature. Or there is the business of how men and women perform in society for one another's benefit: being the fearless protector or the clinging vine, the woman who always understands or the man who is never understood. We have social comedy again when we pit one nationality as well as one sex against another, when the American puritan is ensnared by a continental siren, or when the suitor is German and humorless, and the besought one is French and amused. There is still another social aspect when we add a third person to the situation, a mistress as well as a wife, or a lover as well as a husband; or—for the situation need not be illicit, it need only be triangular—when the wife's old beau or the husband's old flame reappears on the scene. Or there is the man who does not know which of two sisters, or two heiresses, or two widows to marry; or the girl which of a half dozen suitors.

Comedy, indeed, must gain admittance into any part of the world—including prisons and sickrooms and funerals—where people are thrown together. Any institution involving hierarchies and rivalries—for example, a university—is a perfect hotbed of it. There will be everybody's relation to the President or the President's wife; or the President's relation to the President's wife; or to his trustees; all the struggles for precedence and the problems of protocol; the progressives on the faculty and the die-hards; the wives who can't help looking dowdy, the wives who suppose they look chic. For obviously any institution, whether a college or a department store, an artist colony or a country club, provides a cross-section of social types and traits, and brings us face to face with a hundred things out of which comedy is distilled: ambition and pride, arrogance and obsequiousness; a too-slavish following or a too-emphatic flouting of convention; all the stratagems men use in order to outwit or get their way.

And of course comedy becomes purely social in that best known and perhaps best liked of all its higher forms—the comedy of manners. Here we have hardly less than a picture of society itself; here the men and women are but parts of a general whole, and what survives—if we have it from the past—is likely to be known as the Restoration Scene, or Regency London, or Victorian Family Life. Here the drawing room is not merely the setting of the play or novel, but the subject and even the hero; here enter all the prejudices, the traditions, the taboos, the aspirations, the absurdities, the snobberies, of a group. The group, to constitute itself one, must partake of a common background and accept a similar view of life: though there will usually exist some outsider, some rebel, some nonconformist who, as the case may be, is ringing the doorbell or shattering the window panes; trying desperately to get in or desperately to get out; bending the knee or thumbing his nose. Or the comedy of manners will contrast one social milieu with another—the urban and the rustic, the capital and the provinces, Philistia and Bohemia, America and Europe. And in the comedy of manners, ignorance of good form has much the same value that, in straight drama, ignorance of some vital fact has.

And with ignorance of one kind or another we begin coming close to the very mainspring of comedy, or at any rate of comedy in action. For most comedy is born of ignorance or false knowledge; is based on misunderstanding. (Obviously not knowing the truth—though here one might add "until it is too late" —applies to much tragedy also.) At the level of ordinary farce or romantic comedy, the lovers are estranged until a quarter of eleven because the young man misunderstood why the young lady was walking with Sir Robert in the garden. At a higher level, it will not be mere circumstance or coincidence, but qualities of character that block the way. Envy proves an obstruction, or arrogance; or a too-great tendency to be suspicious or to take offense. In *Pride and Prejudice* the very title makes this clear. In Jane Austen's finest novel, *Emma*, there is every variety of misunderstanding, but the greatest misunderstanding of all, and the one that leads to so many of the others, is Emma's concerning her own nature. Emma—so high-handed and so wrongheaded, so often reasonable and so seldom right—is herself a wonderfully modulated comic character. And what matters is not so much the realistic consequences of her mistakes as the assured and benevolent air with which she commits them. And now moving higher still, to Meredith's *The Egoist*, we see self-deluded character constituting, really, the whole book. Sir Willoughby Patterne is the supreme example of self-centeredness in literature—the man who, in his absorption with the creature he is and the role he plays and the impression he makes, can care about nobody else. He tramples on the emotions and even the liberties of all who come his way, only cherishing such people so far as they cherish or pay homage to him. He is stunned by what seems to him *their* selfishness when, appalled by his, they walk out or turn away. And as we watch Meredith's great demonstration of human egoism, as we see with what comic flourishes and farcical leaps and wild extravagant motions it proceeds—as we smile and even laugh—we become increasingly uncomfortable. The more monstrous Sir Willoughby seems, the more we realize that in some sense this man is ourselves. If no one ever misunderstood his own nature worse, no one has ever pointed a moral better. Comedy at its greatest is criticism indeed; is nothing less, in fact, than a form of moral enlightenment.

The Egoist is sometimes declared to be comedy in name only, to be at bottom tragic. I would myself disagree—Meredith carries his theme to so extreme a length as to transform his hero from a man into a sort of sublime caricature, and gives him a purely comic intensity, an intensity quite disproportionate to what it is intense about. If just this is the "tragedy" of most human beings, it must yet serve to expose rather than exalt them; otherwise what shall we call genuine tragedy when we encounter it? Malvolio in *Twelfth Night*, who has also been looked upon as tragic, comes somewhat closer to being so. For pretension with him does partake a little of aspiration; his vanity, moreover, is stung because he is a servant, and stimulated by the mischievousness of others. But Malvolio, like Sir Willoughby, is really too trivial for tragedy, as he is also too priggish. What happens to him seems painful rather than tragic; it is not quite our modern idea of fun.

And this brings up the point that though Comedy has its permanent subject-matter and even its body of laws, it is liable, like everything else, to changes in fashion and taste, to differences of sensibility. One generation's pleasure is the next generation's embarrassment: much that the Victorians shuddered at merely makes us laugh, much that they laughed at might well make us shudder. One always reacts—and quite fortunately— from the vantage-point of one's own age; and it is probably a mistake, and certainly a waste of breath, to be arrogant or snobbish or moral about what amuses or does not amuse one: we may fancy we are less callous than our grandfathers and only be less callous about different things. The cuckold was clearly, in Restoration comedy, a figure to hoot at. Simply for being cuckolded we do not today find a man so comic, or even comic at all: though the moment we add an extra element to his role, such as his elation over cuckolding others, he becomes a comic figure for us. To what extent sex itself is a comic theme must naturally vary with the morality of a particular age: there are times when it seems shocking for a man ever to have a mistress; there are times when it seems even more shocking for a man never to have one. Right in the same age, what is considered virtue by the parson may be termed repression by the psychiatrist; and in such an age, which is usually one of moral transition, we may well find conflicting comedy values. The pendulum-swing of taste always makes it hard for people to know what they really like: if they are in revolt against gentility, they are likely to confuse what is funny with what is merely bold or obscene; if they are converts to gentility, they will be too much outraged by the indecent to inquire whether it is funny. There is nothing at which the Comic Spirit must smile more than our fickle and inconstant notions as to what constitutes comedy. We need not always look back to Shakespeare's drearier clowns as an instance of how tastes change: sometimes we need only attend a revival of what convulsed us ten years before.

CHAPTER II

Ben Jonson

THE Restoration theater has curious antecedents. Or rather, no direct antecedents at all, because for a generation before Charles II was restored to the throne, the playhouses were shut down. The continuity was broken; the Restoration drama had accordingly to hark back for its traditions to pre-commonwealth times; it was like a man with a grandfather but no father. There is thus no gradual, graceful, logical, orderly approach to it; no seventeenth-century flight of stairs up which we move to find the Comedy of Manners waiting for us on the landing. There are no stairs: to reach Etherege and Wycherley after Shirley and Massinger we must make a flying leap.

This might well encourage us to drop the whole notion of ancestry * and begin where the Restoration begins, with the King coming back from exile and the playhouse doors swinging open. And certainly we need not weary ourselves watching the Restoration theater being born. But we ought to have a look at grandfather, not because his grandchildren notably resemble

---

* For a good concise account of the evolution of Restoration comedy, see Chapter I of Joseph Wood Krutch's *Comedy and Conscience After the Restoration.*

him, but because he himself was a great and remarkable man. Ben Jonson set a standard that his grandchildren, though they partly rejected him, partly fell short of. But he all the same established something, transmitted something; and now and again, writing almost a century earlier, he met Restoration comedy on its own terms, beat Restoration comedy at its own game. And always, between him and the Restoration, there is a link, a blood-tie, a question of descent—as with the other comic writers of his age, Shakespeare included, there is not. For in a pre-eminent degree Jonson cared about form, as at its best the Restoration cared about finish. The two things are by no means the same, but each attests the conscious artist. Jonson, again, had not the temperament of the Restoration playwrights; but his, like theirs, was realistic and even worldly. Comedy for him, as for the Restoration, constitutes a view of life and not a kind of idyllic Forest-of-Ardenish poetry. It is not a fraud against real life, but an exposé of fraudulence. And far from being a slope up which we toil to reach the Restoration, Jonson is himself a peak, and a higher peak than any Restoration playwright can rise to. Without him, we should hardly know what Comedy —hard, glittering comedy—can be like at its most creative; without him, we could perhaps not see to what extent Restoration comedy was concerned with surfaces; or how much it lost in weight that it might gain in polish; or lost on the rhetorical side of language to the advantage of the colloquial.

Jonson, it is surely known, was the great classicist, the great classical playwright, of his age. He respected the Unities where most of his contemporaries used the stage as a ship for reckless voyaging through time and space. He pinned his scene down further with logic, where his contemporaries let it rip and blow with imagination. He preferred types to be seen in every street crowd to such shapes as never were on sea or land. He stood for order rather than chaos; for moderation, for sanity. And whatever was not sane or moderate emerged as comedy. When the tail began wagging the dog, when the mania began infecting the man, Comedy might mount the stage. In this attitude is to be found, to a degree, Jonson's famous theory of Humors. Though

Jonson did not invent, he did in a sense perfect, the Comedy of Humors; and he did define it:

> *In every human body*
> *The choler, melancholy, phlegm and blood,*
> *By reason that they flow continually*
> *In some one part, and are not continent,*
> *Receive the name of humors.*

So far Jonson is merely re-stating medieval medical theory; but now he adds:

> *It may, by metaphor, apply itself*
> *Unto the general disposition:*
> *As when some one peculiar quality*
> *Doth so possess a man that it doth draw*
> *All his affects, his spirits and his powers*
> *In their confluctions, all to run one way,*
> *This may be truly said to be a humor.*

This, at any rate, is the law of the Comedy of Humors; and obsession is nine points of the law. Your character is all greed, or sensuality, or snobbery; and to the degree that he craves one thing will not only be foolish about it, but will very likely be wrongheaded about all others.

Two of Jonson's plays, each with "humor" in the title, are more or less dedicated to celebrating the Comedy of Humors; but neither of them ranks with Jonson's best work, and for Jonson's greatness we must look elsewhere. Yet the theory of humors is by no means unconnected with Jonson's greatness, for the theory produced something peculiarly intense and grotesque; and it is very largely through being intense and grotesque that Jonson is great. His own genius ran to harsh outlines, to vivid brilliant coloring. A realist at bottom, he saw that to distinguish the real from the merely conventional one had to use emphatic, even violent methods. A moralist by nature, he *had* to distort: his way of exaggerating was really his way of protesting.

Tradition and the textbooks may be right in yoking Jonson

to the Comedy of Humors; but, as the textbooks are not always prompt to tell us, what is permanent and great in Jonson's comedy has little to do with any humor but one. What galvanizes and unifies the action of the three most distinguished of Jonson's plays; what gives them their dramatic verve, their comic bite; what anchors them to life however wildly they may soar off into fantasy, what gives them the impress of the author however strongly they may bear the look of their age—is an emphasis much less upon mania than upon money. Or if mania there still be, it is a love, a greed, an itch, a driving passion for money. It is the economics of life, not the eccentricities, that we are most conscious of in reading *Volpone*, or *The Alchemist*, or *Bartholomew Fair*. Money, in these plays, is not only the root of all evil but the source of all deception. And this hard, downright sense of money *as* money rather sets Jonson's comedies apart from most later ones (barring those that deal in a stock way with crooks and fortune-hunters or legacies and wills). I do not mean that the importance of the money motive disappears in later comedy; only that there comes to be less emphasis on its economic aspects, and more on its social. Money remains the root of all evil; but, being the root, it is not plainly in view. In Ben Jonson's great comedies, money is equally root and vine; it makes as greedy knaves of gentlemen as of guttersnipes; Volpone's would-be heirs are as wild for having it as the pickpockets of *Bartholomew Fair*. "Get money in thy pocket" is the prime injunction.

Now as comedy—which is to say as society—turns more sophisticated, the money motive necessarily becomes less naked and overt; money becomes the basis for class distinctions and social refinements, for many kinds of pleasure, for many kinds of power. If it still cannot confer birth on a nobody, it can give breeding to his children; it sets the rich against the poor, transforms and reorders society, becomes the basis for marrying into' or out of one's class, for keeping a coach or a country house or a mistress, for abandoning religion or adopting a more fashionable one. Money is the basis of all corruption, but equally the basis of all culture; it makes for the most dissolute society but also for the most lustrous; it perhaps destroys the sense of virtue, but probably enhances the sense of beauty; morals are the worse for it, but manners the better. But in Ben Jonson the emphasis is not yet on what is social and cultural, there is not yet much veneer: money is a concrete and central *fact*.

In a world like Jonson's, where money-getting by any means is the mania of the characters, the comedy will be simple in motive, however devious in method; and will, for the most part, be quite cold and hard. It is this bluntness and singlemindedness that renders Jonson's comedy anterior in feeling to the comedy of the Restoration. As a classicist, Jonson may have inherited the comedy of the ancients, but in practice this boiled down to the unsophisticated, if not indeed crude, comedy of Plautus, and contributed no refining sensibility. As a humanist, again, Jonson stood opposed to intolerance and fanaticism, to all who in the name of some divine decree would bottle up every natural human impulse; he was for learning as against ignorance, for free inquiry as against sanctified superstition. But simply for being a humanist in an age so given to inhuman ways, he had to assert his own values in harshly forcible fashion. He had to simplify, which is to say he had to satirize. The writer of satire, like the writer of melodrama, works in primary colors, and has little interest in delicate shades. But where much satire, and most melodrama, contrasts black with white, Jonson as satirist contrasts black with white only to castigate both. For the contrast is not between goodness and evil, but between cleverness and gullibility, between the fleecers and the fleeced. It is comedy that William Archer described (and derogated) as based on "pure scoundrelism on one side, and illimitable credulity on the other." "Never," said John Palmer, again, speaking of *Bartholomew Fair*, "never did such a gallery of rogues prey so happily upon so complete a company of fools."

There, indeed, is the limitation of Jonson's comic world; it is all knaves and fools. We seldom find in it those other figures—some of them, surely, arch-figures—of comedy: the snob, the coquette, the fop, the bore, the pompous ass, the would-be connoisseur. And that is why Jonson sticks in our minds and memories as a creator of satire rather than of social comedy. Yet Jonson keeps to the right track, for the heart of comedy is always delusion and deception, just as the heart of comedy is a little alien to the human heart—or far oftener concerned with the human brain. Comedy is a matter not of wit alone, but of quick-wittedness; is concerned equally with the triumph or the downfall of cleverness; with how Greek meets Greek and narrowly outwits him; with how the spider lures the fly into her parlor, the reason being often no more creditable to the one than to the other. The intellectualism, the complete anti-sentimentalism, of Jonson's comedy is a very great merit indeed. A world all knaves and fools is, even for comedy, too circumscribed and single-toned. But a playwright overfond of cheats is surely to be preferred to all those who are cheats themselves, who brazenly make over their characters for the sake of happy endings and popular success.

Volpone and *The Alchemist* are both great plays. *Volpone* is the grander, but it is less purely a comedy. It is conceived on a scale that defies working out in purely comic terms, where *The Alchemist* is conceived on a scale that invites to comedy, that nourishes and necessitates it. We are always being tempted to take sides in the matter, to belong to the school that thinks *Volpone* Jonson's masterpiece or the school that thinks *The Alchemist* is. Much the same partisanship arises over other great artists, over *The Red and the Black* and *The Charterhouse of Parma*, or *War and Peace* and *Anna Karenina*, or *Don Giovanni* and *The Marriage of Figaro*. No doubt in a sense, it is a matter of preference, but in each case a distinction is to be made between kinds of merit. *Figaro* and *Anna Karenina* and *The Alchemist* are virtually perfect things of their kind; *Don Giovanni* and *War and Peace* and *Volpone* are not: they are greater, but not as good. While cutting deeper or soaring higher, they are more faulty in structure or less unified in effect. *Volpone* is Jonson's greatest undertaking: *The Alchemist* is his best play.

It is very likely, indeed, the best English comedy—for *The Way of the World* is but the best English comedy of manners. One can hardly begin upon it without quoting Coleridge, that

Oedipus, The Alchemist and *Tom Jones* contain the three finest plots in literature. With *Tom Jones* this has always struck me as going too far, and with *The Alchemist* as not going in quite the right direction; for *The Alchemist* contains no very notable sense of plot. It is more in the nature of an action, if it is not indeed a mere situation richly elaborated upon. Translated into modern terms, *The Alchemist* (so far as plot goes) rather parallels what might take place during a very busy evening in a very accomplished clip-joint. We should see a collection of victims preyed upon in terms of their particular weaknesses, and sometimes used to mislead and defraud one another. Moreover, the sharpers who run the joint are engaged in trying to outwit one another. Jonson's way of developing his essentially straightforward action, the touches and twists he contrives to keep it in constant motion, are admirable. But a *plot*, in the sense of one thing arising out of another, of a marked relation between causes and consequences, of something fortuitous becoming, suddenly, fateful, is just what *The Alchemist* cannot boast. In a way, indeed, it is almost as much treatise as story—a treatise on how rogues operate and victims succumb.

From the moment the curtain rises—from that brilliant first moment which shows three tricksters quarreling, snarling, and angrily throwing up to one another all the facts needed for the exposition—Jonson is a master craftsman and a master showman. Here, as elsewhere, he has the great knack, while developing his story, of exhibiting his characters as vividly as a merchant exhibits his wares. The situation is simplicity itself: during the plague, a citizen of London has fled to the country, leaving his butler in charge of his house; the butler has taken in two confederates, a woman to play any needed female role, a man posing as an alchemist; and the three of them, once they patch up their quarrel, are set to prey upon every sort of victim. To them come a stream of people so dazzled by the thought of wealth as to have shut their eyes to the methods. There is Dapper, a clerk with what might be called a fairly modest greed; he craves a familiar spirit who can make his fortune, and the sharpers assure him that the lady they have in mind, the Queen of

Faery, will be very obliging if he goes about things right—
a small down payment, of course, and his attentions must not be
niggardly. Then comes Drugger, a tobacconist who would like
to expand his business; he, too, can be accommodated. Next
comes Sir Epicure Mammon, a man of far different cut and
breed, who, aspiring on a sumptuous scale, can be victimized at
a handsome rate. Although of no great importance to the action,
Sir Epicure is the towering figure in the play. Interested only in
the sensual and the material, craving the utmost in luxury as a
background for the utmost in lust, Sir Epicure represents philis-
tinism raised to the level of poetry; endows sensuality with the
glow and brilliance of painting. He is his own best spokesman:
dupe no less than slave of a vaulting sensual imagination, Sir
Epicure sees precisely what he wants to see—sees a duchess in
a mere drab. When Doll, the female confederate, is set before
Sir Epicure in the guise of a noble lady, he contrives—once the
alchemist shall have transmuted things to gold—the proper
background for her:

> *We'll therefore go withal, my girl, and live*
> *In a free state, where we will eat our mullets*
> *Soused in High Country wines, sup pheasants' eggs,*
> *And have our cockles boiled in silver shells;*
> *Our shrimps to swim again, as when they lived,*
> *In a rare butter made of dolphins' milk,*
> *Whose cream does look like opals; and with these*
> *Delicate meats, set ourselves high for pleasure,*
> *And take us down again, and then renew*
> *Our youth and strength with drinking the elixir,*
> *And so enjoy a perpetuity*
> *Of life and lust.*

But others follow Sir Epicure into this spider's parlor: two
Puritan divines from Holland, piously seeking gold for good
works, and rationalizing as they seek it. Thus, if a tune is involved, the puritan Ananias remarks:

> *Bells are profane; a tune may be religious;*

and before long they have found divine sanction for becoming
counterfeiters. Just so, in *Bartholomew Fair*, will Jonson's really
great Puritan hypocrite, Zeal-of-the-land Busy, find sanction
for going to the Fair to eat pig. The Puritans of *The Alchemist*
are decidedly smaller figures. Rather better is Kastril, or the
Angry Boy, a brash upstart who is delighted when arrangements
are made for his widowed sister to marry a Spanish count. *Spanish* count—is that better, the sister asks, than an English one?
And Face, the arch-rogue, answers:

> *Ask from your courtier to your inns-of-court man,*
> *To your mere milliner. They will tell you all,*
> *Your Spanish jennet is the best horse; your Spanish*
> *Stoop is the best garb; your Spanish beard*
> *Is the best cut; your Spanish ruffs are the best*
> *Wear; your Spanish pavan the best dance;*
> *Your Spanish titillation in a glove*
> *The best perfume. And for your Spanish pike*
> *And Spanish blade, let your poor Captain speak.*
> *Here comes the Doctor.*

The Spanish count is actually a skeptical friend of Sir Mammon's named Surly, who is sure that all this alchemic talk is
nonsense. Disguised, he dutifully jabbers in Spanish, while the
confederates—pretty naïvely for such rogues—cast slurs upon
him in English. But when he tries to warn the widow against
them, they make him seem the villain, or at any rate a fortune-
hunter. Finally, however, with the house a-swarm with victims,
the cheats are expected to produce results. They begin by offering conventional reasons for delay; then, learning that Sir
Epicure has been indulging his lusts, they blame such premature
misconduct for the complete breakdown of their process. Can
nothing, asks the doleful Mammon, be saved? And Face answers:

> *I cannot tell, sir. There will be perhaps*
> *Something, about the scraping of the shards,*
> *Will kill the itch—*
> *It shall be saved for you and sent home.*

But what puts an end to the fraud, even before the victims can clamor in chorus, is the return of Face's master, Lovewit, from the country. Lovewit being, if not a kind master, at any rate an easy-going cynic, Face dares tell him the truth—successfully gambling that it will more amuse than anger him, and in addition dangling the rich widow before Lovewit himself.

Certainly there is no stature to this comedy; its sharpers are mere cold-blooded rogues, never satanic villains or figures of evil. They go about their work with a kind of sardonic contempt for their victims, with the gusto of clever improvisers, the aplomb of skillful actors. Because their victims are uniformly self-seekers, loving gold not a whit less than the rogues they seek it from, there is no question here of taking sides. We are down to the hard rock of human covetousness; here men are gulled because they are greedy; here the reality is harsh to the extent that the dream is sordid; diamond cuts diamond, and the worst man wins. The worst man wins because he is also the cleverest, combining the best brain with the prettiest wit, the largest daring with the greatest prudence. Because morality plays no part in any of these people's calculations, it need have none in ours. No one hesitates from any twinge of virtue at the outset, no one is remorseful at the end. From start to finish Jonson has caught precisely the right tone. This is always comedy—unsparing and satirical—but pure of its kind, and as rich as constant invention and undepletable rhetoric can make it.

There are, to be sure, two characters in the play who might serve as moral agents: Surly, who sees through the confederates; and Lovewit, who has the power to punish them. But Surly—rather wisely—is just what he is named, and his uses stop with the plot: he is a cog in the machine, not a commentator or Greek chorus. Lovewit's behavior is morally open to question: there are doubtless those who would have him indignant rather than amused, who would not have him forgive his butler, or—still less—continue to employ him; or, least of all, accept the rich widow as a wife. Abstractedly, I think, it is not quite possible to cry down these objections, or at any rate laugh them away. By having Lovewit condone Face's behavior, Jonson may seem to condone it himself; while Lovewit's cynicism doubles the offense. For this is no generous spirit of forgiveness, this is not virtue raising vice from its knees; this is indifference patting knavery on the back. Lovewit loves wit indeed, loves it a little too well; and Face is let off because he is too valuable a servant to lose.

Yet Jonson is dead right in terms of this kind of comedy. Punishment here would be too drastic; punishment—as we shall note in *Volpone*—is rather disastrous even where a true sense of evil exists, for it is one of the axioms of comedy that there be no really painful consequences. Moreover, it is not just part of the joke for Lovewit to act as he does; it is also part of the truthfulness of the picture. Face *is* too valuable a servant for a worldling like Lovewit to lose on moral grounds. We all forgive people who are worth forgiving; and we most of us have a kindness for a scamp who lets us in on the fun, for a liar who does not lie to *us*. Such, says Jonson, is the way of gentlemen, and indeed the way of life. If now and then we hear, faintly, a kind of hyena laughter, we are not even once afflicted with crocodile tears.

Such harsh comedy as this, however, needs to be clothed, as Jonson clothes it, in vigorous language. Jonson proves himself, to begin with, a master of free-moving, quickly intelligible, highly practical verse. Hence Jonson can be as fantastic or ironic or downright as he chooses—as when Mammon, hearing that everything shall be transmuted to gold and silver, says very grandly: "Silver I care not for"; and Face caps the line by answering: "Oh, yes, sir—a little to give beggars." And what can be more splendidly downright than Face's injunctions to Doll as she is about to appear before Dapper as the Queen of Faery:

> *Sweet Doll,*
> *You must go tune your virginal, no losing*
> *O' the least time. And, do you hear? good action.*
> *Firk like a flounder; kiss like a scallop, close.*

When Jonson gets round to the business of alchemy itself, and all the accompanying hocus-pocus, he throws in long mystifying speeches that do, I suppose, slow down the action and are even, in a dramatic viewpoint, tedious. For modern audiences this learned nonsense is often said to be a drawback, even a stumbling-block, to the enjoyment of the play. But surely this is making too much of it, first because—in terms of the whole play —there *isn't* very much; and again, because Jonson's own audiences would have found it—and were meant to find it—as baffling as we do. What could this high-sounding nonsense have meant to Jonson's age when it never, in any age, meant anything at all? To be sure, it might have sounded more plausible when the jargon itself was still current, just as a hodge-podge of psychoanalytical jargon might amuse us more than it will our remote descendants. As satire, all this hocus-pocus about alchemy is rather wearisome now, though as sheer virtuoso speech it can even now be admired.

And certainly the play as a whole can — for its form and language, and even more for its amazing energy, the high spirits that Time has not even begun to dampen.

When we pass from *The Alchemist* to *Volpone*, we feel at once a change in climate. And it is not just that we have shifted from London to Venice; something glittering as well as alien has entered in. *The Alchemist* opens with a vulgar squabble, *Volpone* with a resplendent invocation. *The Alchemist* introduces three sharpers spewing billingsgate, *Volpone* portrays its grandee hero glorifying the realms of gold. We are but two or three steps below the most sublime of all such invocations, Milton's *Hail, holy light;* and we are aware of something not at all un-Miltonic; we feel, indeed, the presence of the grand style. Here is the language of the grand style; and here, in the persons of Volpone and Mosca—of master and parasite, the Fox and the Fly—are a pair of grand-style manoeuvrers. Rich, childless Volpone feigns illness to arouse the hopes of greedy fellow-Venetians who would be his heir; meanwhile Mosca, by assuring each one that he will be Volpone's heir, exacts rich tribute of them all. The scheme is grandiose and perilous, calling for enormous ingenuity and presence of mind; but it is additionally in the grand style for springing from more than just mercenary motives. It is not gold and jewels alone that Volpone craves, but vast power, malevolent opportunities to play cat and mouse with his victims, to torture quite as much as to tempt them. He is a fox only so far as he is wily, and in wickedness very near a fiend. His is the pleasure of making others roar with pain; the manoeuvre, as he puts it, of

> *Letting the cherry knock against their lips.*

And so, in the opening scene, comes Voltore, and then Corbaccio: Corbaccio brings a bag of sequins where Voltore had brought plate. (Corbaccio is deaf, so that much of his encounter with Mosca tends to be farcical.) Mosca suggests that the best way for Corbaccio to become Volpone's heir is to make Volpone Corbaccio's. And Corbaccio, thinking Volpone very ill indeed, agrees—even though it means disinheriting his son. Next comes Corvino, who brings a pearl and a diamond and hears that Volpone is at the point of death and quite insensible. Assured by Mosca that he is the heir, Corvino intimates he won't take it amiss of Mosca to hurry matters a little. Corvino, too, departs: it has been a good morning for the plotters; the fly has coaxed three spiders into his parlor. And it has been a good morning for the playwright; for in this opening act we have Jonson at his most brilliant.

Now the plot begins to thicken, and the plotters to fly higher. From Mosca, Volpone hears of Corvino's beautiful wife and at once longs to see her; sees her, and at once longs to have her. This is not easy; Corvino is so jealous a husband as scarcely to let her out of the house. But Mosca is equal to the situation: he frightens Corvino with the thought that keeping his virtuous wife may lose him Volpone's fortune. There is no struggle; Corvino drags his wife, ahead of time, to Volpone's presumably harmless bedside. When the room is cleared, Volpone leaps at her, a formidable seducer even of a chaste and horrified lady:

> *Why droops my Celia?*
> *Thou hast, in place of a base husband, found*
> *A worthy lover; use thy fortune well,*

> *With secrecy and pleasure. See, behold*
> *What thou art queen of, not in expectation—*
> *As I feed others—but possessed and crowned.*
> *See, here, a rope of pearl, and each more orient*
> *Than that the brave Egyptian queen caroused—*
> *Dissolve and drink 'em. See, a carbuncle,*
> *May put out both the eyes of our Saint Mark;*
> *A diamond would have bought Lollia Paulina,*
> *When she came in like starlight, hid with jewels*
> *That were the spoils of provinces—take these*
> *And wear, and lose 'em;*

But Corbaccio's outraged son saves Corvino's outraged wife from ravishment; and forces Mosca, pleading before the bar of Venice, to use his most brilliant arts to save Volpone and himself from the law. What Mosca does is to "prove" that it was Corbaccio's son who sinned with Corvino's lady. This, the gloating Mosca tells the gleeful Volpone, this is their masterpiece: no more in daring than in achievement can they go farther. But Volpone, crazed by now with power, insists on going farther; insists, in fact, that Mosca inform all Venice that Volpone at last is dead. Only this time, trying to outdo themselves—and outwit each other—they come to grief. Mosca uses the story of his master's death as a way of seizing his master's fortune; and rather than allow him the last word, Volpone peaches on them both, and both are punished.

This is not to summarize the story, but only to highlight it —to indicate less the turns and twists than the bounding leaps of the plot; the tremendous rascality and ingenuity of the conspirators. Subtle and Face, in *The Alchemist*, are thorough-going coldblooded rogues, but their motives are purely mercenary; Volpone's scheming and to some extent Mosca's stratagems spring from motives quite malign. Mosca, to be sure, has his way to make; but Volpone, a grandee of independent fortune, is less impelled by greed, and then only by greed that would transform itself to grandeur. What Volpone wants, and keeps ever wanting more, is to succeed at vast designs of cunning. He would be a potentate, with much the same prerogatives as a cruel, decadent Oriental ruler. His quarry would somewhat resemble himself: they too must be rich, they too must be rascals. His whole impulse is creative rather than acquisitive; he is no mere criminal, but a grand-scale evildoer: other men's disappointments constitute *his* triumphs. His infatuation for Corvino's beautiful wife rolls all his strongest desires into one: here is a woman he passionately longs to enjoy; but a virtuous woman it would give him additional satisfaction to seduce; and a married woman, whose husband it would give him even greater satisfaction to betray. There is nothing paltry about Volpone; and Mosca is no common parasite, but rather—in his own words—a "fine, elegant rascal"; a lithe, deft, stylish fellow whose palaver is as excellent as his plotting. He leaps like quicksilver where Volpone burns like sulphur; he is the playwright of their scheming, as Volpone is the poet. From striving to please his master he comes at last to share his master's pleasures; for more and more, we feel, Mosca enjoys his villains and triumphs for their own sake.

But it is not their evil natures, it is their insatiable desires, that bring master and servant low. They have the same craving for power as their victims have for money. Mosca might master himself, but Volpone grows uncontrollable. It is the very risks that he most seems to enjoy: he plays for higher and higher stakes against longer and longer odds, and is ruined much less from miscalculation than from utter recklessness. Because his cravings can never for long be satisfied, they must compass, in time, his ruin. Mosca, on the other hand, is impelled by greed for his master's money and undone by misreading his master's mind.

Their victims are in some ways more villainous than they are. Vulture, raven, crow—three greedy, three quite unglamorous, birds of prey. Only the ornithologist in real life or the connoisseur of symbolic evil in the arts could much distinguish among them. Corbaccio, being deaf, smacks of burlesque, and is more detestable than Voltore from being willing to disinherit his son, as Corvino is more detestable than Corbaccio from being willing to dishonor his wife. Vulture, raven, crow, they are somehow unforgettable as a group, however uninteresting in themselves or indistinguishable from one another. Here Jonson was handicapped by the terms of his plot. Only Venetians of some importance would have the entrée at Volpone's house or could have any hopes of becoming his heir; this was no free-for-all, but the latest of many plays whose theme was legacy-hunting. That is one reason why *The Alchemist* comes off the better work: its victims are far more entertainingly varied. But even more damaging to *Volpone* than the similarity of vice is the unconvincingness of virtue; for Corbaccio's son Bonario and Corvino's wife Celia are the merest puppets. No doubt Celia's protests against Volpone's ardent assaults are suitably worded, but they leave something to be desired in terms of true intensity.

There are two other defects that cannot be glossed over in *Volpone* before we consider the more vexed question of its ending and general tone. Volpone's three household pets—his dwarf, eunuch, and hermaphrodite—never catch quite the right note of either frivolity or horror. By pleasing Volpone, they may give *us* further insight into Volpone's make-up; and no doubt they add a note of peculiar decadence to the play. But we are concerned with villainy at such a height and on such a scale that these merely offensive creatures detract rather than add; they are like the scratches of a cat amidst snakes that coil and beasts that pounce and birds that swoop down from the sky. Worst of all, they are dull. Even duller is the whole subplot of the play, the business of the English travelers. This subplot alone would make *Volpone* inferior in workmanship to *The Alchemist*.

As for the rightness or wrongness of the play's wellnigh tragic ending, it is not something that can be viewed in isolation. In other words, the question is not just whether so harsh an ending befits a comic play; but whether *Volpone* essentially *is* a comic play. And if Jonson's own theories are to adjudicate his practice, *Volpone* is not in essence comic; for comedy, said Jonson, should "sport with human follies," but not with crimes. Much of the time, here, on a moral basis—and even on a legal one—we are concerned with what must be called crimes; with a man who, if he attains a certain evil grandeur, yet commits vicious and criminal acts. We are concerned with this man's victims, themselves as much devils as dupes; we are concerned with plots involving wronged and innocent people. Corvino's utter baseness—his willingness to sacrifice his wife—becomes comic, it is true, from his having been unwilling, just a moment before, even to show her in public; but it is the about-face that is comic here, the depravity itself goes beyond comedy. The very point of Volpone's downfall, which is not that he cannot calculate the risks, but that he cannot control the need, smacks—beyond any comedy-of-humors mania—of the pathological.

On the other hand, the sight of Mosca and Volpone at work, the sheer brilliance of their performance—such things as Volpone's playing the sick man under Corvino's eyes, or playing the mountebank under Celia's window, or playing the Commendatore in the plain view of all Venice—all this is hard high comedy of the very greatest kind; all this exhilarates us beyond any thought of moral meaning or realistic consequence; all this is too sheerly intellectual for drama, too gaily malicious for tragedy. The truth is that while *Volpone* may burst the mold of comedy, it fits no other mold even so well. Its atmosphere, now glittering now sombre, is an unnatural and impure one; its tone, now outrageously cynical, now sharply moral, is an impure one, too.

Hence it rests on how much we accentuate its tragic elements whether we approve its sombre ending; approve the realistic justice of it, with Mosca and Volpone led away to prison—as opposed to poetic justice, where they might be left empty-handed, suffering as knaves the fate they had plotted for their fools. The whole point about sardonic comedy is that the punishment should fit the crime, not expiate it; pay back the criminal in his own coin, not serve the ends of society. Our last glimpse, as the curtain falls, should still be of the joke, and not of justice. Our thoughts should be traveling backward, say to Volpone's bogus sickroom, not forward to Volpone's prison cell. And yet, such is the nature and stature of the man, that if Jonson's ending seems too harsh, a purely comic one would seem too trivial. A kind of comic Nemesis has overtaken Jonson himself who, from too freely mixing his colors throughout, can achieve no right tone at the end. He has saved the situation all he can by introducing a final ironic twist: Volpone can endure the punishment meted out to him knowing that Mosca's will be a heavier one. The penalty for masters is lighter than that for servants; the ending of *Volpone* is thus sardonic as well as sombre.

Volpone gains and loses from the same cause, from having a size and intensity greater than in any other Jonson comedy—which are at the same time too great for comedy at all. It suffers, like its chief characters, from going too far—from passing beyond something brilliant to something black. But such glittering brilliance against such solid black becomes an ineffaceable memory. The play grows in memory: *The Alchemist* seems better while we are reading it, *Volpone* afterwards.

In any strict sense, *Bartholomew Fair* is not nearly so good a play as *Volpone* or *The Alchemist*. But if it were a better play, it could not boast so broad a canvas. We are, indeed, at a fair, whose rewards and pleasures differ from those of the playhouse. Although they are still chiefly knaves and fools, we are occupied here rather with the people themselves than with a plot. We might better be occupied with a plot; for while at a real fair our bodies may wander at will, in the theater only our minds can, and nothing is more likely to make them than a formless play. Only when a playwright knows how to make his characters genuinely interesting, and his incidents vivid, and his dialogue bright, do we thank him for going about his business the hard way, do we overlook and forgive the absence of plot. But this we can do, I think, with *Bartholomew Fair*, which though garrulous in places and too long on the whole, even after three hundred and fifty years, has surprising energy, and ingenuity, and even comedy about it.

It is impossible not to note how Jonsonian the play is in spirit, however un-Jonsonian in form. When Jonson goes to a fair, he sees very much what he sees everywhere else; he sees, overwhelmingly, knaves and fools. Smithfield buzzes and crackles with life; smells of London and swarms with Londoners;

abounds in all the things that delight and tire the flesh, boasts every kind of trapping and every sort of trap. But it would need a kind of textbook mind to assert that *Bartholomew Fair* symbolizes life itself, or even life in London. It seems to me quite unsymbolic of life itself; there are much too few kinds of people in it—not even enough for a good Morality Play. So far from being life, or London, it doesn't even seem a very true cross-section of a fair. Surely, at a fair, more people would be pleasanter by nature and having a jollier time. The play is simply a cross-section of Ben Jonson's own idea of the world; and this, on the whole, is a very good thing. For if it too much colors the general effect, it also controls it. And so errant and haphazard and anarchic a thing as a fair *must* be controlled: without a guide, however prejudiced, we should make no headway; and, however prejudiced, Jonson proves a wonderfully instructive guide.

For if this too is a spectacle of knaves and fools, of deceit and deception, it has, in a marvelous degree, both verisimilitude and range. Jonson may have but a single theme, but where shall we find cleverer variations on a single theme? He may lack fellow-feeling with the world around him, but who has a sharper comic sense of its outward forms? There are dozens of characters here, most of them talking well, no two really talking alike, and no one talking like Jonson. The hypocritical pomposities of Busy, the expert billingsgate of Ursula, Waspe's acidities, Cokes' rattling nonsense, Littlewit's repetitions, Lanthorne's show-manlike spiel—Jonson's mastery of dialect in a sense rivals his mastery of dramaturgy.

As for the cheating and cozenage, it is through them that the play progresses. Virtually everybody has an end in view. The problem here, in playwriting—as it would be at a fair, in life—is to keep people always in motion; but playwriting has the further problem of constantly bringing people together and then once more driving them apart. There is even the business of getting some of them *to* the fair. In the case of Win-the-Fight Littlewit, who is expecting a child, Jonson ordains that she shall crave to eat pig. There follows the famous scene in which her mother, a convert to Puritanism, questions the Puritan, Zeal-of-the-land Busy, whether one may visit a place so sinful as a Fair for so harmless a reason as to eat pig. Busy being the most striking and sharply satirized character in the play, his first entrance is worth noting:

> DAME PURECRAFT: *O Brother Busy! your help here, to edify and raise us up in a scruple: my daughter Win-the-Fight is visited with a natural disease of women, called a longing to eat pig.*

> . . . . .

> BUSY: *Verily, for the disease of longing, it is a disease, a carnal disease, or appetite, incident to women; and as it is carnal and incident, it is natural, very natural. Now pig, it is a meat, and a meat that is nourishing, and may be longed for, and so consequently eaten. It may be eaten, very exceeding well eaten. But in the Fair, and as a Bartholomew pig, it cannot be eaten; for the very calling it a Bartholomew-pig, and to eat it so, is a spice of idolatry, and you make the Fair no better than one of the High Places. This, I take it, is the state of the question: a High Place.* (And so on, with Busy finally deciding that pig *can* be eaten at a fair.)

So ends Act I; with Act II, we are at the Fair among people with wares to sell and wiles to spread—among ballad-makers and pastrycooks, wrestlers and pickpockets. Here gather, meet, move on, and continually re-form the little knots of visitors: Zeal-of-the-land Busy and his group; the foolish Bartholomew Cokes, with his tutor Waspe, his sister Mistress Overdo, his sister's ward Grace Wellborn; Winwife—who, like Busy, is a suitor of Win-the-Fight's mother—and his friend Quarlous; while, alone and disguised, there skulks Adam Overdo, a justice of the peace who seeks first-hand knowledge of the doings and misdoings of the Fair.

Of doings and misdoings there is no end. Pig is eaten and pockets are picked; busybodies are turned into laughing-stocks, a fool and his money are soon parted, a husband and his wife are soon parted; and while the husband preens himself as a playwright, the wife disgraces herself as a bawd. It is Jonson's old, constant, inescapable theme: let him for a moment attempt a character who is neither knave nor fool—in this case Grace Wellborn—and she is neither alive nor interesting, either. The one other kind of person with whom Jonson can succeed, because it is the one other kind he can believe in, is the hard-bitten, soured soul, the misanthrope like Waspe: Waspe, the tutor and not-vigilant-enough watchdog of the nincompoop Bartholomew Cokes. With his chip-on-the-shoulder surliness, Waspe is enjoyable. When Littlewit bids him be civil, he answers:

> *Why, say I have a humor not to be civil; how then? who shall compel me, you?*

Waspe is pure "humor"—or rather, pure ill-humor; a character that Jonson happens to be satirizing, but would fundamentally sympathize with. For in Waspe we have that social paradox, the man who is hired for his superior talents and occupies an inferior place.

But Waspe is an exception—if he *is* an exception—to the company of rogues and fools, for he quite possibly belongs with the fools, as Adam Overdo almost certainly does. And Jonson's using so varied and heterogeneous thing as a Fair to divide humanity into but two categories is as much the philosophical weakness as it is the structural virtue of the play. In *Volpone* or *The Alchemist* the plot only calls for rogues and fools. But here Jonson has seized on one of the few things that may be allowed to symbolize life itself, and has merely exploited it to express a view of life. But even if one saw life as harshly as Jonson saw it, a Fair is an unsound place to look for evidence. Doubtless nowhere could one more easily squander one's money or be bilked of it, or act silly, or cut capers, or be led astray. But, after all, one goes to a Fair a little intending to play the fool: one hopes to flirt, one means to get drunk. We are no more to be graded for vice by how we act at a Fair than we are to be graded for virtue by how we behave in a church. It may be disgusting to get drunk, but it is also fun. There is, perhaps, something grim about folly, but often something very gay about fools. What is wrong is that Jonson went to the Fair to moralize; used it for satire rather than comedy.

But having condemned it as too one-sided and, as I would think, too long-drawn-out, one has said the worst; on its own terms it is animated, bustling, very possibly brilliant. Nor, if Jonson somehow ruled out gaiety, was it from any condemnation of cakes and ale; here in the person of Zeal-of-the-land Busy, Jonson gave Puritanism its forty whacks. For his Puritan is not simply unattractive, is not merely fanatical: he is also a transcendent hypocrite, the best and most forceful of his kind on the English stage. It is sufficient tribute that he makes us think of Tartuffe, though once we have done so, we can only think less of Busy.

In passing to *The Silent Woman*, we begin to pass from Jacobean to later comedy. If *The Silent Woman* contains much that seems old-fashioned even in Jonson, and actually combines two practical jokes out of ancient Greece, it yet varies its entertainment with a display of manners, of the gallantries, the fripperies, the fashionable life of the town. Here, too, Jonson is less heavy than usual and less harsh. He desires, as he says right off, to please "not the cook's taste, but the guests'." This aim, to be sure, is never a very sound one, and almost never, among men of high talent, leads to complete success. But if the play suffers from Jonson's desire to be likeable, it prefigures the Restoration in its efforts to be light. This is as near to froth as a playwright full of bile could come. Here is no satirist who would castigate, merely a jokester who would amuse. Here, as with the Restoration, the plot is even more trivial than it is elaborate; but the trimmings are redeemingly lively and gay. Others, to be sure, have called the plot wellnigh perfect (certainly it conforms to the Unities of both time and place); but the plot as a whole, or rather the play as a whole, has no inner unity, no characterizing pigmentation.

The comedy that emerges, from one Greek joke's meeting with another, has to do, first, with an old noise-hating recluse who marries a babbling creature in the belief that she will never open her mouth; and, again, with an old man marrying a young girl who, as it turns out, is a boy. Morose is put in double jeopardy: the silent woman is neither silent nor a woman. Such double practical-joking, far from begetting anything that smacks of real life, suggest a rather low level of farce. Impersonation, of course, whether of boys pretending to be girls, or vice-versa, was a favorite device in a period of all-male casts; but though that may explain its popularity then, it hardly enhances its value now. Nor does Morose himself—who seems not just misanthropic but also mean, and hates noise not least because it so often signifies fun—raise the level of the play above that set by the plot. Morose ought to be more human or more inhuman, more victim or more villain. We don't mind seeing him baited, as we do Malvolio, with whom he is sometimes compared; but we don't much enjoy seeing him baited either. His really wanting to prevent his nephew, Sir Dauphiné, from becoming his heir, further loses him sympathy, for his attitude shows a kind of needless rancor. On the other hand, his plot to oust Dauphiné strengthens Jonson's story, for it is Dauphiné's counterplot that carries the story forward.

The story is ingenious enough, even though neither of its practical jokes proves sufficient. (It is the silent woman suddenly babbling that we relish, not the babbling itself; while her being not woman but man helps straighten things out at the end rather than mix things up en route.) And Epicene himself is less man *or* woman than mere god-from-the-machine—a means whereby Morose can be divorced rather than the audience diverted. Thus, from the cook trying to please the guests, we get a clever but far too mechanical plot; a trim but extremely inconsequential play. Moreover, the subplot—the business of the duel between Sir Jack Daw and Sir Amorous La Foole—intrudes yet a third, and *Twelfth-Night*-ish, practical joke into the proceedings. We demand more of Jonson, as it would seem that Jonson demanded more of himself. And in truth, in *The Silent Woman* he gave us more. He turned what was never a green and living tree into a kind of glittering Christmas tree. There is a lack of sap about the play, but an abundance of sparkle. Perfect the plot may be, but Jonson turns away from it for his best effects. He is always great when he can amplify or exaggerate a small idea; when upon a minimal realistic base he can build a spreading fantasy: it is one of the talents he shares with Dickens. To give a modest example: after the Silent Woman begins to babble, Morose pins his hopes on her going to sleep—only to be told that she talks ten times worse in her sleep, and snores like a porpoise! And in the same way, Jonson can catalogue or enumerate to brilliant comic effect. Here is Mistress Otter inveighing against her husband:

> *I'll commit you to the Master of the Garden, if I hear but a syllable more. Must my house or my roof be polluted with the scent of bears and bulls, when it is perfumed for great ladies? Is this according to the instrument, when I married you? that I would be princess, and reign in mine own house; and you would be my subject, and obey me? What did you bring me, should make you thus peremptory? Do I allow you your half-crown a day, to spend where you will, among your gamesters, to vex and torment me at such times as these? Who gives you your maintenance, I pray you? Who allows you your horse-meat and man's-meat? your three suits of apparel a year? your four pair of stockings, one silk, three worsted? your clean linen, your bands and cuffs, when I can get you to wear 'em?*

This is as precise in its detail as Defoe, and as engaging as Dickens; and with this we are on our way to Etherege and Congreve, for though the plot has been borrowed from the ancients, this specific picture is drawn from the age.

And, indeed, Jonson's own genius for detail can blend with the sovereignty of detail in the comedy of manners. Thus, when Truewit outlines for Morose how fiercely a wife would torment him, he pictures for *us* what a fashionable wife of the times might be like: and when Truewit takes up the subject of the wooing of women, he might be any sophisticated Restoration blade:

> *If you appear learned to an ignorant wench, or jocund to a sad, or witty to a foolish, why, she presently begins to mistrust herself. You must approach them i' their own height, their own*

line; for the contrary makes many that fear to commit themselves to noble and worthy fellows, run into the embraces of a rascal. If she love wit, give verses, though you borrow 'em of a friend, or buy 'em, to have good. If valour, talk of your sword, and be frequent in the mention of quarrels, though you be staunch in fighting. If activity, be seen o' your barbary often, or leaping over stools, for the credit of your back. If she love good clothes or dressing, have your learned council about you every morning, your French tailor, barber, linener, etc. Let your powder, your glass, and your comb be your dearest acquaintance.

Let cunning be above cost. Give cherries at time of year, or apricots, and say they were sent you out o' the country, though you bought 'em in Cheapside.

But there are other reasons why *The Silent Woman* beckons us toward the Restoration. Two of them are plain enough: the scene of *The Silent Woman* is London, the subject is in great part sex. One mark of Restoration comedy is that the reality of London quite equals the artificiality of the plot. Half the secret of the comedy of manners lies in the fact that while there is more rouge than flesh to the characters, the world they inhabit is recognizable and familiar. We might almost say that in such comedies the people cannot be real and the places have to be. Real—and most often fashionable; there must be references to the "right" places—or the wrong ones—to shop or dine at, to gamble or drink in. For a contemporary audience, such references are not only an enjoyable snobbery, but valuable short-cuts. *We* would know exactly what today's playwright wished to convey by referring to the Stork Club or the St. Regis, or the Ivy and the Savoy Grill. But when several centuries have passed, the reference will probably perplex to the precise degree that it once shed light; we may try to guess, but the name may be more imposing that the thing, and what we take to be a palace may emerge a pub, and what sounded the essence of gentility may be quite beyond the pale. We may thank God for that race of burrowers who set us right in footnotes.

It is not just the sense of London, however, that gives *The*

Silent Woman its Restoration stamp. *The Alchemist* is laid in London, without suggesting Restoration comedy at all. But in *The Silent Woman* there is great concern with sex on something like Restoration terms—in terms, that is to say, of intrigue and gallantry. The Collegiate Ladies, with their hard, frivolous, licentious natures and their knowing comments suggest a new style of amorousness, veneered rather than lusty, callous rather than carefree. Sir Dauphiné's relations to them, again, show not a particle of warm-blooded responsiveness, not to speak of romance. About *The Silent Woman* there is a kind of coldness, a fashionable want of heart, not elsewhere found in Jonson: elsewhere people, though vicious, are intense; though inhuman, have fanatic desires. Whatever Mania is, it isn't cold: yet even Morose—perhaps because malevolence is what chiefly impels him—has rather a cold air. And we are among people, too, whose social milieu, though not clearly defined, is yet not irrelevant: people well enough placed for sexual dalliance to go hand-in-hand with social leisure. We can sniff here the life to come.

Money, which is Jonson's great theme, still underlies the action; but no longer dominates it. For of course it is Dauphiné's craving to be Morose's heir (and fear that he won't be) that sets the whole plot in motion. Rather than not inherit, Dauphiné will go to devilish lengths; and rather than make Dauphiné his heir, Morose will gamble on matrimony. But the terms differ greatly from those in *Volpone* or *The Alchemist*, and the tone differs even more. On Dauphiné's side we get no sense of villainy; it is all done, rather, in sport; it is the story of youth at the mercy of crabbéd age, of one who loves life at the mercy of one who hates it. That, of course, is the way to take the sting out of a Dauphiné's craftiness and darken the figure of a Morose; that is part of the scheming of playwrights rather than of their characters; it substitutes a convention for a conviction, it means that the cook is pandering to the taste of the guests. Yet we might notice that the money-motive is precisely what Ben Jonson *added* to the plot. The silent woman who became a babbler, the woman who was all the time a man: these Jonson borrowed. But the nephew plotting to inherit his uncle's fortune,

Jonson himself thought up. His theory of humors will not take us far with him, and did not take him far himself: it is but a small crystallization of his general mastery of the fantastic, the hyperbolic, the grotesque, of what made Jonson a great satirist and a great rhetorician. The heart of his work, the hard realistic implacable core round which the tangle of extravagance grows is money. It represents God and Devil, in an age when both were vividly menacing. Much that was comic in Jonson's time lived on, and much else came into being. But one thing went out of English stage comedy for good—intensity. The one man who might have brought it back, though doubtless too impurely, and at too great a cost in sentimental melodrama— a man, at any rate, who passionately loved the stage—was Dickens.

CHAPTER III

Etherege

An author's being wellborn is decidedly no proof that his work will be well written. It is true that two of France's great writers were dukes; that James I of Scotland wrote a charming love poem; that Lady Mary Wortley Montagu wrote admirable letters; that Byron and Shelley and Dryden had genius. But the wellborn oftener tend to write like Queen Victoria, who actually underlined hundreds of words she had better omitted. Considering their opportunities for leisure and culture, there are perhaps fewer good high-placed writers than we should imagine; but considering their opportunities for enjoyment and self-indulgence, there are more than we might expect. Writing a good play or novel takes almost as much time and labor as it does talent. Nor is there much social incentive among the well-born. Society doesn't mind if its members write skillfully, but it minds even less if they don't. It is rather pleased should one of its kind be witty; but it scarcely expects him to be. Most of the great society wits—a Sheridan, a Sydney Smith, an Oscar Wilde —have been outsiders; and in the end it is perhaps easier to buy wit as one does cloth than to make it at home.

But in all this the Restoration was rather different. Many of its wellborn people were witty; many, even, were talented. Society not only repeated all kinds of good remarks; it coined them. Society not only went to the playhouse; it tended to write the plays. And this means, by and large, the most dissipated and cynical part of society—the very people who stayed up late breaking all the commandments; who drank and gambled when they might have been reading and writing; and who, for that matter, were dead and buried when they should have been at the peak of their careers. No question about it, they led shocking lives and wrote shocking plays. But equally they led stylish lives and wrote stylish plays; and were as witty when alone with their pens, as in company, over the wine. And there is something rather remarkable about a group of wastrels who should be almost as concerned with the portrayal as with the pursuit of pleasure. But they were; and as a result, these gentlemen-authors produced a most indecorous literature, yet a real literature of a kind.

Lord Rochester, Lord Dorset, Sir Charles Sedley, Sir George Etherege, the Duke of Buckingham—and Dryden, though he was so much more than a gentleman; and Congreve, though he came so long after the rest. Never, certainly, have we been so forcibly reminded that the Poets Corner is only a stone's throw from the House of Lords. And it is with the atmosphere created by these men that we must begin any examination of Restoration comedy; for though artificial in itself, it mirrors much that is real. These men wrote, more than we may imagine, about the sluts they knew and the rakes they were and the childish, brutal pranks they played; about their own foppishness and heartlessness, their wish to dazzle and need to ridicule. Strictly autobiographical these plays are not, but they perhaps come as close to autobiography as to fiction. Rochester and Etherege, for example, took part in a notorious prank that began with tossing fiddlers in a blanket and ended with one of their victims dying of his wounds. The marvel is that in coming close to autobiography, they yet managed to come even closer to art; that they should have known—for that in the end, is what it comes down to— what to do with words. But they did, and all the more remarkably for refusing to work very hard; for insisting that they were gentlemen, amateurs, dilettantes who wrote when they had nothing else to do. Obviously they were poseurs; but just as obviously, they were not plodders: they worked more than they pretended, but much less than most people who have worked as well. The result is as we might imagine: often careless, often capricious, sometimes thin and plagiarized and faked; but in addition to its merits, it had only the amateur, not the professional, vices.

These men are so much the symbols, and so little less the actual comedy voices of their age, that we, like the textbooks, must begin with one of them; with Etherege, whose *Comical Revenge*, or *Love in a Tub* has most often the honor of ringing up the curtain on the Restoration stage. It is one of a very few honors that can in all conscience be conferred upon the play, which is neither very good in itself nor very typical of its period. The date is 1664. Most of *Love in a Tub* could be dated much earlier and assigned to a much less distinguished hand; yet it gives evidence of both its author and its age, and contains just enough talent to explain the great success it had when it was first brought out. Like so much youthful work, it is a pastiche; there are four distinct elements to the plot, and they conflict far more than they ever combine. One of the four must have creaked even in the 1660's; another is straight out of Elizabethan comedy; a third is a trivial interpolation. But the fourth element is substantially new, and sounds the note that is to reverberate, or at least tinkle prettily, throughout the age.

The perennial plot is technically the principal one. It is sheer balderdash about young lovers, and enjoys the depressing honor of being done in verse. The heroine, Graciana, had been plighted to a cavalier officer named Bruce; but while Bruce was long away, she fell in love with Lord Beaufort. In time, of course, Bruce comes back, and Graciana's suitors, being both the soul of honor, must duel over her; and Bruce almost die of his wounds; and Graciana renounce Beaufort from a sense of guilt. But Graciana has a sister with a passion for Bruce, so that instead of no marriages there are eventually two. What is most tedious about this is less the plot itself than the statuesque effects compelled upon it by heroic couplets.

The second element in *Love in a Tub* has no relation to the first; characters in the two groups hardly so much as meet. The second element concerns two sharpers out to rook an upstart simpleton, and is the stock-in-trade, indeed the dominant subject matter, of countless Elizabethan comedies. It is a holdover, where the romantic plot is sheer hand-me-down; it is done nicely at times, with a certain relish and even a certain Restoration air; and it gains by contrast, being done in prose. The third element is chiefly notable for giving the play its title, and tells how an insolent French valet is put in a tub while drugged and asleep, and must thereafter go about with the tub on his back. This is no more than a prank or crude piece of vaudeville; while the servant himself, talking outlandish dialect, is as dreary as he seems superfluous.

What remains—the story of the wealthy widow and Sir Frederick Frollick—is substantially new, and alone does credit to the author. Here, amid the romantic waxworks, the Elizabethan stereotypes, and the crude and dismal slapstick, there enters, in just the right clothes, at just the right gait, with just the right swagger in his walk and right banter on his lips, the Restoration gallant. Here is a figure that reels home drunk today at dawn, and fetches up an amour or an imbroglio tomorrow; who keeps a woman, goes upstairs with a wench, and flirts archly and easily with a widow, and at length marries the widow. The widow, for her part, is eager to catch Sir Frederick, who has money and position. The real point, however, is not the sort of characters they are but the bantering relationship they achieve, the lightness and insouciance of their give-and-take. There is nothing scabrous or gross or leering about it; it remains froth without scum. One is always as conscious of something social as of something sexual, of a play of minds and a matching of wits. There is a true realistic basis for Sir Frederick and his widow, and they achieve a true comedy effect. Theirs are modulated human voices; all the other people use falsetto, or frigidly orate, or talk impossible stage dialect.

In his next play, *She Wou'd If She Cou'd*, Etherege—and the Restoration with him—begin to come into their own. The dif-

ference between it and *Love in a Tub* is more than strict stage
merit will explain. In terms of plot and character, parts of *She
Wou'd If She Cou'd* seem old, as other parts seem borrowed. But
in terms of the play as a whole, there is a good deal more that
is new, and what there is seems a great deal more important.
Here we find that quality that especially typifies and glorifies
Restoration comedy—airiness. Artifice, which at the outset used
stilts and then its feet to walk on, has been given wings and
begun to fly. One of the great paradoxes of Restoration comedy
here first asserts itself: though almost all the conversation and
almost all the plot are concerned with sex, the human body has
almost no *physical* importance. Sex is a springboard for wit, for
social make-believe, for intellectual dalliance; becomes now a
kind of game, now a kind of spelling-bee, now a kind of dance—
most of all, a kind of hare-and-hounds, with the chase far more
important than the capture. Sex is an obsession without being in
the least a passion. And because no one's heart is in it, sex in
Restoration comedy is at its worst thoroughly nasty; but at its
best, volatile and airy and gay. It runs a great gamut—all the
distance, one might say, from Watteau at his most charming to
Hogarth at his most brutal.

The best parts of *She Wou'd If She Cou'd* have this bright,
brisk airiness. The best parts concern two young ladies, Ariana
and Gatty, and two men about town, Courtal and Freeman.
And here we might first say that though the rest of the play has
very little merit, it does have a certain compactness. The story,
though complicated, doesn't sprawl; and the other characters,
though too familiarly outlined or fumblingly treated, have their
interesting or entertaining moments. Gone, at any rate, are the
worst aspects of *Love in a Tub*. There are no romantic lovers
spouting noble impossible sentiments in correctly corseted
rhyme; in fact, there is no rhyme. There are no separate plots
that lack even a nodding acquaintance with each other. There
are no crudities like the joke about the tub, and no characters
like the valet who carries the tub about. Here, the plot lines,
rather than not meeting at all, perhaps criss-cross too often.
But often amusingly. In Lady Cockwood, the "she" of the title,

Etherege had a chief character for keeping the plot in motion, as well as promising in itself. He did not handle it too well, but the Lady Cockwood type will always hold our attention; we are always alert to the sort of married woman who, whether over-vain or oversexed or both, must have a second man on her string; the sort of married woman, moreover, who has reached a certain age and was never at any age a belle. Lady Cockwood, for reasons of plot as well as character, is as mercilessly portrayed as the type can well be. She is not just a hypocrite who exploits to the full all her husband's slips from grace—for that, of course, makes good comedy; she is a spiteful, malicious woman who, to further her own intrigues or queer the pitch of other people's, callously involves whom she will. She is a little too rasping for the good of the play, and a little villainous where she might better be feline. But she mars the play's tone rather than its movement; and she has her excellent moments, as when—on the point of misbehaving herself—she catches out her husband and becomes the essence of injured virtue.

Lady Cockwood's husband, Sir Oliver, is conventional enough; but offers a measure of conventional fun. One of those clumsy, not-very-bright-even-when-sober, and not very often sober, country gentlemen on a visit to London, he has only the will, not the wit, to be a man about town; and not the graces, but only the wherewithal. Easily pleased, easily flattered, easily fooled, he is an eternal type, and perhaps too beery and noisy for comedy that aspires to elegance.

But the four lovers strike just the right note. They are so well matched as pairs that it means little if we never know which girl, at the end, is matched with which man. For what matters is the style of the courtship—if the right word is not campaigning. The two young ladies are wise after their kind—knowing, yet girlish, pert but not imprudent. They have wit, and spray their talk with it; they have charm, and splash it about: above all, they know how to mock at men in that sprightly way by which a girl shows not her malice but her mettle. It is precisely here that the quality of airiness is so decisive—on the one hand, for esthetic reasons, so as to balloon the play up into a region where everything seems to float and glide; and again for psychological reasons, so as to give these girls a touch that frees them from every taint. It is a question, with them, not of virtue but of grace: what counts is not how far they are flesh and blood, but how far they transcend it. And yet they are not girls meant for entirely elegant comedy: we come upon them not wearing pearls in the ballroom but wearing masks in the park. They are not mere jeunes filles, but the English translation of the phrase, with its change of meaning—young fillies; their uncle, indeed, always calls them Sly-girl and Madcap. This is important; they are minxes and flirts with just enough of the ingénue to make them charming; and with that basic innocence which, having nothing to be reticent about, sees no need for reticence.

There is less to say of the men, who are drawn well but to a familiar pattern. What matters is that they are a sufficient match for the girls, that they come in on cue and know the right answers. But because *they* must profess devotion where the girls may pretend to doubt; and because the girls are more of an age and the men for all time, the men at moments seem like a piano accompaniment rather than an answering voice. Nevertheless, the thing as a whole is a true duet of the sexes. Here is the first meeting in the Mulberry Gardens—so fashionable as to be "the only place of refreshment . . . for persons of the best quality to be cheated at":

Enter the Women, and after 'em Courtal at the lower Door, and Freeman, at the upper on the contrary side.

COURTAL: *By your leave, Ladies—*
GATTY: *I perceive you can make bold enough without it.*
FREE: *Your Servant, Ladies—*
ARIA: *Or any other Ladys that will give themselves the trouble to entertain you.*
FREE: *'Slife, their tongues are as nimble as their heels.*
COUR.: *Can you have so little good nature to dash a couple of bashful young men out of countenance, who came out of pure love to tender you their service?*
GATTY: *'Twere pity to baulk 'em, Sister.*

ARIA: *Indeed methinks they look as if they never had been slip'd before.*

FREE: *Yes faith, we have had many a fair course in this Paddock, have been very well flesh'd, and dare boldly fasten.*

(They kiss their hands with a little force.)

ARIA: *Well, I am not the first unfortunate woman that has been forc'd to give her hand, where she never intends to bestow her heart.*

GATTY: *Now, do you think 'tis a bargain already?*

COUR.: *Faith, would there were some lusty earnest given, for fear we should unluckily break off again.*

FREE: *Are you so wild that you must be hooded thus?*

COUR.: *Fy, fy, put off these scandals to all good Faces.*

GATTY: *For your reputations sake we shall keep 'em on: 'slife we should be taken for your Relations, if we durst shew our Faces with you this publickly.*

. . . .

FREE: *A good Face is as seldom cover'd with a Vizard-Mask, as a good Hat with an oyl'd Case: and yet on my Conscience, you are both Handsome.*

COUR.: *Do but remove 'em a little, to satisfie a foolish Scruple.*

ARIA: *This is a just punishment you have brought upon your selves, by that unpardonable Sin of talking.*

GATTY: *You can only brag now of your acquaintance with a Farendon Gown, and a piece of black Velvet.*

. . . .

GATTY: *Truly you seem to be men of great imployment, that are every moment ratling from the Eating-Houses to the Play-Houses, from the Play-Houses to the Mulberry-Garden, that live in a perpetual hurry, and have little leisure for such an idle entertainment.*

COUR.: *Now would not I see thy face for the world; if it should but be half so good as thy humour, thou woud'st dangerously tempt me to doat upon thee, and forgetting all shame, become constant.*

FREE: *I perceive, by your fooling here, that wit and good humour may make a man in love with a Blackamore. That the
Devil should contrive it so, that we should have earnest
bus'ness now.*

COUR.: *Wou'd they wou'd but be so kind to meet us here again
to morrow.*

GATTY: *You are full of bus'ness, and 'twould but take you off
of your employment.*

ARIA: *And we are very unwilling to have the sin to answer for,
of ruining a couple of such hopeful young men.*

FREE: *Must we then despair?*

ARIA: *The Ladys you are going to, will not be so hardhearted.*

This has a real Restoration swing about it; and the play, in
general, brings in a good deal about manners and fashions,
whether as social tidbits or satirical targets. Thus, when Sir
Oliver asks after certain strumpets, he is told: "Tis term time,
and they have severally betook themselves, some to their cham-
ber practice and others to the place of public pleading." This
brand of worldliness bears Etherege's trademark: the deeper,
more philosophic worldliness of a Ben Jonson, which doesn't
merely fizz and foam but bites like acid Etherege quite lacks.
(It is of course alien to airiness.) Etherege is no real satirist,
but largely a banterer; his satire stops, really, with the kind of
people—fops and the like—who, merely by existing, satirize
themselves. His wit is never very searching or brilliant, only
quick, easy, and well turned. But that has its own kind of merit:
it seems characteristic of those who utter it, rather than put into
their mouths.

In his last and most famous play, however, Etherege strikes
various notes that we do not quite expect. Written eight years
after *She Wou'd If She Cou'd*, *The Man of Mode* is one of the
more important Restoration comedies, and as interesting for
what is esthetically wrong with it as for what is right. Here
stands forth the comedy of manners in classic and often glittering
guise: here is the fashionable world of Restoration London re-
vealed with so sharp a sense of detail that we still catch its full

fashionableness today. If Jonson's *The Alchemist* is a kind of treatise on the ways and wiles of rogues, *The Man of Mode* is a kind of handbook on smart London life—on how to behave and misbehave, avoid scandal or advertise it, make love or seem to make it; what to wear, where to go, when to leave; how, quite literally, to add insult to injury; how to deceive a parent, a mistress, a lover, a friend; how, when practicing the lures of a spider or the stings of a wasp, to exhibit all the brightness and gaiety of a butterfly. No play could be frothier in its portrayal of manners; and no one a better figure of fun, a more delightful idiot, than the man of mode, than Sir Fopling Flutter himself. We shall say more of him later; what should be said here is that, along with the gloves-and-fans, the fops-and-fiddlers side of the play there is another, a colder and more brutal side. For if half *The Man of Mode* seems painted on a screen, in what were always delicate and now are slightly faded colors, another half— or almost half—seems mercilessly transcribed from life; seems like naked realism only very lightly veiled beneath the gauze of comedy. What alone sheathes the words and keeps them from stabbing outright is the stylish highbred rhythm of the prose. Etherege's Dorimant is not only a real rake, but a case-hardened worldling; and less hotblooded, in the end, than coldblooded. Mrs. Loveit is no ordinary mistress who resents being deceived or cast aside; hers is real erotic passion for Dorimant, real jealousy, real helplessness over her situation. Dorimant has, to be sure, a cynical Restoration wit, and Mrs. Loveit an accomplished Restoration waspishness, but the pair themselves are drawn to the life (if Lord Rochester was the model for Dorimant, that only makes him more authentic, not more real). The presence in all this of Belinda—who proves false to Mrs. Loveit from loving Dorimant, as he proves false to her from loving Harriet—adds a certain cynical harshness to the picture, and is needed for portraying Dorimant at full length; but it adds a touch of staginess as well.

Esthetically, you will have observed, there must be something amiss here: gay comedy and harsh realism are nestling under one blanket; what had seemed to be done in sport seems suddenly to be done in earnest. When we lose the sense of the *game* and are made mindful of the stakes, something has happened that is out of place in artificial comedy; and there can be no talking away the fact that beneath all the froth of *The Man of Mode* lies more than a drop or two of hemlock. Etherege blundered artistically by mixing realism and comedy, much as Fielding did in *Tom Jones*. But creatively Etherege, like Fielding, probably gained more than he lost: if less pure as a work of art, *The Man of Mode* is a bigger, more expressive piece of writing.

And if it fails to be quite a model for the emerging comedy of manners, it remains a most satisfying example of it. Here, to begin with, are those three favorite figures of artificial comedy —the rake, the coxcomb, and the scandalmonger. Medley, Etherege's scandalmonger, is not quite enough so; there is not malice enough to his prying, not wit enough to his malice. But Dorimant is one of the best, because one of the truest, of all society rakes; and Sir Fopling Flutter one of the best, because one of the most splendidly imaginary, of all coxcombs. From his first entrance—which is almost as long delayed as the celebrated first entrance of Tartuffe—he is one of the grandest fools in Christendom.

It is Sir Fopling's great merit, that however often he may allude to London or Paris, he himself has no existence in the real world. Only a master of the most delicate style could have made him come alive—or rather not come alive—in the theater. He must be all affectation and absurdity, yet somehow float, not mince. Anything emphatic would misrender him; anything merely effeminate would prove his ruin—the shoe-pointing, handkerchief-dangling, nose-wrinkling fellow who is standard for such parts is all wrong. So far as he can be made flesh at all, Sir Fopling is the offspring of an orchid and an idiot. Mere wit is almost dull when set against some of Sir Fopling's fancies: "I sat near one of those fellows at a Play today," he tells Mrs. Loveit, "and was almost poisoned with a pair of Cordivant gloves he wears." "Pox o' this apartment," he cries, going into Lady Townley's, "it lacks an antechamber to adjust oneself in." And he is perhaps best at the last, when he decides to give over courting Mrs. Loveit: "An intrigue now would be but . . . to throw away that Vigour on *one*, which I mean shall shortly make my Court to the whole sex in a ballet."

In terms of himself and the play alike, Sir Fopling is mere decoration: a play-within-a-play almost, for the other characters are as much diverted by him as we are. Though of very unequal value, these others form a representative group; representing in part the London society of their time, in part the London stage. The other men of the piece, Old and Young Bellair, are fairly stock: Old Bellair, here the heavy father, there the elderly beau; Young Bellair, a half-rakish, half-romantic man-about-town, never above sinning but not beyond virtue. He is a kind of dead center for the play. He isn't heartless like Dorimant, or bloodless like Medley, or all beer and no foam like his father, or all foam and no beer like Sir Fopling. But if he lacks excesses, he lacks individuality as well, and bulks far larger in the plot than in our memories.

The three principal women have more character—and less charm—than we might suppose of Etherege. There is no mere ingénue among them, Harriet being, like the girls in *She Wou'd If She Cou'd*, too pert. She has charm at moments, but never their charm, or *their* high spirits either; and though she and Young Bellair, in the scene where they pretend to be in love, are playing an even more elaborate game than Ariana and Gatty with their gallants, Harriet, we feel at times, is displaying not her mettle but her malice. It is Dorimant, in his relation to Mrs. Loveit and Belinda, who makes us feel this; for Dorimant is a real man who casts a real shadow, and causes Harriet to be more than merely lively. Harriet and he catch the sunlight at the end: but with Mrs. Loveit his relations are all storm, and with Belinda all gray skies. Belinda can sniff her fate from the very start, from the way that Dorimant treats Mrs. Loveit:

> *He has given me the proof which I desired of his love,*
> *But 'tis a proof of his ill nature too.*
> *. . . I sigh to think that Dorimant may be*
> *One day as faithless and unkind to me.*

And much later, after they have been to bed together:

> *"What does that sigh mean?" Dorimant asks her.*
> *"Can you," she answers, "be so unkind to ask me? Were it to*
> *do again . . ."*
> *"We should do it, should we not?"*
> *"I think we should," Belinda answers—and goes on: "The*
> *wickeder man* you, *to make me love so well."*

There are no rose-colored glasses, no grace of distance or
haze of poetry about any of this. There is the sense of a very
hard man who knows his own strength and charm; and a woman
—two women—who, though knowing what he is, are helpless.
They berate him together, but betray each other for love of him.
Both having lost him at the end, Mrs. Loveit indulges in what
we might call the morality of regret: "All men are Villains or
Fools; take example from my misfortunes, Belinda; if thou
wouldst be happy, give thyself wholly up to goodness." Stock
advice, and as much inspired by sour grapes as a bitter heart,
but one is not untouched. Etherege himself was perhaps not
quite unscathed, for he too knew that life was not as he had tried
to live it—all beer and skittles. He strikes no very deep note,
nor seems more than momentarily concerned with anything beneath the surface, or near the heart, or beyond the power of a
new pretty face or fashion to smooth away. But like all those
others of his age whose watchword was pleasure, whose motto
was *Carpe diem*, he was haunted a little by the knowledge that
the night cometh. The frivolous and pleasure-loving, in their
own way, always must be: they have ever less to fall back on,
to look forward to. There is no emotion (in the usual sense) in
Etherege's plays; but there is a kind of faintly elegiac apprehension that evokes more than the plays themselves can be said
to express—as there is equally this morality of regret, born not
of any guilt for having sinned, but only of the forlornness that
has come in the wake of the sinning.

Something like this is to be found, or at any rate felt, in *The
Man of Mode;* something that without the realism of Dorimant,
Mrs. Loveit, and Belinda we would not have. But it should not

be over-stressed. Much oftener, much more dominantly, the play is gloves and fans and fops and fiddlers; an achievement of light, cool, easy but now foaming and even iridescent prose; a catalogue of sharp, gay, vivid details of London social life; a capturing of attitudes, a playing of jokes. That is what is most characteristic of Etherege and most valuable: for, if a minor figure, he is immensely accomplished in a field where it is not particularly easy to be accomplished at all.

CHAPTER IV

Wycherley

Wycherley follows Etherege, and they are most alike in being most unlike the other comedy writers of the Restoration proper and in being the two best men at their trade. But they are not greatly alike for all that, and their coming together may only the more conveniently set them apart. They have one further similarity, however: neither of them wrote much—Etherege turning out just three plays, Wycherley four. So small an output seems remarkable only of Wycherley: in Etherege we constantly feel the gentleman author, the courtier who is a good deal of a fop, and we would be surprised that any one so elegant should also prove industrious. But Wycherley is in very different case. He led, to be sure, much the same life of pleasure; he got involved with one of Charles II's best-known mistresses; he married a countess whom he met in a bookshop and who kept an eye on him even when he went to a tavern—he had to sit by an open window that she might be certain he was merely drinking. But though Etherege and Wycherley led much the same kind of life, they were different kinds of writers and different kinds of men. Etherege is clearly a minor writer, Wycherley essentially is not. Wycherley has a much more vigorous talent and much more violent emotions; he cannot, like Etherege, keep life under tissue paper in a bandbox; he cannot even keep life inside a drawing room or the confines of a park. His age and place in society led him to write for the theater with little restraint and with consistent coarseness and license. But in a later age he would almost certainly have turned novelist, and been more at home in the world of Fielding and Smollett. He was like them not cynical; like them robust rather than dandyfied; like them touched with humor rather than wit; like them, essentially a social critic rather than a social chronicler. A moral misfit in his own age, wallowing in sinfulness and stammering out repentance, he displays some of that self-consuming, self-poisoning rage that we associate with Swift. He is psychologically the most interesting of the Restoration comedy writers, and potentially the most significant. Yet only two of his four plays have any of the interest of major literature, and one of the two is to my mind a failure. Wycherley was just once able to master his age.

Wycherley professed to have written his first comedy when nineteen. This is possible only if we understand that it was substantially rewritten much later; it was not in any case produced till he was over thirty. Beyond the fact that internal evidence compels a later date upon it, it never seems much like the writing of nineteen. It has a coldness and a harshness born of experiencing life rather than of the shallow pretensions and assumptions of youth; and its best writing has a smack and briskness, even a smack and bite, that nineteen seldom attains to. I make the point, not to suggest that *Love in a Wood* has much merit, but only that it has such a lack of youthfulness. Its faults outweigh its virtues: it is tiresome, at any rate, rather oftener than it is enjoyable—but in a dull slow-paced professional way rather than an uncertain and immature one. Wycherley already knows how to write a play of sorts; how to handle dialogue; how to contrive those misunderstandings that keep the plot moving and delay the dénouement. He knows the tricks—only too well, it may be: one reason why *Love in a Wood* is but fitfully enjoyable is that there is too much of everything; too many characters, too many speeches, too many intrigues, too many asides. The whole thing seems mismanaged less by awkwardness than by excess: the multiple relationships, the need to shuttle from this one to that,

rob the play of pace; while the plethora of words takes the edge
off the wit. There is talent and even skill in this first play of
Wycherley's, yet after a time it exhausts our interest and even
our patience.

There is no need to summarize the play; and there is probably
no way to. Among other things, there are five separate ro-
mances, four of them glaringly unromantic. For such multiple
courtship, one would have to go to *As You Like It* and its lovers
wandering about the Forest of Arden. Here, too, the lovers wander about in the open air; not only is the play's title *Love in a
Wood*; its subtitle is *St. James' Park*. But it would be hard to
think of two plays more dissimilar in spirit than Shakespeare's
and Wycherley's; or of anything more pastoral than the Forest
of Arden or less so than St. James' Park. Each play, it is true,
contains one element that might better belong to the other.
Shakespeare's Jaques is bilious enough to have turned against
the world from having seen it lived on Wycherley's terms; and
Valentine and Christina, the two faithful ardent lovers of *Love in
a Wood*, descend from even more extravagantly idyllic comedies
than *As You Like It*. But where Jaques is of great help to *As
You Like It*, Valentine and Christina are a hindrance to *Love in a
Wood:* Wycherley makes them so conventional and stagey that
they have nothing idyllic about them, only something operatic.

For the rest, we are among people who have few virtues and
scant grace. They are not merely profligate, but treacherous;
not merely inconstant, but unkind; they behave as dishonorably
to their own sex as to the opposite one; and though never did a
play end with more people on their way to the altar, never was
there less feeling that marriage meant happiness. The very basis
for marriage among these people is curiously uncivil. As the
deplorable Dapperwit says to the still more deplorable Gripe:
"If you will rob me of my wench, sir, can you blame me for
robbing *you* of your daughter?" Seldom, even in Restoration
comedy, does one find that one's mistress has become one's
mother-in-law.

Old Gripe, moreover, had begun by lusting after Dapperwit's
wench; he had next been framed, broken in upon while trying to

seduce the young lady; then been blackmailed into giving her a large marriage portion; finally been led to think that as long as he had given her so much money, he might as well marry her himself. With his hypocrisies and his blood-sucking, Gripe is a stock character with two uses: in a melodrama, he can be a villain; in a comedy, a victim and a butt. Wycherley does pump a certain life into him; his scenes with Mrs. Joiner, the matchmaker who plays him false, are brisk and lively. Then there is Lady Flippant, most desperate of widows, on the lookout for a husband. Marriage is her one object in life, and a pretended dislike of marriage her one stratagem. But nobody is fooled by it, just as nobody is attracted by her. To be sure, she is married off at the end (in the general mêlée of misalliances) to a fortune-hunter who has not had good hunting. And, in line with the play, she is a hard satiric butt who appals rather than amuses us; there is a kind of furiousness and ugly passionateness of purpose about her not usual to the ordinary comic husband-hunting widow; most of her is straight out of the comedy of humors, and the rest is realistic. There is also the egregious Dapperwit, who professes to help Sir Simon get Gripe's daughter while all the time intending her for himself. Only once does he let self-interest lag; during the amusing moment when, rather than not complete a fancy figure of speech as the man of wit he is, he risks being caught out with Martha. This is a good touch, though scarcely in character; for Dapperwit is much more blackguard than fop. And indeed the whole play is less amusing than it might be, from frequently giving off a sense of hard scheming as well as foolish strut; of human faithlessness as well as sexual infidelity. In one way it comes as a relief not to find Lady Flippant merely silly in her husband-hunting or Dapperwit merely silly in his pretensions. But as everything else is excessive, so is the tone. *Love in a Wood* has often the harshness of a Ben Jonson play without the trenchancy or stature.

Yet *Love in a Wood* is an instructive play: it shows us a Wycherley colliding with his age rather than coming to terms with it. There is so much that he seems to feel must be satirized, must be stigmatized, and he goes at it somewhat in the style of a muckraker. If this is to be true comedy of manners, he must moderate his tone; and if his people are to be more fun for us, they must also be for him: there must be less animus and greater animation.

Wycherley's second play, *The Gentleman Dancing Master*, is very much simpler than *Love in a Wood*, and also more entertaining. With some indebtedness to a play of Calderón's, Wycherley has woven one of his own where things take place on such unconvincing terms that we must almost admire his impudence in expecting us to accept them. The story concerns a girl of fourteen kept behind closed doors by her hispanophile tyrant of a father till it comes time for her to marry her francophile fop of a cousin. The girl talks the cousin into bringing round a young Englishman that she may *pretend* to flirt with him; and when the Englishman is caught out by her father, she passes him off as her dancing master; and so on. The "and so on" actually contains the worst bits of impudence—thus, when the coast is clear for the girl and the Englishman (who have naturally fallen in love), the girl suddenly balks for no reason whatever. But it doesn't much matter that the father has to be considerable of a fool and the fop completely an idiot; for we are not once asked to be convinced, but only to be diverted. The treatment is everywhere as fantastic as the effect is farcical.

But farcical in comedy-of-manners terms, which means that the absurdities lie as much in talk as in action. The characters tend to write little essays about themselves; there is more embroidery than cloth to their roles; the father with his adoration of everything Spanish and the cousin with his adoration of everything French wind up like catalogues rather than characters. Their two manias do much less to enhance than to extinguish each other; and in the theater I would think that the play would seem hopelessly longwinded. But neither there nor in bookform would it seem boorish: with far more farcical situations than in *Love in a Wood*, Wycherley has managed to be far lighter in tone. None of the cliché-adjectives about Wycherley—coarse, high-spirited, brawny, racy—apply. The reason is obvious: beyond its altogether artificial plot, *The Gentleman Dancing Mas-*

ter is concerned with foibles, not vices; with manners, not morals; with deceptions that work out to every one's advantage, with characters who play set roles and spout set speeches: the heavy father, the silly coxcomb, the dragon-ish, duenna-ish aunt.

But though, thanks to its comedy-of-manners side, the play is a good deal airier than most farces (and most Wycherley), the air is not fresh air. The whole thing is almost as stale a joke as a plot. We have no sense, as we do in Etherege, of observing manners at first hand and even, on occasion, for the first time. Because Hippolyta is shut up in her father's house, we cannot help being shut up with her; but it might be any town house in any town in any bygone time. What we miss is the delineation of particular manners, of a particular society; the whole thing is curiously stock and old-fashioned; and for once the coarsest of the major Restoration comedy writers comes off, by Restoration standards at least, as rather tame.

I say by Restoration standards, because the well-known scene in which Hippolyta's maid throws herself at Hippolyta's fiancé is exactly like low French bedroom farce. Nothing could be more downright, more classical, more clinical in its humor. Nor is the scene near the end, when Mrs. Flirt lays down conditions for being kept by the fop, precisely tame, either. It is worth quoting, if only for anticipating at a raffish level a similar scene at a level so infinitely finer—the scene, of course, where the lady is Millamant and the subject not maintenance but marriage:

> FLIRT: *Then separate maintenance, in case you should take a wife, or I a new friend.*
> MONS.: *How! that too! then you are every whit as bad as a wife.*
> FLIRT: *Then my house in town and yours in the country, if you will.*
> MONS.: *A mere wife!*
> FLIRT: *Then my coach apart, as well as my bed apart.*
> MONS.: *As bad as a wife still!*
> FLIRT: *But take notice, I will have no little, dirty, second-hand chariot new furbished, but a large, sociable, well-*

painted coach; nor will I keep it till it be as well known as myself, and it come to be called Flirt-coach; nor will I have such pitiful horses as cannot carry me every night to the Park; for I will not miss a night in the Park, I'd have you to know.

MONS.: *'Tis very well: you must have your great, gilt, fine painted coaches. I'm sure they are grown so common already amongst you, that ladies of quality begin to take up with hackneys again, jarni!—But what else?*

FLIRT: *Then, that you do not think I will be served by a little dirty boy in a bonnet, but a couple of handsome, lusty, cleanly footmen, fit to serve ladies of quality, and do their business as they should do.*

MONS.: *What then?*

FLIRT: *Then, that you never grow jealous of them.*

MONS.: *Why, will you make so much of them?*

FLIRT: *I delight to be kind to my servants.*

MONS.: *Well, is this all?*

FLIRT: *No.—Then, that when you come to my house, you never presume to touch a key, lift up a latch, or thrust a door, without knocking beforehand: and that you ask no questions, if you see a stray piece of plate, cabinet, or looking-glass, in my house.*

MONS.: *Just a wife in everything.—But what else?*

FLIRT: *Then, that you take no acquaintance with me abroad, nor bring me home any when you are drunk, whom you will not be willing to see there when you see sober.*

The Gentleman Dancing Master is a minor play and, if successful at all, the most minor sort of success. Wycherley here would seem to be marking time and even to be playing safe; or perhaps, having hissed at vice and spat at treachery in *Love in a Wood*, he was momentarily relaxed and in a mood to be playful.

With *The Country Wife* we pass altogether out of the hothouse and breathe, not indeed country air, but the true air of Restoration London. This is a play about which there has been a certain disagreement. Mr. Dobrée treats it unequivocally as a masterpiece; William Archer, equally given to superlatives, called it "the most bestial play in all literature." The fact that two men of unusual critical discernment should hold such divergent opinions argues that the play has, at least, very positive qualities. And I think we can say that it represents all the qualities, whether favorable or frowned upon, for which Wycherley is known. It is vigorous and often brilliant; it portrays a society almost wholly lacking in either conscience or heart; and with almost no interruptions and no inhibitions, it is occupied with sex. For once, there is almost no concern over money, ro fop for decoration, no scandalmonger to spew bile, no old maid or widow to drip acid. There is one gentleman who prides himself on being a wit, but only as that should put him above being jealous.

Probably men will argue forever over what is the most compulsive of human hungers; but there can be no argument that it is one of three. Either, as Balzac insists, it is money; or as La Rochefoucauld contends, it is vanity; or as the Freudians and at this point Wycherley would say, it is sex. I would myself argue for vanity, from whose demands there is simply no let-up, and which dictates a good deal of our feeling about money and sex. But that is by the way: what is worth noticing is that these three hungers dominate the writing of comedy. What makes men more knavish than money, or more foolish than vanity, or more brutish than sex? What makes men lie more to themselves than vanity; or to others than money; or to women than sex?

If we halt briefly to discuss the role of sex, not in life but simply in literature, it is because in literature—as opposed to mere reading-matter—sex reflects as well as represents something, and can be treated in as many ways as there are human philosophies and artistic forms. The treatment can be predominantly romantic or realistic or naturalistic; or puritanical or hedonist; or lyric or heroic or tragic; or comic or satiric or farcical. It is not always referred to as sex; in its more exalted aspects it is called ecstasy; there are times when it is called madness; there are countless times when it is called sin. Like all things that comedy is ready to pounce on, it is something that many people have an impulse to hide. Almost the whole genteel tradition in literature is concerned with putting draperies over our three great hungers—vanity, money and sex—and rose-colored glasses on us.

My main reason for adverting to all these attitudes toward sex is to suggest that sex cannot be profitably dealt with in literature without reflecting one of them. It cannot be dealt with simply as a commodity and possess any value; I would even think that it cannot be dealt with simply as a commodity and possess much lure. For when it seems to be treated so, as in the average movie or best-seller, it is *not* offered as a mere commodity—but as rather a pipe dream or forbidden fruit. Even for sex to seem pleasantly pagan it needs a touch of poetry about it. When an Elizabethan writer asks, what can be lovelier than a young man and a young woman alone together in a green bower of a May morning, we think, very physically and directly, of sex: but of sex in the perfect setting, and of sex at the perfect age. It is charming poetry. But a middle-aged man and a middle-aged woman alone together in an apartment hotel of a January afternoon are not poetry: without some attitude toward their relationship, without their seeming comic or pathetic or frustrated, one would scarcely read on.

Sex is the mainspring of Restoration comedy for more reasons than one. As is obvious, so much profligacy under Charles II was the natural result of too much repression under Cromwell. And in literature even more than in life; for it had probably been suppressed even more in literature than in life. The theaters had been closed down for a generation—a generation, be it remembered, when there were no novels. At the Restoration, sex —always the most interesting subject to the largest number of people—would come back into literature with a rush, and with a total lack of restraint. And it would do so all the more, for being the most interesting of subjects to the King: the one man who now could act as censor had no wish to. And sex bulked so large not only for being an imperious human appetite, but because it helped express an emerging social attitude. The Puritans were everywhere now portrayed as hypocrites, and as hypocrites, above all, in sexual matters. Hence a crusade against hypocrisy arose; from having pretended to virtues it did not possess, society now pretended to vices. But the more common intellectual mode was to pretend to nothing: one's place at court, one's place in society, was helped rather than harmed by one's being a gambler or a drunkard or a rake.

Thus, though there may have been prudential motives for a wellborn young girl to remain chaste, or for a married woman to remain faithful, of moral pressure there was very little; and there was even less moral pressure on anything else. Sex, to Restoration society, had become a kind of ubiquitous game, where it was something of a disgrace to be cuckolded, but none whatever to cheat; and all this is mirrored and no doubt magnified in Restoration comedy. But a second point to remember, hardly less important than the first, is that the great bulk of Restoration comedy is concerned with the leisure classes. Its people, with nothing but time on their hands, had every incentive to dalliance and every opportunity to dally. Wherever they went, it would seem—to the playhouse, to the park, to balls and masquerades—it was with an eye to an adventure or an assignation. The very fact that society women went masked indicates not only what they themselves contemplated but what the whole age countenanced. A world of false faces, moreover, scarcely suggests a world of true hearts. It was additionally a world of made marriages, where there was no love even at the outset, and where a woman most valued a husband because she might more safely, now, acquire a lover.

It was an age of gallantry—one that distrusted virtue, one that misdoubted love. And, in good society, it was so much an age of leisure that the joke is at the expense of those who lacked leisure. The butt of these comedies is almost always some alderman or City knight who is still concerned with making money and has not the time, or always the inclination, to watch over his wife. And as portrayed by these gentlemen-writers, he is often socially snubbed in the same breath with being sexually deceived. Sometimes, to be sure, the cuckold is simply middle-aged in a group of people generally younger; but, again, he is far less often a middle-aged man of birth than a middle-aged man of business. Hence, for the purposes of a Wycherley or an Etherege, he is doubly comic. In our present society, a business-man of fifty is the solidest of citizens. In Restoration society, he was near neighbor to a villain: he was an upstart who wore horns.

We ought not forget, for it has much to do with the sover-eignty of sex, that in point of age Restoration society was a curiously youthful one. Lords and ladies were often dead, or mad, or diseased at fifty; most of them had lost their looks much earlier; and their reputations earlier still. And young people, bred up to the pursuit of pleasure and given to realize how short would be pleasure's span, would be peculiarly heartless as well. If any one had told a typical Restoration young couple to look to their elders for guidance, he would have been answered with a horse laugh—and told to look to their elders himself (if they still were alive or at large).

Of all this *The Country Wife* is the epitome. It portrays not simply a society dominated by sex, but a society whose sexual activity is the key to its general composition. The curtain goes up on Horner; and Horner is the center of the play. Just back in London from France, he has thought up a great scheme (though Terence thought it up first). A notorious rake, he will pretend to have met with disaster in France and been rendered impotent. He will make a butt of himself as a way of making secret con-quests of a host of women, and of making cuckolds of their husbands. He will be a worse menace, and have the greater em-pire, for seeming harmless; and while being publicly scoffed at, will secretly gloat. There is more than method in his stratagem: there is malice. He is to sex what Volpone is to gold; and, as with Volpone, the game itself means as much as the rewards. But the rewards will be great, too; and Horner is not least amused by the smug, contemptuous way with which husbands *thrust* him into the company of their wives, as a harmless fellow to gossip or play cards with. This co-operation from the hus-bands is the cream of the jest. Horner, even more than Volpone, lacks conventional vanity; he is as willing to seem impotent as a smart gambler is to seem a dub or a crack diplomatist to seem a duffer.

So Sir Jasper Fidget—a bustling man of affairs in this world of gaping leisure—thrusts Horner upon his lady wife; and she is no bad match for him. She is one of the most finished portraits of a truly lecherous and conniving woman to be found: so proper a lady that when Sir Jasper speaks of "the naked truth" she chides him for using such a word as "naked"; and to Horner, when their talk turns free, she protests, "Come, let's not be smutty." Nor is this mere crude satire. It goes deeper into human nature, into what might be called the compartmented self: Lady Fidget has superficially become what she wants others to think she is; she brings to mind somebody's remark that the greatest hypocrite is the person who does not know he is a hypocrite. As one can smile and smile and be a villain, so the Lady Fidgets can shudder and shudder and be a slut. And she keeps suitable company, as Horner finds out: in no time he has got himself a harem.

In this panoramic study of sex, Horner is flanked by two men of his acquaintance, who are at extremes to each other. Pinchwife is the violently jealous man: enough of a town rake to know all the ways of town women, he has married an ignorant country girl and is determined to stand guard over her, to suspect every move she may make and every move made toward her. At the other extreme is Sparkish, who, engaged to Pinchwife's sister, refuses to be jealous on any account, to be suspicious for any reason. Psychologically speaking, Sparkish takes the wiser course; for Alithea, his fiancée, is a decent and honorable girl who feels she cannot deceive any one so trusting (where Pinchwife's country wife is driven as much by resentment as by desire to emulate city ways). But Wycherley was in a mood, as both prankster and moralist, to punish the trusting and the jealous man alike; to deprive Pinchwife of a faithful wife because he cared too selfishly, and deprive Sparkish of a wife far above his deserts because he did not really care at all.

As a sort of Vanity Fair of sex, *The Country Wife* is probably without a rival in Restoration or any other period of English literature. We can have nothing but praise for the fullness of the picture; nothing but praise for the force. Much of the time, moreover, the play romps wickedly from scene to scene, with a vital comic gusto, a tremendous farcical abandon. If Pinchwife with his jealousy, and Sparkish with his refusal to be jealous, are foils to each other and targets for Wycherley; so Lady Fidget, with her accomplished dissembling, and Margery Pinchwife, with her rapturous naïveté, offer an even livelier contrast; while Alithea, the nearest the play comes to a true heroine, is by no means wishy-washy. *The Country Wife* has, besides, considerable verbal explicitness. "Women of quality," Horner remarks, "are so civil, you can hardly distinguish love from good breeding, and a man is often mistaken." And Horner, at the end, says to Lady Fidget:

> *Faith, madam, let us pardon one another; for all the difference*
> *I find betwixt we men and you women, we forswear ourselves at*
> *the beginning of an amour, you as long as it lasts.*

And we get a whiff of the fair-dealing of the age in Quack's remark: "As at first a man makes a friend of the husband to get the wife, so at last you are fain to fall out with the wife to be rid of the husband." The play is full of those similes that Wycherley is fonder of than skillful at: "A woman masked, like a covered dish, gives a man curiosity and appetite" or "Marrying to increase love is like gaming to become rich; alas! you only lose what little stock you had before."

If epigrams are not Wycherley's forte, certainly plausibility isn't. Perhaps one needn't gag too much over the characterization of the country wife (who seems almost as knowing at moments as she seems naïve at others) for she is a woman, and this is a farce. And conceivably some defense can be made for Sparkish's utter refusal to be suspicious of Harcourt or jealous of Alithea—the defense that he is a comedy-of-humors character, whose mania is a *lack* of jealousy. But at least once in the play, no defense is possible: Harcourt's dressing himself up as his non-existent priest of a brother is not only incredible but puerile. Yet this masquerade is at least at the expense of an

insanely unjealous man, where Margery's dressing up as Alithea
and getting Pinchwife to lead her all the way to Horner's, is at
the expense of an insanely jealous one—and of her own husband
to boot! One need not adduce all the evidence of this sort. The
important fact is that it is so glaring and frequent that it does
more than affect the play's plausibility; it badly impairs its tone.
This is not a new fault in Wycherley—*The Gentleman Dancing
Master* taxes our credulity quite as much. And the fault is easy
to understand, if not to forgive: for Wycherley is among those
robust writers with whom it is the constant movement, the com-
posite effect, that counts; he is not dandiacal like Etherege or
elegant like Congreve. He is quite the opposite—as man and
writer alike, he runs to extremes, to excess. As a sex comedy,
The Country Wife might almost be called lurid. No one seems
to have reached out toward London life with a greater sense of
enjoyment than Wycherley, or afterwards to have recoiled from
it with a greater sense of disgust. He is the great pagan of
Restoration comedy; but he is also the great Puritan.

It was not frustration that made a moralist of him, but satiety;
not lofty thinking but loose living; not an appeal to ethics but a
recoil from experience. He was a full-blooded man first, and
only a bilious one afterwards. And as man, so was the playwright. He must first create freely and robustly; and only then
harshly and mordantly criticize. The two sides of him really
present one picture, but in different lights and with opposite
effects, like a photograph and a negative; and they sometimes
give a twofold value to a single quality. Certainly, up to a point,
the thing that for centuries has most made *The Country Wife* a
scandal has also most made it a sermon. There is no use pretending that Horner's famous china scene is not fully as indecent
as it is amusing. There is no use pretending that a comedy that
turns upon a rake's making out he is impotent is not appealing
to a very definite side of its audience. We may be past the Victorian reaction of a Macaulay, who compared Wycherley to a
skunk, or the Edwardian reaction of a William Archer, dubbing
this "the most bestial play in all literature"; we may be past it
in tolerance because, for one thing, we have got past it in in-

sight. But neither can we accept it as a mere invitation to smack our lips, and in the same breath shrug our shoulders. The question is not one of prudishness but of proportion; and though the fun far outruns the smut, the smut must—if only because it can seem so calculated—give us qualms.

But the thing, as I said, that for centuries has most made *The Country Wife* a scandal has most made it a sermon. The play is so indecent because Restoration life was so indecent. We are appalled because we were meant to be appalled; Wycherley never intended us to be enraptured. The gusto with which he painted Horner should not lead us to suppose that he meant him for a good fellow; he meant him for a bad fellow, as certainly as Ben Jonson meant Volpone. Though Margery is not without a certain appeal, we are not to suppose that because *she* was unfortunate in having Pinchwife for a husband, we would have been fortunate in having her for a wife. To the extent that the characters sharpen their wits against one another, this is legitimate and traditional comedy enough; but to the degree that they harden their hearts against all that is fair and honorable in life, this is harsh, protesting satire. No doubt a certain sort of prude could only be disgusted by this play without ever being amused. The most tolerant of us, on the other hand, could hardly be amused without ever being disgusted. But, for too long, what is revolting in the picture has been glibly confused with what is salacious. Who, however much amused by *Gulliver's Travels*, is not sometimes disgusted? But salaciousness is there not much in question—though bestiality is—hence even your prude will allow that *Gulliver* is amusing and Swift a moralist.

However Wycherley may have misused sex in *The Country Wife*, he was sound in making it the pervasive fact of his play. For through sex alone could he show what he wished to show, reflect what he wished to reflect; with sex alone could he find the right key to a callous, cold-hearted, dissolute Restoration society. Money, no doubt, made possible their way of life; but these leisure-class people were overwhelmingly concerned not with making but with spending it. Ambition doubtless played a great role in their scheme of things, but not in their day-to-day existence. These people are not, after all, the great nobility, but only the lesser fry. It was physical pleasure they cared most about—which is to say, their *own* pleasure. It wasn't simply what they did to each other, it was how they did it; not out of weakness or necessity, but out of all lack of affection and principle. We may suppose that *The Country Wife* exaggerates, but not that it misrepresents. For all that it romps like the liveliest farce, it is a serious play, a key play. One can study textbooks and source material and documents in the British Museum—as no doubt one must—to become an expert on Restoration facts. But half a library of all such things probably counts less than *The Country Wife* if one would become an expert on Restoration feeling. It hardly seems to me the masterpiece it does to Mr. Dobrée; but nothing could be more vigorously expressive, or more central to its period.

In *The Country Wife*, Wycherley not only penetrated to the center of his world, he remained close to the center of comedy also. He is not too angry to keep others from being amused; and whatever its ultimate meaning, the play is in mood a farce— much of the time, in fact, a roaring and lively farce. In his last produced play, however, Wycherley went completely out of bounds. Starting off in *Love in a Wood* with an excess of material, he wound up, in *The Plain Dealer*, with an excess of emotion. In it he lashes out too violently at the life he knew too well; too violently, indeed, to preserve the sense of that life. The play's reality crumbles beneath the playwright's rage. The picture we see painted, beyond seeming incredible, keeps calling attention to the man who is painting it. Wycherley is so anxious to indict, so determined to punish, that he wildly, feverishly, portrays all manner of crime.

Many people, to be sure, regard *The Plain Dealer* as Wycherley's masterpiece—more people, it may be, than regard *The Country Wife*. And certainly in some ways it is a staggering performance, a work crammed with vigor and talent, harsh satire and savage bite. But—at however impressive a level—it seems to me a failure as art, a failure as comedy. Under our very eyes we see its force splintering into violence, its wine turning to vinegar. For anyone to be effectively *appalled*, he must feel a simultaneous sense of horror and of truth; he must accept what only a little earlier he could scarcely have imagined. That is what we do in *The Country Wife* and fail to do here. For in *The Country Wife* we are offered a picture of a shocking but actual society, where here we are given the vision of an enraged and half-hallucinated man. Wycherley wields his club with massive force here, but with wildly faulty aim.

He begins—and so may we—with the figure of the plain dealer himself. We will postpone for the moment all comparison between Wycherley's plain dealer, Manly, and Molière's misanthrope. For this is very much Wycherley's own play; and Manly is created, not indeed in Wycherley's own image, but out of his black thoughts and lacerated moral emotions. Manly is already disgusted by the shams, the duplicities, the indecent self-seeking of London society. A sea captain who prefers honest rough weather to treacherous calms, he has acquired the sea's roughness along with its honesty, and a sea captain's confidence in his own best judgment along with his need to judge. Manly is so proud of being frank, he never asks whether he may not be brutal; is so proud of having a mind of his own, he never wonders if he may not misread things. "Now I speak ill," he says, "of most men because they deserve it; I that can do a rude thing, rather than an unjust thing." You see the virtue of his position; you see also what vast encouragement it gives him to be rude. He has reached the point of being as bilious as society is tainted; and would be not glad, but sorry, to have his opinion of it disproved. He is a little like the man one sometimes meets who thinks all literary or music critics either stupid or crazy or corrupt, so that he increasingly regards himself as infallible.

Or rather, there is *one* music or literary critic whom our man makes an exception of and swears by; just so Manly exempts from his indictment Olivia, who is his fiancée, and Vernish, who is his friend. These two he wholly admires and trusts: indeed he has bestowed all his money on Olivia—"I can never doubt," he tells Freeman, "her truth and constancy."—"It seems," Freeman answers, "you do; since you are fain to bribe it with

money." And of course it is Manly's fiancée and his friend who
are destined to betray him. So far our story is familiar enough,
and its irony is, if anything, too familiar. Yet it could be persuasive; and we could accept equally the poetic justice and the
human injustice of the story. But Wycherley was treating of no
ordinary betrayal, and of no ordinary victim. His Olivia is not
just a spotted worldling, treacherous because greatly tempted,
or unfaithful because easily lured; his Vernish is not one of those
worldlings by education and weaklings by nature who have
neither the moral starching nor the personal stamina to hold
firm. By people such as these, sadly lacking in character, a man
of great strength of character might easily be fooled: strength
can never quite comprehend weakness. But Olivia and Vernish
are not passive betrayers, or even clever compunctionless self-
seekers; they are utter villains, who do not betray Manly simply
for gain, but betray him gloatingly and malignantly—and in
partnership. Olivia, in particular, not only commits every infamy against her suitor; she would also inflict every indignity
on him—through hating him outright, as it were, rather than
through feelings of guilt. Olivia has with some justice been
called another Vittoria Corombonna; and when a comedy writer
is brought into comparison with a blood-and-horror writer like
Webster, conceivably the Comic Muse has strayed off her own
preserves.

But if Olivia and Vernish are no passive betrayers, Manly is no
easy victim. When he learns how Olivia has used him and what
she thinks of him, we get some notion of how hellish and furious
can be a gentleman scorned: Manly, still raging with desire for
Olivia, and now aching for revenge, plots to possess her under
cover of being some one else, and then to publish his having had
her to the town at large. Thus Manly, on being made a victim,
turns villain himself; and despite his hatred of dissembling, turns
complete dissembler.

To be sure, Wycherley might have meant to show how, in
the very act of resisting the corruption of his age, Manly so
strongly felt its pressure as to be himself corrupted. But we feel
that Wycherley meant no such thing—not just because of the

alacrity with which Manly embarks on retaliation, but because of the alacrity with which Wycherley lets him, in succumbing to his baser self, regain the upper hand. Manly gets revenge indeed, gets back his money, gets back his right to feel that among all the depravity of London rare angels do exist. He wins, at the end, Fidelia; or rather she, poor girl, wins him, having followed him around in men's clothes for years—saying nothing and being lovesick; shipping before the mast and getting seasick; enduring Olivia's endearments when she took Fidelia for a man, and Vernish's when he learned she was a woman. Fidelia, I would imagine, has times without number been compared to Shakespeare's Viola; but the comparison is even more incongruous than it is inescapable; and Fidelia throws the play even more out of kilter than its white devil of an Olivia does.

But Fidelia is also enlightening; for Wycherley, in bringing so selfless an angel into his noisome world, is committing Manly's mistake; is himself providing so wild an exception to the rule as to raise doubts about rule and exception alike. It at least helps to *characterize* Manly, that, with so low an opinion of society in general, he should yet have so exalted an opinion of his fiancée and his friend; but it entirely stigmatizes Wycherley that of a society so monstrous he should predicate a single exception so angelic. You may urge that Fidelia is much what she is because of the role she must play in the plot; but somehow, in situations like these, blunder begets blunder, and in the very plot he chooses the author is really plotting against himself.

For, among other things, *The Plain Dealer* is rather absurd as a result of being set down in rage. The whole thing suggests a man, and a comedy writer, and a satirist, and an artist, who has lost control. He has seen so much of Restoration society that he cannot stomach any of it. Out of a satiety of worthless pleasure has come an excess of revulsion; the pagan in Wycherley feels such nausea that he is in a rage against himself; and the Puritan in Wycherley can only turn it into a rage against society. Wycherley's mood, like Manly's, is not just one of indignation, but of revenge; and like Manly's, his revenge is misguided, intemperate, and a reflexion on himself. There is no incident, no character, no turn or twist of plot, however vicious, however unsuited to comedy, however unintentionally comic, that Wycherley is able to forego. He paints, as a result, a picture of really lurid infamy—not from wanting to be melodramatic, only from having to be mordant. Again and again, and harder and harder, he lashes out at Restoration society; but less and less do the blows tell, does the body bleed. For instead of feeling the Restoration's hatefulness we simply feel Wycherley's hate. And when Wycherley sets about striking a balance through Fidelia, no balance is possible; being at one extreme, he can only rush to the other; against pitch black he can only set pure white.

From any point of view—comic, realistic, tragic—the final point about Manly is not the mere rightness or wrongness of his attitude, or the goodness or badness of his nature, but the violence of his methods. Moderation he looks upon as compromise; conventional good manners as hypocrisy; social adjustment as personal surrender. The pattern of extremism is always the same: the exception must be made as white as everything else is black. Out of disgust for all other political systems comes a fanatical faith in Communism; out of a sense of the incorrigible wickedness of this world comes some zealotic formula for achieving Heaven. And with it, as with Manly, is born the self-righteousness that can embark upon revenge in the belief that it constitutes justice.

Wycherley *might* have intended Manly as a Horrible Example; unfortunately he projected him as his own alter ego. Wycherley is himself fanatical here: under the guise of comedy, he resorts to melodrama; in a black mood for realism, he goes so far that nothing whatever seems real. The play can be very powerful at its best; it can be fascinating and brilliant, but never sound. It is not so much hoist by its own petard as shattered to bits by its own dynamite. The whole thing, in a way, is extraordinary. For if there is any cliché of clichés about the Restoration, it is that it represents a world of cynicism, of people who raise their eyebrows and shrug their shoulders and turn their backs. And here is a play wrecked by all lack of commonsense, of skepticism, of proportion; here at the very fount of Indifference juts up the tousled head of Fury.

It is the sadder failure because there is in the play force enough for half a dozen successes. Although one does not respond as one should, one is certainly not unresponsive; one knows at least what Hazlitt meant when he said that whoever reads *The Plain Dealer* must be the better for it afterwards. And it would be mere extremism on one's own part to ignore or minimize the elements in the play that survive or stand outside its extremism. Thus Freeman, who acts as Manly's confidant (if a plain speaker may be allowed one) is a scamp but no scoundrel, one who—in his own words—"sides with all, but will suffer for none"; while Olivia's cousin Eliza is a decent human being unfortunately granted a very minor role. And the subplot, involving Freeman with the Widow Blackacre and her son, seems much more amusing than it is generally allowed to be, or than such things generally are. The Widow, with her lawsuits and law talk and law French, may be a hand-me-down from the Comedy of Humors, and plainly we could do with less of her, but she is sometimes quite funny, and a fair caricature of a certain aggressive, hard-riding type of businesswoman. One enjoys the way love, or any other subject, always makes her drag in the law: when Freeman proposes marriage, she answers, "I'll no more hearken to your foolish love-notions than to offers of arbitration . . . I that am a relict and executrix of known plentiful assets and parts"; and when she threatens to cut off her son, "If you do that," she tells him, "farewell the goodly manor of Blackacre, with all its woods, underwoods and appurtenances whatever!" She may be running loose out of Ben Jonson, but she is yet not out of place, as Fidelia is outside Shakespeare. But we cannot take leave of Wycherley with either of these un-Wycherley-like women; or even with this powerful bad play. To be sure, he wrote only one very good one; yet he bulks large in terms of Restoration comedy, as would any man so vigorous, so clear of sight if awkward of stance, so molded and marred and maddened by his age. He is one of those writers who, with a hundred faults, yet have a kind of stature. He must be found lacking; but he lacks what, had he had it, would have made him great.

The Plain Dealer derives of course from the *Misanthrope* of Molière; but if we speak now of *The Misanthrope* it is not just because of this blood relationship. A vast number of Restoration comedies are related to Latin comedies or Elizabethan comedies or French comedies. Some are related to two or three: Wycherley's own masterpiece, *The Country Wife*, is part descendant of Molière's *École des femmes*, part of his *École des maris*. But for the most part this business of genealogy seems to me quite barren and unrewarding: to be much concerned with it in life is to be a snob, and to be much concerned with it in literature is to be a pedant. Yet there are times when it is less a matter of our seeking out the relation of one play to another than of having it forced upon our attention. There are times when the difference between the two plays will constitute the difference between the two playwrights; when the difference between two playwrights suggests the difference between two cultures or between perfect and imperfect, mature and immature art. One cannot read *The Plain Dealer* without being put in mind of *The Misanthrope*; but less because of their likenesses than of their differences. Those differences not only carry us to the heart of the Restoration, they carry us to the very heart of comedy. Besides, can we possibly shut Molière out of the Restoration picture? Quite the least of it is that a dozen Restoration playwrights were borrowing his plots. Far more important is that they were unable—or unwilling—to preserve his spirit; that he was too alien for them, and too civilized for them, and too profound. And never more civilized or profound than in *The Misanthrope*; as nowhere so much as in *The Plain Dealer* was Wycherley unbalanced and savage.

Wycherley calls his Manly a plain dealer, Molière his Alceste a misanthrope. Alceste, too, hates shams and cannot bear the frivolities and frauds of society: he is morally no less than personally disgusted; consumed indeed with spleen. And his greatest disgust is less for the outright knaves than for those who, instead of coldshouldering the knaves remain on good terms with them: that is how Alceste's friend Philinte behaves; and unfortunately how the woman Alceste is in love with does. Unlike Wycherley's Manly—who imagines his Olivia to be everything good till she is proved to be everything evil—Alceste is aware of Célimène's limitations. *His* way of deceiving himself is to think she is the victim of the society she lives in, and that his love will work a change of heart in her, and lead her to wish for a change of scene. Meanwhile, approve of her present conduct or not, he is in love with her.

Wycherley's Manly has to grapple with a perfect she-devil, as at the end he is rewarded with an angel of light. But Molière's Alceste is involved with no one so vile and with no one so virtuous. Célimène is simply a worldling, a woman with many charms who enjoys having men admire them; a witty woman, who knows how hard it is to be witty without also being unkind; and how hard it is to be well-mannered without also being insincere; and how hard it is to enjoy life without sometimes being tarnished by it. Célimène, without too much approving the way of the world, is willing to accept it; for by temperament, by education, by femininity, she far prefers an urbane society however corrupt, to a virtuous wilderness however pure. At the same time, she is not without her own values and preferences: she much prefers Alceste to the fops and fair-weather friends who hang about her, and she stands ready to marry him. But Alceste is not willing simply to marry her, or even to reform her by slow degrees: as an unalterable condition of marriage, he demands that she renounce society and live with him in solitude. This she refuses to do, and he accordingly—and quite abusively —breaks with her.

The story, or if you prefer the lack of one, has almost nothing in common with *The Plain Dealer*: the similarity lies in the situation at the outset and in the nature of the two heroes. And we may certainly allow to Wycherley a frequent power and boldness, a distinct theatrical vividness, quite lacking in Molière— because alien to Molière, quite undesired by him. For Molière did not create his misanthrope in the same savage mood with which Wycherley created his plain dealer—to lash out, despite his own misdeeds, at all the evil-doing of the age. However moral Molière's purpose, he could never have adopted Wycherley's immoderate ways—his lurid twists of plot, his extravagant forms of villainy, his black-and-white view of mankind. An Alceste, to Molière, represented something very dubious indeed —something, to say the least, quite as dubious as Célimène did. The clash between them is not between right and wrong, but between two views of life, two kinds of natures, each with the defects of its virtues, each valuable at the expense of the other. Doubtless Célimène is too willing to compromise: but Alceste is too determined not to. Célimène, smiling at people one minute and ridiculing them the next, is plainly two-faced; Alceste will practice no wiles, but too much enjoys making other people wince. Célimène, out of vanity, goes with people who are unworthy of her; Alceste, out of conceit, finds almost no one worth going with. Célimène doesn't love Alceste enough to give up the world for him; but Alceste really resents loving Célimène at all. Moreover, the same aspects of fashionable society that have made Célimène conform have made Alceste rebel. About all they really have in common is that each is a superior person of his kind; and that, of course, only doubles their differences and their difficulties.

What makes *The Misanthrope* the very highest comedy is not the story it tells but the attitude it expresses; the understanding it brings to the conduct of both these people, and the questions it raises—not in print, but in our minds—about human conduct in general. There is much to be said here on both sides, but not quite enough on either. Ill-natured, self-righteous, intolerant, happy to lose a lawsuit he ought to have won because now he has all the more reason to lash out at human iniquity, Alceste forfeits not only much of our liking but a real measure of our respect. He is not only sour but selfish, and not so much strong-minded as fanatical. Célimène, on the other hand, though charming, witty and graceful, is questionably easy-going and quite needlessly treacherous: fashionable society has defeated her in one way, as it has defeated Alceste in another. She is as selfish as Alceste—though sweet where he is sour. But then, her sweetness is mere insincerity. And so it goes, now the one up, now the other: though most of us would find more to approve of, as well as like, in the lady. Nor does this rest only on most of us being readier to make terms with life than be intransigent about it. It rests partly on Alceste's setting up so much severer standards than Célimène, and yet performing, on the whole, less well.

We may take such sides as we choose; the point is that Molière does not take sides,* does not satirize, except with minor characters. He simply states. He knows, to be sure, very well— and means for us to know—that fashionable society is the real culprit. But fashionable society is hardly the basis of *The Misanthrope:* it rather constitutes the barrier between hero and heroine. It is they who are the basis; the superior man and woman whose differing virtues beget differing vices. And surveying the two of them, each so superior, each so far from perfect, we ask ourselves at length just what constitutes the best and soundest conduct, just how possible it is to achieve a set of virtues that carry no weaknesses in their train—how to be firm but not rigid, or flexible but not frail, wellbred without being hypocritical, honest without being acrid, witty yet not malicious, kindly yet not soft; how to live *in* the world without becoming a worldling, or out of it without becoming a crank. It is, to say the least, appallingly difficult: the student of ethics, the seeker after the good life, must almost certainly conclude that there exists no rose without thorns. And anything so impossible to amend it would be pointless to rail at. This is no subject for satire; only one for comedy, or for tragedy.

Molière understood this and perfectly dramatized it as an idea; which is the real drama of *The Misanthrope*, and which explains why Molière dispensed with plot. Doubtless *The Misanthrope*, as a play, is somewhat thin and static: but we may feel sure that, as not only the greatest comedy writer of the age but also its leading actor, Molière willed it so. He was mounted here above the merely dramatic; above even the critical; the comedy of *The Misanthrope* is philosophic, and indicates more than words can express. And the lack of emphasis and coloring

---

* It is true, however, that the moral "problems" concern Alceste.

matter, the easy and untrumpeted approach, is one proof of how civilized Molière himself could be.

Certainly no two plays so much alike at the outset as *The Misanthrope* and *The Plain Dealer* could wind up much farther apart. Their divergence is very instructive. It yields a contrast, to begin with, between comedy at its most unruffled and olympian, and satire at its most sulphurous and enraged. Where Molière is not fighting at all, Wycherley is actually fighting himself—and losing the fight, for all his prowess and strength. But quite as much as we have a contrast between the comic and the satiric spirit, we have one between moderation and excess, between the most perfect feeling for proportion in Molière and the most hopeless want of it in Wycherley. The world of *The Misanthrope* seems a completely social one; that of *The Plain Dealer* comes to seem more and more animal. As an animal world, it is often livelier, crueler, more immediately absorbing, but it will not do as a serious criticism of human life. Where the high comedy of *The Misanthrope* stands at the very borders of tragedy, the harsh, curiously maudlin satire of *The Plain Dealer* actually, I think, crosses the frontiers of melodrama. To smile, even as sadly as Molière does in *The Misanthrope*, is still to smile, if only a very little about the eyes; but to bare one's teeth like Wycherley cannot be passed off as to laugh. The lesson here is not simply that between moderation and excess, between one of the greatest of French artistic virtues and one of the worst of English artistic faults. It is equally that one cannot write comedy when one is in a mood of self-hatred born of self-indulgence. For comedy refuses to scream as an alternative to sobbing; and even satire balks at whiplashing other men's hides as a masked way of beating one's own breast.

CHAPTER V

Dryden

JOHN DRYDEN is not only a master; even after three centuries, he is in many ways a model. He is a model of a certain kind of criticism, of a certain kind of satire, of a certain kind of verse, of a certain kind of prose. In whatever he might do there was a fine vigorousness: he knew how to make sentences and couplets march to the sound of fife and drum; his very ridicule has a bracing, out-of-doors effect. But the temptation must be resisted to talk about Dryden in general; we must confine ourselves to the writer of plays—indeed, to the writer of comedies.

Although that, if we are to sample him in any useful way, is just what we cannot do. He seldom wrote comedy as we nowadays understand it, or even as the Restoration generally understood it; and such comedy as he did write in a "pure" vein— *Sir Martin Mar-All*, for example—belabors single ideas like a comic strip. Dryden's famous *Marriage à la Mode* is a comedy with a non-comic side to it; his *The Spanish Friar* is a heroic drama with a comic subplot. Jack of all trades and master of many though Dryden was, stage comedy never sat easily on him. At first blush it seems odd that so great a master of satire, with so keen a sense of the absurd, could not frisk and romp on the stage, where absurdity can play so large a part. But it was perhaps the stage as a medium that hampered him—for the Restoration stage has a strikingly indoors quality, at odds with Dryden's own outdoor vigor. To be sure, much Restoration comedy is laid in parks and pleasure grounds, in Hyde Park and St. James's Park, Spring Gardens or the Mulberry Gardens (three of these four haunts, in fact, form either the title or the subtitle of plays). But what goes on in them still smacks of the drawing room, or invites to the boudoir; the fops dawdle and mince, the men-about-town ogle and strut, the ladies glide along, whispering and wearing masks; it seems much the same indoors as out. It is tempting to speculate on how Dryden's great successor in satire and rival for first honors at it, on how Pope might have shone at writing the comedy of manners; Pope who is so su-premely an indoor poet and a town poet, Pope who excelled even Congreve, who indeed excelled everybody, at this kind of polish; who had, if a less airy, then a more brilliant wit, if a less temperamental, then a more intellectual worldliness; who could be divinely elegant and diabolically cruel. Pope was probably too concise for stage comedy, as Dryden was too rugged; yet if one were asked to find a spiritual third for Etherege's *Man of Mode* and Congreve's *Way of the World*, would not one really find it, rather than in anything behind the footlights, in Pope's *Rape of the Lock*?

Only a row of footlights separates *The Man of Mode* from Pope's *The Rape of the Lock*; but between *The Man of Mode* and Dryden's *The Spanish Friar* there stretches a vast gulf. *The Man of Mode* and *The Spanish Friar* do not perform the same function in the theater; they spiritually do not inhabit the same age; they literally do not speak the same language. Etherege's Sir Fopling suggests lace ruffles, and Dryden's Torrismond seems clad in chain mail. Dorimant is a high-society rake, Dominic a low-comedy rascal. But it's not that between *The Man of Mode* and *The Spanish Friar* there is all the difference between night and day; it's rather that there is all that differ-ence between one half of *The Spanish Friar* and the other.

Of course there was nothing new about the scheme of *The Spanish Friar*: the very trouble is that there was something out-moded and old. The comic subplot, or co-plot, or second plot, is one of the most familiar characteristics of Elizabethan drama. It is also one of its least forgivable blemishes. At its worst, as in Middleton's *The Changeling*, the *idea* of comedy is as out-of-place as the comedy itself is grisly. *The Changeling*, and many other Elizabethan plays with comic subplots, are tragedies; *The Spanish Friar* is on the other hand heroic drama. And for the mingling of heroic drama with comedy there is an outstanding, indeed a supreme precedent—Shakespeare's *Henry IV*. And *Henry IV* is certainly a triumph of a kind, though scarcely a triumph of playwriting. Falstaff not only bestrides the play, he distorts it, he destroys its balance. It takes two evenings to get him off the stage and Prince Hal onto the throne; and the pageant of history is halted time and again while the fat knight sneaks furtively, or waddles heavily, or swaggers boozily across the road. Yet, in addition to all its Shakespearean glories, there is even something to be said for the logic of *Henry IV*. Its heroic and comic halves possess a certain genuine psychological point and provide a valid philosophical contrast. Falstaff and the Prince are cronies, the Prince is roistering as well as royal, raising with one arm the sword of heroic drama, with the other the tankard of tavern comedy. So long as Falstaff and Hal are of one mind, the play is pretty much one play: *Henry IV* does not begin as two halves, but bifurcates only as it proceeds. And the two halves are dramatic in that they contend with each other over whether Hal shall be a playboy or a prince. Moreover, the comic and heroic halves that merge over Hal stand eternally apart, challenging each other, in the persons of Falstaff and Hotspur. For Falstaff represents the comic approach to life, as Hotspur the heroic. Hotspur burns

> *To pluck bright honor from the pale-faced moon*
> *Or dive into the bottom of the deep*

while Falstaff asks: "Who hath honor?" and answers himself, "He that died o' Wednesday"; and it is against these philosophic extremes that Hal achieves his bright and balanced destiny.

But if even in *Henry IV*, with all its magnificences, we feel the two parts uneasily jostling each other, what can we expect in the many plays where there is so much less validity and merit? Shakespeare, moreover, began by looking at history, not by concocting a plot; but what can have possessed men of ability, men of Dryden's stamp, to go in for this sort of left-hand, right-hand playwriting? What except catering—whether consciously or not doesn't matter—to popular taste, to the taste that not only deprecated too tragic an ending, but got restless with too serious a story, or simply felt better treated if given two stories for the price of one? There is of course a little more to it, something that makes a little more sense. It was not simply *comic* relief, narrowly regarded, that audiences craved, but the relaxation of coming upon mere human beings after too long a sojourn among heroes, the relief of dropping into colloquial prose after a long spell of rhetorical verse. Artistically there is no justifying this two-plays-in-one; psychologically there may be. The trouble grows out of the very nature of heroic drama, which, more than any other form of writing, runs to hifalutin and stilts, and which, more than any other form, runs the risk of turning preposterous—in a word, involuntarily comic. Thus, heroic drama deflated itself by voluntarily introducing comedy, and all the more by introducing it at a deliberately low level.

I offer this as mere speculation; but something of the sort must account for the long sway the comic subplot exercised, over not only audiences but playwrights. Most such playwrights doubtless adopted it chiefly because it had always been there; but Dryden, who is probably the best writer of pure heroic drama in English, came in time to see that he had blundered. Late in life he was to say that "though the comical parts of *The Spanish Friar* are diverting, and the serious [parts] moving, yet they are of an unnatural mingle, for mirth and gravity destroy each other." They do not necessarily, but certainly they do when following the method of *The Spanish Friar*, which is not one of mingle at all, but of the merest alternation. It is much as though one were to put the *Eroica* on one gramophone, and musical comedy tunes on another, and alternate the two at three-minute intervals.

As heroic drama, *The Spanish Friar* tells one of those involved, inflated, wellnigh impossible stories of burning conflict between love and duty—the sort of thing that seems at home in the French drama, with its classic diction, statuesque attitudes, and great set speeches or *tirades*; but which in English either goes up in purely romantic flame or never takes fire at all. In *The Spanish Friar* Queen Leonora—whose father had usurped the throne—is pledged to marry one of her generals, Bertran, but falls in love with a more triumphant general, Torrismond. She allows Bertran to murder the King her father had deposed, ostensibly to tighten her hold on the throne, actually in the hope that an enraged populace will seek Bertran's blood and set her free to marry Torrismond. But just as she and Torrismond are passionately united, Torrismond discovers that he is son to the murdered King, and has in substance married his father's murderess. The situation is clearly untenable—one in which, in all seasons, filial duty must rebuke connubial passion; and, on the lady's part, a sense of guilt ruins all hope of happiness. It is very tragic, or almost so: for after the Queen has renounced her throne and renounced her love and made anguished preparations to take the veil, it turns out that the old King is still alive.

I have synopsized the story as perhaps the quickest way of criticizing it. Everything is present that should be: the most exalted personages, the most feverish passions, the most fiendish dilemmas, along with the most satisfactory of endings. Except for Dryden's use of alternating current, the story-telling is rather better than the story; there is suspense; and one is genuinely surprised that the King still lives, even if also a trifle annoyed. But what saves the play as heroic drama, what gives it the stamp of talent if never the stamp of truth, is the proficiency and energy of its verse. It is rhetorical, no doubt, and has fire but no warmth, a ringing tone but small reverberation. It can thrill but not touch us, rise to a crescendo but not drop to a whisper. But that is not so much to disparage as to define it; its job is to express heroic drama, not human drama; something whose great virtue is its size, and great drawback its hollowness. If you cannot adequately express heroic drama without to some extent exposing it, that is a risk that must be taken with *anything* essentially theatrical. The theater's great aim is to achieve an effect—to startle us like a pistol shot, to stir us like a trumpet call. But along with its passion for being effective goes a marked indifference toward telling the truth, and that passion and that indifference stand forth particularly plain in heroic drama. All this Dryden understood, and his verse fits all this like a glove. It offers us pat but trenchant give-and-take—

> —*How can my hand rebel against my heart?*
> —*How could your heart rebel against your reason?*

It gives us at times real eloquence, at times accomplished hi-falutin. If at its worst it seems hackneyed and stagy, at its best it is truly and splendidly Drydenesque:

> *My joys are gloomy, but withal are great.*
> *The lion, though he sees the toils are set,*
> *Yet, pinched with raging hunger, scours away,*
> *Hunts in the face of danger all the day;*
> *At night, with sullen pleasure, grumbles o'er his prey.*

Linked as it is to competent story-telling, the verse makes the heroic side of *The Spanish Friar* still pleasant to read.

In contrast to his heroic drama, Dryden offers the most unheroic comedy imaginable. Where there was verse, there now is prose; where romantic passion, lechery. Where every one struck attitudes, every one indulges now in hocus-pocus. We shift from a brave, highminded soldier to a fat, self-seeking friar, from Hotspur's world to Falstaff's; and the two worlds are never, as they are in Shakespeare, merged. They are at most bridged, by making one of the Queen's best warriors also one of Spain's best libertines. One Lorenzo is attracted by a jealous old usurer's pretty wife; and the friar, who is the lady's confessor, becomes Lorenzo's go-between. Time and again Lorenzo and Gomez's wife hoodwink old Gomez, but never for quite long enough to cuckold him. Time and again the fat friar is caught out red-handed as their accomplice, only to lie his way

or defy his way out of it. Dryden attacks his humorous scenes
with the same energy he employs on his heroics; and in prose,
as in verse, is never at a loss for words. Verbally, the wit lacks
a certain lightness and speed, and is likely to be drawn out for
more than it is worth. As comedy of situation, with the jealous
old husband always turning up in time to spoil the fun, all this
is without freshness and subtlety alike. What remains is the
friar, with his ponderous waddle, his itching palm, his smooth
tongue and unscrupulous wits. It is easy enough to call him
Falstaffian—he is fat, fairly clever, and a rogue—but it serves
no useful purpose. Dryden's friar has no large amount of wit
in himself, nor is he the least cause of wit in others. His hypocrisies can make us smile at times, as when he groans over his
"legs crippled with often kneeling"; but how far that falls short
of " 'Tis my vocation, Hal; 'tis no sin for a man to labor in his
vocation." At the very most Friar Dominic has Falstaff's quick-
wittedness without his charm; and in any case is an accomplice,
never a companion. And though both are cynical, Falstaff represents an understandable philosophy of life, where the friar misrepresents one. It is one thing to be so much a worldling that
you cannot be a man of honor; it is another to be so much a worldling that you only pretend to be a man of God.

Falstaff, besides, is not a type, but a supreme figure of comedy;
where the friar *is* one, and an obvious satiric butt. Much more
than in Falstaff shall we find his counterpart in the smug fat
cleric hugging the side of beef in Hogarth's *Calais Gate*, and
for the good reason that Dryden and Hogarth were seeking the
same effect. They were satirizing the lax, piggish type of priest:
the satire, in Hogarth, is made in one stroke, and the point of it
is economic—his gluttonish priest is set against his starving
soldier; in Dryden, economics goes arm-in-arm with immorality: his friar is corrupt, and for money will wink at vice and
even wave it on. *The Spanish Friar* was regarded, on Dominic's
account, as anti-Catholic, and was proscribed when James II
came to the throne; only to be revived under Mary, when Dryden had himself become a Catholic. How specifically Catholic
the friar is meant to be, and how much just any venal cleric,

one cannot be sure, for the age was rife with sectarian feuds, and Dryden himself a pretty reprehensible opportunist. What we *can* feel in Friar Dominic is the sense on Dryden's part of getting in his licks. The all-too-worldly friar is a commonplace of fiction, a standard butt of satire. Dryden knows Dominic's comedy value, and usefulness to the plot: but seems too bent on making him a figure of ridicule to convert him into a figure of fun. And in this low-comedy atmosphere, he ought to be a figure of fun.

I must admit, I prefer the heroic side of *The Spanish Friar* to the comic; its humor has nowhere the vigor of its verse.

In *Marriage à la Mode* we have again two plots, but here the verdict is the opposite one: the comedy half far excels the serious half. The serious half is, indeed, altogether deplorable, with no gift of story-telling or power of verse, and with a plot no less silly than dull. Here again we move among royalty, again of the kind that has seized rather than inherited the throne. Here again, though this time for a princess rather than a prince, there is a hateful struggle between love and duty. This time the lovers converse in couplets, which have a way of blanketing passion. We somehow become too fascinated by the rhymes to take much interest in the romance. But the whole plot is stagy and full of stilted attitudes and tragicomic posturings; worse still, there is no suspense.

The first thing to note, as we turn to the comedy side of *Marriage à la Mode*, is how radically it differs from that in *The Spanish Friar*. It is as genuinely comedy of manners as anything we might choose from out the whole Restoration. The characters, the plot, the talk, above all the theme, are exactly what the comedy of manners invites. Nothing could be more artificial, more worldly, in a sense more stylized; nothing have more piquant possibilities or a more fashionable air. The one thing that, in this sense, sets the play apart is its taking place in Sicily rather than London, among people named Rhodophil and Melantha rather than Sprightly or Lady Fondle. But Sicily was compelled upon it by the serious half of the plot, and it is no more Sicilian than a painted backdrop makes it.

The play's title—*Marriage à la Mode*—pretty much sets off its theme: while the opening song is even more explicit:

> *Why should a foolish marriage vow,*
> *Which long ago was made,*
> *Oblige us to each other now,*
> *When passion is decayed?*
> *We loved, and we loved, as long as we could,*
> *'Till our love was loved out in us both;*
> *But our marriage is dead, when the pleasure is fled:*
> *'Twas pleasure first made it an oath.*

Doralicé and Rhodophil have been married three years, which—in the sophisticated view of their world—is too long for love to have lasted. So, because *his* eye tends to wander, and hers to flirt, they find—or at any rate fancy—that they are out of love. Just then Rhodophil's friend Palamede returns to Sicily from abroad, having been commanded by his rich father to marry an heiress he has never met. On arriving, he comes upon Doralicé, not knowing she is Rhodophil's wife; while Rhodophil has begun to philander with Melantha, not knowing she is Palamede's heiress. For a time these misunderstandings are exploited for plot purposes, but soon the two men learn the truth and are disposed to fall out over it. Only if they do, it will be harder for each to have access to the other's wife. The intrigues continue, even to having the women dress up in boys' clothes; but at the end neither lady has sinned, both men have found they can be jealous, all four realize that their rightful mates are perfectly satisfactory ones, and grasp that the price of philandering—after marriage—can far exceed the pleasure.

The comedy in *Marriage à la Mode* follows a real thematic development: we have not only a reversal in terms of plot, but an advance in terms of "idea." We start off with an affectation—that love and marriage are incompatible, and that not to accept the fact is unsophisticated. The ensuing plot is in the nature of high farce; but the dénouement consists in stamping out affectation and facing truth. Dryden's is not a romantic ending: his point is not that one's wife or husband is the one real love, marriage the one happy state. It is not, again, a moral ending: the characters are not brought round to reverencing their marriage vows, to feeling that conjugal love is noble, illicit passion base. It is a purely realistic ending: the people decide that the game isn't worth the candle; there would be too much risk, uncertainty, jealousy; and as they all find their mates attractive, why embark upon being unfaithful?

It is a triumph of good sense rather than virtue; but yet one that gives virtue the helping hand she almost always needs. The play may well prove a deterrent to vice, but it is far more truly an exposé of pretense. We can feel sure that in Restoration days the counterparts of our Sicilian quartet took a somewhat bilious view of marriage, partly because that was the fashionable view, partly because it suited their book. If they could make themselves feel that marriage destroyed love, and that marriage without love was a farce, they could philander with a clearer conscience and a lighter heart. *Marriage à la Mode* tends to show up the shallowness of the first view and the downright fraudulence of the second. The appeal is not to righteousness but to reason; and the whole point is that Dryden is a man who is serious—not about morals, but about sex.

Before the end of the play is reached, Dryden rings all the changes possible on the sheer comedy of the situation. For all their sophistication and fine talk, his ladies and gentlemen are forced by the plot to be peculiarly obtuse at moments. At times Rhodophil doesn't recognize his wife's rather childish stratagems; at times, indeed, he doesn't even recognize his wife. One wonders at such moments—so easily could women dress up like boys and not be caught out—whether it is the human body that has changed, or only the clothes. But of course it is the conventions of comedy that have changed: in an age that completely accepted the soliloquy and the aside, it was not hard to believe that a man wouldn't recognize his wife when she wore a mask. And though all these scamperings and sashayings seem skittish now, this willingness to accept absurdity for the fun that was in it may have made for more fun than we have today. We, perhaps, can't even visualize it all, for we depend for our antics on timing and pace, where theirs depended on style, on something akin to ballet. People hiding in a shrubbery, or behind a screen, even lovers pushed into closets, might still, so to speak, dance their parts. The very clothes they wore, the very roles they played—of fop and gallant and fine lady—enabled them to be exuberant without ceasing to be stylish. Today our farce-comedy must be rattled off, the exits and entrances must follow a time-table, the jokes must crackle, the situations build, the curtains clatter down; there is exuberance enough, but virtually no style at all.

And the ladies talk and sniff and gossip stylishly, too: Doralicé, even when dressed up as a boy, can talk as prettily as a book: "You are an admirer of the dull French poetry," she says to Melantha, "which is so thin, that it is the very leaf-gold of wit, the very wafers and whipped cream of sense." Which brings to mind Melantha's own passion for things French, her being yet one more Francophile in the list, but the first female one. With Melantha, Dryden comes closest to pure fun and farce, and he adds some bright touches to the handling of her type: she forces her maid, for example, to fetch up as many elegant French words as she can each day, and exchanges old clothes for the maid's new phrases.

There is true point, and sound development, and some very polished writing to the comedy side of *Marriage à la Mode:* one can only confess that it fulfills all the conditions and understands all the aims of the comedy of manners; while the man who wrote it had, unquestionably, genius. I must for all that admit that I find it lacking in salt—that there seems something a little flat, or forced, or heavy about many of its scenes. Mr. Dobrée, one of the few writers on the period in whom one can have any confidence, troubles me a little by his very high opinion of the play, but reassures me, also, by analyzing how Dryden falls short. Dryden has a talent, says Mr. Dobrée, equal to Etherege's or Wycherley's, but "no specific comic flavor to impart to his use of it. His essence, after all, is in his diction." And that is very much it: the ingredients are excellent, but there is not yeast enough, not savor enough. The play lacks just what that laughed-at French poetry has—"the very leaf-gold of wit, and wafers and whipped cream of sense." In elegance and polish, the dialogue often equals Etherege and challenges Congreve; yet it is literary where theirs is colloquial; it is prose where theirs is talk. What is missing is that special touch, that sixth sense, that makes one pianist or tennis-player so much superior to another who is otherwise his equal. To be sure, the comedy here must suffer from being involved with such wretched serious stuff; yet it comes to more than that. Dryden wishes to be gay, believes in being gay, but cannot long contrive to be. No one could make words march as he did; but words that should skip, and splash one another with water, and mock while they seem to caress, and elude while they seem to consent—these were not his forte. And there are frequently, perhaps, just two or three words too many, the want not of a writer's ear, but of a playwright's. Then, too, Dryden has planned his jokes rather better than he actually pulls them off, which perhaps explains why *Marriage à la Mode* sounds better summarized than when read. It wasn't more talent Dryden needed; at times one almost feels it was more triviality. A streak of the fop and cynic and snob can carry an Etherege up like a balloon, where a Dryden's far solider qualities have the drag of an anchor and chains.

CHAPTER VI

Thomas Shadwell

THOMAS SHADWELL slinks from one generation to another, like a man between guards. On one side of him walks Ben Jonson, whom he had the bad judgment to imitate; on the other walks Dryden, whom he had the worse judgment to outrage. Every one knows Dryden's pulverizing lines:

> *Shadwell alone of all my Sons is he*
> *Who stands confirmed in full stupidity.*
> *The rest to some faint meaning make pretence*
> *But Shadwell never deviates into sense.*

These are hardly the words one would choose for one's tombstone, yet they are almost all the tombstone Shadwell has. In any group study of Restoration comedy you will find his name; in any group picture of Restoration playwrights you will see his face. But it is certainly not necessary to read him to appear cultured; it is more than enough to know that, besides never deviating into sense, Shadwell was the continuator of the Comedy of Humors, and wrote as much like Jonson as he was able. I hope I can show that Shadwell is a good deal better than he sounds. To be sure, nobody could sound worse; and the one advantage of so deplorable a reputation is that it must leave any one who investigates it agreeably surprised. One begins by remembering what Dryden said about Shadwell, and by visualizing him as a ponderous Jonson. And then one opens, let us say, *The Squire of Alsatia*. There is no telling, after half a dozen pages, how good it will be as a play, but certainly it has life as a picture; and as Alsatia was a part of London where criminals enjoyed a kind of sanctuary and went briskly about their business of fleecing the innocent, the play is a useful and picturesque social document. Here is Belfond senior, a young gentleman up from the country, green as grass, ripe as a plum for plucking, and immensely taken with a gang of crooks he supposes are men of quality and whose lingo he takes to be the fashionable language of the town. When Cheatly remarks that the coal is coming, Belfond says "Coal?"—to be told that coal is money—the ready, the rhino. And so on:

CHEAT.: *The prigster lugged out in defence of his natural, the captain whipped his porker out, and away rubbed prigster and called the watch.*

BELF. SEN.: *"Prigster lugged out, natural, porker, rubbed"— admirable! This is very ingenious conversation; you're the purest company! Who would not keep company with the wits? Pox o' the country, I say!*

HACK.: *But, squire, I had damnable ill luck afterwards. I went up to the gaming ordinary, and lost all my ready, they left me not a rag or sock. Pox o' the tatts, for me! I believe, they put the doctor upon me.*

BELF. SEN.: *Tatts, and doctor! What's that?*

SHAM.: *The tools of sharpers—false dice.*

HACK.: *Hark you; prithee, noble squire, equip me with a couple of megs, or two couple of smelts.*

BELF. SEN.: *"Smelts!" What, shall we bespeak another dish of fish for our dinner?*

SHAM.: *No, no; megs are guineas; smelts are half-guineas: He would borrow a couple of guineas.*

BELF. SEN.: *"Megs, smelts!" Ha, ha, ha! Very pretty, by my troth. And so thou shalt, dear captain; there are two megs:*

*and, I vow and swear, I am glad I have 'em to pleasure you;
adad I am!*

This is almost as good an education for us as it was for Belfond; it is like listening to some seventeenth-century Damon
Runyon or Walter Winchell. In fact, so long as Shadwell remains inside Alsatia, he too can claim sanctuary—from dullness.

The play is one of several adaptations of Terence's *Adelphoe;*
it is the story of the town brother and the country brother,
the one tame, the other wild, the one bright, the other dull.
While the town brother has been given a very civilized London
bringing-up by his uncle, the country brother has been badly
kept down, so that when he runs away to London he is in a
mood to throw off all restraints. The play is a complicated
farce involving not only the two young Belfonds, who are mistaken for one another, but also the two elder ones—the father
and uncle; together with sharpers, sluts, and two highly respectable girls with two highly respectable fortunes. Sex and
money both figure strongly in the plot, and even love plays a
sizable if shadowy role.

The plot has often the tediousness that goes with over-compli-
cation. Thus, while the rural brother is burning up the town,
even the seemlier brother is involved with a mistress he has
discarded, a nice young girl he has debauched, and an even
nicer girl he yearns to marry. Indeed, all the people in the play
lead very active lives, which is scarcely to the play's advantage.
But though there is too much plot, of a ponderous old-fashioned
sort, it is quite decently contrived. Shadwell is a sound enough
craftsman; he does make you wonder what comes next—and
it *does* come next, not two acts farther along. William Archer,
in his brilliantly exasperating *The Old Drama and the New*,
refers to the play as "pure Ben Jonson." Nothing really could
be more impure Ben Jonson. But Shadwell, like his master before him, has at least learned his trade, and has borrowed his
master's trademark and created characters in a comedy-of-humors style. Unfortunately, one of the real weaknesses of the
play is the weakness of its character-drawing. Of four Belfonds,

you might suppose that one would come to life, but the two from the country act like a hotheaded boor and a harebrained booby, while the two from the city converse like utter prigs. Actually it is the booby who (thanks to his delight in the lingo of Alsatia) is the best fun; but he is not much fun for all that. And though the crooks are more interesting, if only because their profession makes them so, there is nothing really individual about them. Compared to Jonson's nimble scoundrels, these are mere stage crooks—though collectively, as denizens of Alsatia, they have a certain picturesqueness. But Shadwell is not, like Jonson, haunted by the overwhelming reality of money. Shadwell knows that money is the basis of a good scheming plot. But Jonson knows it to be the fulcrum of society, believes it to be the root of all evil.

And of course between Shadwell and Jonson there is a gulf of language, for Jonson, if not quite a great master of nervous colloquial speech, is one of the greatest of all masters of rhetoric; where Shadwell can never rise above tolerable everyday prose, and sometimes sinks below it. It would be idle to compare the language of two men when it could only be a contrast. Leaving Jonson out of it, however—and he can be left out of Shadwell more than tradition indicates—there is perhaps more to be said for Shadwell's prose than has been said. If it is seldom very sharp, or rich, or vivid, or any of the things by which prose is distinguished, it is seldom very turgid, or languid, or lumpy, or any of the things by which prose is debased. It does its work, not always so briskly as it might, but often with the ring of real speech (though living speech—a very different thing—is preferable in the theater). It also contains a not unenjoyable kind of wit—never elegant or inspired, but with the smack of honest repartee, such as any reasonably quick person might make. It is, I suppose, exactly the kind of thing we think good enough off the stage but not good enough on. Thus when young Belfond's father, seeing his son's discarded mistress in a fury, cries out: "Here's a son for you—here's the effect of whoring," the son answers: "No sir, 'tis the effect of not whoring; this rage is because I have cast her off." This is not very witty, but it is exactly what a somewhat quick young man, in real life, might say.

The chief merit of *The Squire of Alsatia* hasn't much to do with the stage; it consists in setting forth the social life of the period. Shadwell's exposition seems intended less at times for his own audience than for posterity. Thus Sir William, describing his trip home from Holland, says:

> *I finished six weeks before I expected, and had time to come by the way of Flanders, and see that country. . . . And from Newport I came to Dover; and riding post from thence, I took a boat at Southwark, and landed just now here at the Temple.*

Doubtless, hearing this, Shadwell's contemporaries nodded their heads, for just so would *they* have traveled; yet it somehow seems written to inform us, ages hence. The whole play teems with realistic detail, though of course there can be no *creative* quality of realism when a playwright indulges in all the mechanical operations of farce. But through the interstices of the farce-plot, we can get genuine glimpses of prosperous middle-class life. As for the life inside Alsatia, here alone Shadwell achieves real vivacity. The Alsatia scenes are properly raffish, and at their best have the undeniable appeal of underworld life. Shadwell gives us rather more of them than we actually require or enjoy, and he adulterates their realism with the stagy, where he should enrich it with something imaginative. There is more factual truth here than art, but there is not enough of either. I cannot agree with Allardyce Nicoll when he says that we "shrink in horror from the picture" that Shadwell presents. Certainly its implications are horrible enough, and the real Alsatia was an undoubted cesspool of crime and vice. But Shadwell's Alsatia is a place where through the demands of the plot people who might be real are very little more than puppets. If anything should horrify us, it is that Shadwell put this world to such facile and tawdry uses, that whatever the implications of it, the actual effect is not horrifying enough. Out of a comparable world, any number of English writers—Dekker under Elizabeth, Defoe under Anne, Dickens under Victoria—have contrived something far finer *and* more horrifying. In Shadwell, the real brutality of Alsatia is blurred by the mere stage villainy, and is blunted further because Shadwell lacks the verbal mastery to make each incident tell.

Shadwell missed the chance to write a truly valuable play about Alsatia because he could only be truthful to the degree that he was reportorial. Indeed, what is good about it only suggests how much better it could have been, and what is bad, or conventional, or contrived, only seems more glaringly so by comparison. In *A True Widow* we find Shadwell using material that is less interesting, but more of a piece and more his own, and the general result is more satisfactory. On the stage *A True Widow* failed where *The Squire of Alsatia* hugely succeeded, but the failure becomes understandable if, as Saintsbury declared, it was because the play exposed the practice of wellborn men keeping—instead of marrying—girls of decent family. No doubt even in such an age large parts of the audience would have been too much disconcerted to be entertained. For on other grounds the play meets the fashionable requirements of the age very well—and better than Shadwell himself customarily does. If character is treated along the lines of the comedy of humors, the tone and writing are much nearer to the comedy of manners. There is certainly as much chatter and persiflage as there is action and plot; the characters inhabit a world—half mercantile and half highborn—that the comedy of manners delights in; the coxcomb and the wit preen and display themselves, as is *de rigueur;* there is a good deal of mere mannerism, such as we find in Etherege, along with a good deal of sheer mania, such as we look for in Jonson. The plot is neither conspicuously old nor conspicuously new: Lady Cheatly's pretending to possess a large fortune as a way of marrying herself and her two daughters off is good Restoration comedy enough; while her accomplished rascality and some of the things it gives rise to, hark back—and rather heavily—to Jacobean days.

But if he did it by intention, Shadwell was wise in blending the two forms of comedy. The genuinely light touch, the instinctively elegant turn, that are the soul and secret of the comedy of manners, lay quite beyond him. But he could contrive a fashionable enough imitation of the real thing; he could achieve a sort of rough-and-ready elegance: which, though not enough for pure comedy of manners, could considerably freshen up a comedy of humors. And though not—in terms of Etherege or Congreve—the real thing, it was—in terms of actual society —nearer to the real thing. As in *The Squire of Alsatia*, the flings and retorts are at just about the level of pert real-life conversation, and are sometimes rather engaging just because they are. This is to explain, not to extol, them. In a good comedy of manners, we expect a finer wit than we encounter at a dinner party. In Shadwell, we find just that wit: hence, though we are sufficiently entertained, we don't listen for what will next be said: we only wait for what will next be done. In a good comedy of manners, we also expect more airiness, more unreality. It is one of Shadwell's limitations that he cannot achieve a successful level of artifice, that his artifice is never graceful enough, and often not artificial enough: it draws us back to real life. This is in itself a fault, but so uncommon a one as also to be a kind of virtue. Our laughter comes freely— but not so appreciatively as to impede the flow of the story.

In the same way, though Shadwell gives us no Sir Fopling Flutter, his coxcomb is entertaining enough, for a time; and so is his poet; and so is his sportsman. The poet pretty well describes himself while chattering about a new play:

> *I saw it scene by scene, and helped him in the writing. It breaks well, the protasis is good, the catastasis excellent. There's no episode, but the catastrophe is admirable;*

and Shadwell achieves something better with him when his poet tells how he weighs himself before he sits down to write, and again when he gets up. On the old-fashioned comedy-of-humors side, Shadwell achieves at least one mild success, in the person of Lady Cheatly's brother, Lump. Lump is a type that every age and virtually every satirist has a go at—the methodical, literal-minded, efficiency-worshipping philistine; but Shadwell, for a wonder, mounts Lump on a broomstick and lets him sail off humorously into space. Lump insists that any wise man mnst have his day planned even fifty years hence, and when questioned, he answers: "Let me see . . . the 6th . . . the 6th. I take physic!" "What!" asks his sister, "sick *or* well?" Lump suggests Jonson less than he does Dickens.

There is another good character in the play: Lady Busy. Here we come to the business of gentlemen keeping respectable girls rather than marrying them—for her ladyship is nothing more nor less than a procuress. For once, Shadwell, in character-drawing and dialogue alike, manages to strike the right note: Lady Busy is a combination of grande dame and saleswoman. Now she snorts, now wheedles; here, like the Devil, she cites Scripture to her purpose; there, like the Devil, she unrolls seductive visions. There is just enough of humorous exaggeration and satiric fancy brought to bear to get her off the ground, to make her real rather than realistic.

In terms of subject-matter, the play seems a little too downright and sordid for comfort: it is not just that young ladies were kept, but that their mothers took a hand in the keeping, and that their elders and betters played the role of go-betweens. Here we come upon a side of Restoration life that has no real counterpart in ours; here what might pass for worldliness in one age fails to qualify in another. For there is no suggestion that these girls took the step either from sheer financial need or from already having gained a bad name; they agreed to be kept, they went at being kept, very much as they went at being married. The great argument was the substantial sums of money they could come by—enough to make them secure and independent, however much it might leave them stained. And apparently, with enough money put by, they could in due course marry and lead quite respectable lives. Shadwell's play clearly reveals that the whole arrangement was owing less to a disregard for morals on the women's part than to a distaste for marriage on the men's. Clearly the men-about-town of those days valued their freedom, and needed a real incentive—such as falling passionately in love or making a decidedly advantageous match—to make them marry. In an age notorious for infidelity, they would not relish the idea of being cuckolds; or still less, of becoming fathers to children not their own. In Stanmore, the gay blade who refuses to marry, Shadwell is dealing with a special Restoration type; for Stanmore is neither the extremely cynical rake who is half villain, nor the confirmed bachelor who is half crank. He is a genuinely realistic figure; and it is through such sidelights that Shadwell helps to portray and even explain his age. The lovers of the age were quite as much realists, for that matter, as the rakes. Says Bellamour to Isabella:

> *I know my duty and your worth; and would time stand still,*
> *I could be content to gaze upon that face and not tempt you;*
> *but our love is frail, and we must take our pleasures while we*
> *may.*

He says it with as much grace as Shadwell can ever attain to; but he means it as men everywhere meant it in that age, faced with the thought of dying young. It was because it was so vivid an apprehension that it became the constant burden of their poetry—of Herrick's best-known poem, of Marvell's best-known poem, and of how many others.

There is something diluted and over-extended about *A True Widow*; the talk, if there is to be so much of it, needs to be brighter; the coxcomb wears out his welcome, the man of wit turns into a bore, the sportsman gets on our nerves. We could wish, too, that the play did not so frequently give in to the stage shams and conventions of the age. Shadwell was so good a copyist, it is regrettable that he copied what he saw in the theater along with what he caught in the streets and the houses of his friends. But in need though it is of both scissors and file, the play proves entertaining and even illuminating. After reading it, it becomes impossible to dismiss Shadwell or even condescend to him.

Of *Bury Fair*, which is traditionally regarded as Shadwell's best play, one cannot say anything like so much. Indeed, barring bits and pieces, and possibly a character or two, one finds it hard to say anything good at all. From a glance at the criticism that sets it above Shadwell's other (and unseemlier) plays, one feels pretty sure that it enjoys its primacy not because it gives the most pleasure, but because it gives the least offense. No female character in the whole course of the play comes close to being debauched, and two male characters speak out in the strongest terms against debauchery. There is no talk, anywhere, of keeping or being kept; the talk itself is far seemlier than elsewhere in Shadwell; and the whole thing, if not quite a model of gentility, is yet no outrage upon it. And it might really be refreshing to encounter this sort of thing for a change, were the play not otherwise so inferior. But it most certainly *is* inferior: in the language of our own stage, half the characters are what is known as cut-ups, and much of the action is the merest shenanigans.

Thus there are *two* practical jokers in *Bury Fair*, and one young lady disguised as a page and in love with her master. The comic momentum springs from one of the practical jokes, which turns on passing off a French barber as a French count. The romantic apparatus consists in having two close friends find themselves in love with the same girl; it all ends happily, however, because the girl has a sister—the very young lady who is disguised as a page. The chief satiric butts are a rich woman and her daughter, who dote on all things French and high-toned, and are completely duped by the barber.

Aside from snatches of dialogue or a bit of characterization, the whole thing seems not unlike one of those operetta librettos that have been watered down from some long-forgotten farce. For what it is, it is perhaps acceptable enough, agreeably written, competently put together, full of respectable borrowings from Elizabethan times. But for what it is, it is entirely too well-behaved; if it is to be no naughtier, then it ought to be wittier or livelier or wilder; if it is not to be coarse, it ought to be polished. Instead it is tame and longwinded, with the satire almost as obvious as the pranks are juvenile. In play after Restoration play, the fops and coxcombs are ridiculed for worshipping French customs. Obviously, and with good reason, the Francophile was as easy a satirical target as a certain kind of Anglophile is in America today. It was the age of French supremacy in everything from warfare to cosmetics, when the court of Louis XIV represented form and *ton* to all the world. But the joke here, of making a count of a barber, and letting a pair of society women dote on him as a count, is of the very crudest sort. No doubt the trick did well enough, as popular fare, in the seventeenth century. But even then, the touch must have seemed extremely broad and the inspiration pretty belated; and Shadwell's consistent glibness must have betrayed, even to his contemporaries, the hack in him.

For that, most of all, is what was wrong with him: he was a hack. He seems to have had no real social or intellectual or moral convictions, no esthetic compulsions. He had considerable natural talent of sorts; he had a fairly well developed theater sense. But he was incapable—for one reason—of the finer effects in writing because he was uninterested in them. He drew on Alsatia, with all its sordidness and depravity and squalor, quite without feelings of any serious kind—feelings of a Hogarth, of a Goya, of a Gorki, of a Villon; simply with the feelings of a Sunday-supplement writer who had lighted on good copy. He miscalculated, in the box-office sense, when in *A True Widow* he chose to write of kept women; but again, one feels he wrote about them because he saw them around him, not because he had any strong feelings on the subject. His best qualities in the end are a very sharp eye and a keen but unselective ear. He shows neither heart nor lack of it, neither conscience nor absence of one; he can be witty but wit is not his forte; he can strike most of the attitudes and sing most of the refrains of his period, but he originates none of them. His realism is the best thing about him, but even it reproduces Restoration life faithfully because Shadwell has no sense of how that life might be heightened, or intensified, or metamorphosed into art. He gives us a useful photograph because he doesn't know how to paint an organic picture.

And so, in talking about Shadwell's plays, one singles out this particular merit or that particular fault; or praises the plot; or deplores the style; or notes what derives from Middleton or what does not too much differ from Etherege. But one finds no sense of progression in him, no getting to the heart of the matter, for, being the work of a hack, the matter has no heart. Shadwell isn't even preëminently a craftsman or preëminently an amateur. Still less would one call him a satirist, or a moralist, or a dandy, or a wit. All the same, he had his virtues, his rather numerous virtues, and what we feel about him, and lament, is hardly so much a sense of barrenness as a sense of waste.

CHAPTER VII

Aphra Behn

THE name of Aphra Behn will never possess the dignity of other women writers—of Fanny Burney or Maria Edgeworth. I suppose, in fact, it will always be notorious. That she was the first Englishwoman to earn a living by her pen must always be overshadowed by the story of how she earned it—by all but outdoing the men at indecency. But she competed with men on grounds far less notorious. One way or another, Aphra Behn had a good deal of ability. If, in the end, hers was not a distinguished achievement, the trouble lies in her need to earn her living rather than in how she earned it. The trouble lies in having to write for money, in becoming—like Shadwell—a hack. No doubt as a popular playwright she made abundant use of that always popular ingredient, sex. But it is not overindulgence in sex that limits Mrs. Behn's achievement; her treatment of sex may well be her most distinctive virtue. Where she falls short is in not giving her work, enjoyable and energetic as it can be, enough artistic purposefulness, enough seriousness—even low seriousness. She uses formulas and recipes; and though she sometimes imparts a flavor of her own, it is too faint. Mrs. Behn adds something to the gaiety of nations, but very little to the wisdom, and this is a pity, because she might have done both. Whether much of her life, as we know it, is legend—whether or not she went to Surinam, or there was ever a Mr. Behn, whether she had few lovers or many, whether she passed a season at Court and caught the eye of Charles II, she obviously lived a full if highly bohemian existence; she obviously had a friendly heart and an adventurous soul, had indeed what Bagehot called an experiencing nature. And she had the sharp eye and keen ear and facile tongue to turn her experience to real account. But the need to make a living hampered the ability to probe disinterestedly at life.

If we first look at Mrs. Behn with *The Town-Fop, or Sir Timothy Tawdry*, we shall not be much impressed. Half the time we are in a Restoration London that is all too recognizable; half the time we don't seem to be in Restoration London at all. The best scenes are by no means brilliant; the worst are contemptible. In exchange for some agreeable and at moments quite well-turned prose, we must put up with poetry that is often feeble and oftener out of place. There are perhaps three entertaining characters; the others are either sheer stage types or sheer impossibility. We want to know how the story comes out, but that, frankly, is about all we do want to know.

If *The Town Fop* has any special quality, it is indeed that it hasn't any, that we may take it to represent the dead level of Restoration comedy, as one comedy or another of the past ten years on Broadway—say *John Loves Mary*—may three centuries hence stand forth as typical entertainment of today. Each will have behind it the sense of an age rather than an author, or, more precisely, the sense of an age in terms of its hackwork. Both plays are written from formula, in deference to the taste— or lack of taste—of the time; occasionally, each may say or show something real in spite of itself, or in defiance of its main objective. At the moment, the author of *John Loves Mary* seems to operate a smoother-running machine; Mrs. Behn, on the other hand, seems capable of better writing, and interests us rather more because, where the author of *John Loves Mary* is always a hack, Mrs. Behn has become in places a social historian.

Like so much hackwork in every age, Mrs. Behn's play uses

anything that may prove effective, with no thought for the total effect. In the midst of trying to make the audience cry, the hack cannot resist whatever might make it laugh. He sees nothing wrong with trying to exalt his readers one moment and scandalize them the next. The hack has no conscience because he has no convictions; and though he is much given to talk about bad taste, by bad taste he means something that offends the audience's—rather than his own—sensibilities (and that hence may react against him at the box office). In the case of *The Town Fop*, Mrs. Behn did nothing worse than try to please, and conceivably even tried to preach. But the fact remains that she made no attempt to arrive at any settled view of human nature, that she mixed the most florid emotion with the most unblushing cynicism, aware that most audiences were fond of sugar and even fonder of spice. Mixing elements so complaisantly can be worse in the end than merely alternating them: the two halves of *The Spanish Friar* are quite intended to offset each other, to represent poetry and prose, the heroic and the lowdown. To us it seems absurd to skip baldly back and forth, but at least each half is the more sharply perceived through its utter unlikeness to the other. Mrs. Behn's method retains the incongruity while losing the sharpness. It blandly mixes characters that are entirely hard-headed—for whom love is entirely a question of sex, and marriage entirely a question of money—with characters of such pure and passionate ardor that, if they cannot marry their adored one, they would just as soon kill not only themselves but any available bystander.

Now both kinds of people do exist, and could no doubt be contrasted to excellent effect, as in no very different way a Falstaff and a Hotspur are contrasted, or a Don Quixote and a Sancho Panza. But that requires a certain awareness and a certain irony that are altogether lacking here. One gets no feeling that in *The Town Fop* Mrs. Behn is contrasting anything at all, even sugar with spice. In the process of rewriting another man's play, she is mixing an old Spanish-style comedy of intrigue with a modicum of plainspoken Restoration realism. Characters like Bellmour and Celinda strike attitudes out of date for generations, and never native to England, while Sir Timothy Tawdry is one more ridiculous and ridiculed Restoration fop, and Betty Flauntit—that peculiarly Restoration figure, the kept woman— is a bit of comic realism that proves truly interesting and alive.

The main story here—and we need not linger over it—tells how young Bellmour, though he and Celinda are rapturously in love, is ordered by the uncle who controls his estate to marry his cousin Diana—an attractive girl much in love with him but whom he does not and, as it turns out, need not love in return. But before the uncle relents, Bellmour goes about in a state of the utmost discouragement, dividing his time between duels and bordellos, while the despairing Celinda dresses up as a man and captivates the spurned and rather irritable Diana. Nor is Friendlove, in the dual role of brother to Celinda and suitor to Diana, less occupied with matters of romance and revenge. This side of the story is mostly set down in deplorable blank verse, and none of it has anything to do with Restoration England. Mrs. Behn adds to it the town-fop from whom the play gets its name: Sir Timothy is also a suitor for Celinda's hand but only because their parents desire it. He is the usual bundle of attitudes, the usual butt for laughter; he goes about with two sycophants, Sham and Sharp, whom he abuses when aroused and makes use of for his dirty work. Despite his bullying, Sir Timothy is of course a coward, loud for the challenge, late for the duel. Mrs. Behn has given him one rather individual touch—of gaining courage through anger, and knowing it. With women he is thoroughly selfish, but not notably shrewd: Betty Flauntit, whom he keeps, has more ways of making a monkey out of him than most wives would; and he acquires a wife without wanting her when one of his henchmen, under pretense of calling in a fake parson to fool the girl, fetches a real one to fool Sir Timothy. When he learns the truth, Sir Timothy makes the nearest thing in the play to a witty remark: this, he says, is his punishment for never going to church, for had he, "I might have chanced to know the parson."

As a figure of fun Sir Timothy is easily surpassed by a large number of Restoration fops. But he is not entirely without interest, and what, in one sense, is wrong with him is in another his crowning virtue. If Sir Timothy were more comic, we should laugh at him the more and look the less; as it is, though what we look at fails to seem real, it does at moments go to the heart of the matter. It does—rather than acquaint us with the surface attitudes and idiocies of the fop—indicate that whole race of men who go through life obedient, not to their own desires, but to the fashions. Sir Timothy is not, in other words, the key to the age; the age is the key to Sir Timothy.

It is for Betty Flauntit that we must keep our real praise, for in her, with her mixture of something spirited and something shameful, of leading a hard life and driving a hard bargain, of scorning common prostitutes in the very act of descending to their level, we have one of those stage characters in whom the comic and the realistic so coalesce that they are said to come alive. Hear her upbraiding Sir Timothy:

> *Forgive me!—Who shall forgive you your debauch'd Whoring and Drinking?—marry, ye had need so, you are such a Ruffler, at least if y'are every where as you are at home with me—No, Sirrah, I'll never bed with you more; here I live sneaking without a Coach, or any thing to appear withal; when even those that were scandalous two Ages ago, can be seen in* Hide-Park *in their fine Chariots, as if they had purchas'd it with a Maidenhead; whilst I, who keep myself intirely for you, can get nothing but the Fragments of your Debauches—I'll be damn'd before I'll endure it.*

No doubt it is just this kind of speech that got Mrs. Behn her bad name; none the less, it is for just this kind of speech that she still deserves to be read. She had a great many failings, but a writer can be pardoned them who can capture the exact point at which the lewd becomes the ludicrous.

Mr. Allardyce Nicoll has suggested that Mrs. Behn was not quite without a purpose in writing this play, that her using— here as so often elsewhere—a forced marriage, constitutes a protest against that unhappy practice. I doubt it. I am sure that Mrs. Behn was against forced marriages, as people are against cannibalism or cancer, but it is hard to believe that any writer who really sought to protest against them would use methods like these, where the situation is even more forced than the marriage. Bellmour's uncle is completely arbitrary: his motive is not the social-economic one that, for better or worse, underlies forced marriages in general. Moreover, had Mrs. Behn had any profound conviction about the evils of forced marriages, surely she should have pictured one, and shown how Bellmour's and Celinda's lives were shattered. So unprofound were her convictions that though, in the play from which she adapted hers, the original of Celinda died of a broken heart, she herself manoeuvred a happy ending. I fear that Mrs. Behn belonged to the one class of people who really favor forced marriages: I mean popular playwrights. If people in plays could always marry whom they please, either audiences would have to go home at the end of Act I or stay on to be shown the evils that emerge out of love matches.

The matter of forced marriage turns up again in *The Lucky Chance, or An Alderman's Bargain*, and is used—along with almost everything else—more plausibly. *The Lucky Chance* is a far better comedy than *The Town Fop*, though a far more farcical one. It too is wonderfully lacking in purpose or meaning: once more Mrs. Behn is plainly concerned with amusing an audience, and quite unconcerned with how. But here she largely rids herself of an outworn plot of intrigue, here her blank verse is both curtailed and improved, here there is a genuine sprightliness to story and dialogue alike. At odd moments we are given first-rate glimpses of manners; in Gayman's landlady, Mrs. Grimes, we have perhaps an even better character than Betty Flauntit; and though, today, the play—from its abundance of hocus-pocus —could only be done as farce, or rather—owing to its indecency —could hardly be done at all, it still combines good humor with high spirits.

Whatever may be the underlying theme, the visible subject-matter is clearly sex, and we cannot fail to note how Mrs. Behn warms to her subject. I say this approvingly, for the warmth of the approach carries over into the play, and gives it a saving

exuberance. Without this exuberance, a play treating indeli-
cately and incessantly of sex, leading us in and out of bedrooms,
harking back to the tricks and stratagems of the *Decameron,*
must grow ponderous from over-complicating the plot, must
grow tedious from never varying the subject-matter, must grow
nasty from making the merest commodity of sex. Thanks to
possessing this exuberance, *The Lucky Chance* proves very entertaining. In addition, sex itself seems to acquire, on the Restoration stage, a slightly different character. It seems both a little
more farcical and a little more real; something that the characters find quite as enjoyable as the audience, a source of fun
rather than a subject for wit. It is easy to say that, being a
woman, Mrs. Behn outdid the men of the age in her efforts to
write like a man, that wherever they introduced three assigna-
tions, she would feature four. There is perhaps some truth in
this. But there is perhaps more truth in something else: that the
men of the Restoration did not write about sex as men commonly
do; for *them* it was more a subject for wit than a source of fun,
something in their ink rather than their blood. We may be
astonished at times that their fops can be so virile, but we are
just as astonished that their rakes can be so foppish. Now at its
best—I am speaking of comedy—this is all to the good. In
comedy, it is not the animal aspects of sex, but the human ones,
that can be most soundly exploited, and not the personal but
the social aspects of sex that can arouse the most civilized laughter. There is also involved the whole question of a proper stage
artifice, a proper literary art. Etherege is a more important and
artistic writer than Aphra Behn, and not least because he treats
sex as a springboard where she treats it as an end in itself.

But where Restoration comedy is not at its best, where sex
becomes a theme for inferior wit, for third-rate social comment,
where we get all the atmosphere of a hothouse and none of the
roses, Mrs. Behn can prove a good deal more refreshing and,
at *her* best, a good deal more amusing. She may at least claim
that she is not a "suggestive" writer if only because she is so
explicit; she may claim to be more upright than her contemporaries about sex simply for being more downright. She cares

about sex, and though we may smile at the thought, we ought also to be impressed by it. She may, in *The Lucky Chance*, bang away at sex for all it is worth as box-office, with the pertinacity of a literary procuress. But she goes at it with gusto too, even with feeling; there is real indecency in the play, but also real desire. For her, as for her characters, sex is not just something to be witty about. For her indeed—as a woman—it is something, even amid the wildest farce, to be serious about. For a woman, even in that age, "Gather ye rosebuds" was not the main objective. A woman had to find security and happiness in marriage, or had—for so long as she was able—to gather guineas and sovereigns.

It is the merit of *The Lucky Chance* that, high-spirited as it is, it does cause us, here and there, to react; does lead us, now and again, to reflect. Of *The Town Fop* I have said that it carries the stigma of real hackwork, having only the sense of the age about it, and not of the author. Something better can be said of *The Lucky Chance:* here we do feel a sense of the author; here what is lacking is something much rarer still—the sense of the artist. But the artist might almost be out of place here: what would Taste, or Restraint, or Proportion, be doing in this galley? Or a sound conception of life, when the fun rests on a complete exaggeration of it? As the comedy proceeds, it turns more and more to farce; as the farce proceeds, it gets more and more old-fashioned. Two young and very desirable young women are married to two old aldermen; plainly the aldermen must be tricked and defeated. So we are shown young Gayman hidden in a chest, and young Bellmour dressed up as a ghost, and young Bredwell in the guise of the Devil. And that only sets off the hocus-pocus; before we are through, one of the old men will throw dice for his wife, agreeing to be cuckolded rather than lose three hundred pounds, and one of the young men will marry one girl dressed up as another.

At times we shall have too much of it—too much hocus-pocus, unseemliness, improbability. But on the whole it is quite good fun, with even some passably good wit. There are really amusing touches—such as old Sir Feeble using baby-talk to his already thoroughly miserable bride. One of the virtues of Mrs. Behn's being a woman is that she makes the contrast between her old men and her young ones not just a convention of Restoration comedy, but a fact of life.

The City Heiress, or Sir Timothy Treat-All is a very rewarding play, no less as revelation than as reading-matter. It shows what Mrs. Behn was capable of doing—and why, simultaneously, she was incapable of doing it. It shows to what extent she was a mere mechanic and copyist, a mere creature of her age, but it shows her, no less, sounding a truly individual note. Here again, as in *The Lucky Chance*, the author makes herself distinctly felt; here again, amid borrowed plots and cut-to-measure bawdry, we feel sex to be a living thing, and desire something that stirs the characters rather than the plot. For Restoration comedy in general, sex simply opens the way to laughter; for Mrs. Behn it plainly has something to do with love.

Thus, though the play is often set apart as a thrust at the true-blue Protestant Whigs (with Sir Timothy identified as the anti-Catholic Earl of Shaftsbury who sought to keep the future James II off the throne), the key-character is not Sir Timothy but his nephew Tom Wilding. Wilding is perhaps just one more Restoration rake—in the sense that a rake seems as indispensable to a Restoration play as a butler to a drawing-room comedy. Nor is Wilding much individualized: he is profligate enough to want to ruin the reputation of any woman who goes with him; he is penniless, and at the mercy of an uncle's whims; he has altogether conventional dash and high spirits. The important thing is that three women are very much and very believably in love with him—and in love with him just as he is, whether telling them lies that hurt or speaking truth that hurts them more. Diana, whom he keeps, has no illusions about him; nor has Charlot, the City-heiress whom he marries; while Lady Galliard, the widow he pursues with real desire and has his way with but refuses to marry, has them least of all. But they love him anyway, and we believe that they love him anyway. His struggle with Lady Galliard—a woman for whom to capitulate is to sin, and to sin is to suffer—constitutes a kind of amorous debate between the sexes, as well as a moral debate about sex, which rises impatiently above the usual artifices of Restoration comedy.

To bring back the theme sounded earlier, Mrs. Behn cared about sex. She might play it up for all it was worth as bawdry and hence as box-office, but for herself, in the end, sex is real, sex is earnest; the woman and the writer are alike in their refusal to purvey amorous apparitions as substitutes for flesh and blood. It was her luck, good or bad, to live in an age that permitted her to be frank—though as a woman she was fiercely attacked for daring to be; but it is only her frankness that coincides with the age: her feelings are all her own. We are sometimes inclined to miss the point about the Restoration, and to think that sex was an obsession with it. But it wasn't so much obsession as fashion. People were supposed to be immersed in it and unsqueamish about it, as in most other ages people are supposed not to be. A married lady without a lover was treated with scorn, felt like blushing. Sex was not passion, but a fashionable game you were expected to know how to play, as you are expected to know how to play tennis or bridge. In society there was probably a good deal more virtue concealed than exposed, but on the stage it was almost required that sex be featured and that sex be frank. A Restoration comedy-writer attempted other subjects at his peril. Now it is very rare for sex—as a subject for the most outspoken and yet frivolous sort of comedy—to be so brazenly the fashion. Following Restoration times and throughout the eighteenth century, sex was very greatly diluted with sentiment, and was more and more forced to respect appearances. Sex was still acknowledged as a fact during the eighteenth century, but it was no longer elevated into a fashion. During most of the nineteenth century, of course, it was not even acknowledged as a fact, but kept in the dark as a kind of shameful misfortune: so soon as it caught the limelight, it changed its name to scandal. Only in the 1920's—some 250 years after Mrs. Behn—did sex enjoy any of the freedom, or attempt any of the frankness, it had during the Restoration. But even in the 1920's it was something one could openly *talk* rather than laugh about; its vice was exhibitionism rather than callousness; its language was far more the solemn jargon of Freud than the mere levities of Noel Coward.

Actually there has never been among English-speaking people another period that had quite the Restoration's cold-hearted attitude toward sex. To the extent that emotion is incompatible with high comedy, or sober truth with witty make-believe, this was all to the good. To the extent that sex is the best of all subjects for light comedy, it was in itself perfectly sound. But to the extent that you *had* to write about it—as much to seem sophisticated as to be successful—it came to seem mechanical; and to the extent that everybody wrote about it, it got to be stale. And, never endowed with much lure, if it was to capture audiences it had more and more to sneer at virtue or be steeped in vice. By becoming such a staple, it must have made plays that lacked its attitude seem tame, but without necessarily making plays that had it seem lively.

Amidst all this Mrs. Behn perhaps provided the one real shock—which was to make sex seem like sex. Possibly that— more than her being a woman—explains why she was abused where equally bawdy Restoration playwrights got off scotfree. If so, the shoe is now on the other foot, and though we cannot acquit her of indecency, of coldheartedness and a cynical outlook we can. And at her best, we can certainly praise her too. Reading *The City Heiress*—with its vivid love-making, its satirical thrusts, its brisk farcicality, its contrast between Sir Charles drunk and Sir Charles sober—one no longer compares Mrs. Behn with the author of *John Loves Mary;* one does not, indeed, quite know with whom to compare her. She can take all the hurdles set her by her profession; only somehow not make the last and decisive leap, the leap into literature. Her great fault was not that she was morally but that she was artistically too easy-going; not that she happened to shock, but that she attempted to please.

CHAPTER VIII

Congreve

With Aphra Behn ends the first generation—the true generation—of Restoration playwrights; and we must now, as it were,
simultaneously cross a stream and climb an eminence; move forward to the 1690's, and upward to Congreve. England in the
1690's is a somewhat changed place: William of Orange, with
Mary, is on the throne—a brilliant but cold, sickly, boorish
man with no love for the theater, with none for London. There
is no court life worth speaking of, no air of low morals and high
style. It is difficult to determine whether fashionable people are
at heart any better than they once were, but at least, now, they
pretend to be. The Restoration had got itself a very bad name,
and the theater had got itself a worse one. It was increasingly
under fire; and during the 1690's Jeremy Collier was to launch
his sharp and celebrated attack on it, his *Short View of the Immorality and Profaneness of the English Stage*. Congreve was not
spared in this attack; indeed he helped precipitate it; and it
would be idle to suggest that he worked on a more moral plane
than his predecessors. He is no more shocked by what he sees
than was Etherege or Shadwell, and on occasion he himself can
be just as shocking. But because he was so much finer an artist,
and the stage now so much less of a bear garden, there is a
certain refinement in tone. Burke said of Marie Antoinette's

court that "vice itself lost half its evil by losing all its grossness." Burke, there, was dangerously suggesting that esthetics can do the work of morality, was rather implying that it is only half as ill-behaved to poison your uncle artistically as to fell him with a meat-ax. In real life, it may be just the other way round; but in literature, an elegant, high-bred depiction of vice must have, for a while at any rate, a genuine lure.

Congreve does, in any case, stand apart from the earlier generation of Restoration playwrights, Etherege excepted, as distinctly in tone as in talent. It is very largely a matter of the prose itself: in the literary sense he is always a patrician, a master of the kind of writing that has breeding without stiffness, style and at the same time ease. Etherege has ease and airiness, a sort of fashionable rattle, a sort of constant fizz: he is the best kind of "smart" writer, a Noel Coward who is not sentimental and vulgar. But he is not endowed with such style and breeding as we shall find in Congreve; while too, despite his own gather-ye-rosebuds sense of how swiftly pleasure fades, he lacks any deeper intimations. With Congreve appears not simply the literary patrician, but the almost too civilized worldling. I don't know whether this is a second-generation phenomenon, but it is hard to imagine so fine a flower as Congreve springing out of uncultivated soil. The point, in any case, is that Congreve does not represent a period, but a tradition. He does not just mirror Restoration manners; he embodies the civilized point of view. Actually, it is the Restoration that makes him just a little less than completely civilized—that tarnishes him with a certain shallow cynicism, a certain merely fashionable sophistication. Of the completely civilized man we require something, in the final reckoning, that Congreve never quite gives us. We do not expect him to raise his voice, but we expect him to do more than raise his eyebrows. He need not be warm-hearted, but it must not be a sense of indifference that he conveys, it must be a kind of serenity. It is what we find in La Bruyère. But in worldliness, in an ability to appraise life in the very act of savoring it, in a fine appreciation of tangible civilized benefits —the brightest talk, the best champagne, the most charming women—in all this Congreve is certainly a master. It is as easy to over-praise the type as to underpraise it: I would here merely identify Congreve with it, the more so as we must hereafter associate him with the Restoration playwrights.

Congreve's first play, *The Old Bachelor*, was produced when he was just twenty-one, and it at once captured the town. It is not hard to see why, at least in terms of a London audience of the period. For plainly what had happened was that a bright and witty new playwright had arrived on the scene, but nothing unfamiliar in the way of playwriting had arrived at all. The plot, the characters, the situations, the general atmosphere, the interminable amorousness, were all in the most accepted style of the times. Thus the audience was in a position to be constantly dazzled by the writing without once being disconcerted by the play. Congreve, far from clashing with what had been done before, had merely done it again with a polish all his own. *The Old Bachelor* is not creation but brilliant re-write. It stands as a play in much the same category in which Pope's *Essay on Criticism* stands as a poem: where Pope re-glazed a body of worldly maxims and moral precepts, Congreve re-clothed stock characters and routine situations.

It is simpler to put the pieces of *The Old Bachelor* together as though it were a picture-puzzle than to summarize the play. In Heartwell, the old bachelor of the title, we have the stock figure of a surly, reluctant, indeed unwilling lover of women. He owes something to Ben Jonson's Morose and something to Wycherley's Manly: he, like them, is for all his misanthropy and mysogyny a dupe of both sexes. Congreve draws him, however, with a lighter hand, and contrives to brighten and differentiate him a little by showing that he can no more resist women than he can stop railing against them. As for the other principal lovers, Bellmour, being the most generalized, is perhaps the least exactly imitated—he is the regulation young rake, the sprightly man-about-town, fit to conquer any attractive woman and win for himself, whenever it shall please him to marry, a sufficiently suitable wife. Belinda, the wife he finally wins, is rather pert but affected, one more précieuse such as Jonson foreshadowed, Molière immortalized, and almost every satiric playwright had somewhere a go at. Belinda has, however, a touch of the mettlesomeness that culminates, for Congreve and Restoration comedy alike, in the figure of Millamant. Ariminta, like Bellmour, is too much a mere type to have a specific ancestry: she is essentially the heroine who plays hard to get. Vainlove, who finally captures her, is a little more uncommon, being paired off against her as a young blade who wants only what he cannot have. "By Heaven," he cries, "there's not a woman will give a man the pleasure of a chase." "Ah, come with me and refuse to be my love"—that is his motto, and that is Ariminta's method. In the two of them Congreve contrives the sort of situation that is his by temperament rather than inheritance, and that consorts well with elegant and even high comedy. It is somewhat a pity that two characters so promising can catch no more of the limelight.

But Congreve was taking no chances—or, as it turns out, was hurting his chances—in *The Old Bachelor*; he tossed in everything. In Sir Joseph Wittol we have the young gentleman of small parts and weak understanding who is ubiquitous—whether as gull, fop, booby, or country cousin—after *Bartholomew Fair*; and in his companion Captain Bluffe, we have simply the bragging coward as old as Plautus. Finally, in the case of Fondlewife and Mrs. Fondlewife, with Bellmour for a third, we have the ardent lady, apprehensive cuckold, and accommodating gallant that are a Restoration staple. The specific situation here perhaps most resembles that in *The Spanish Friar*. Although rather more fun that it is usually allowed to be, it is fun at a purely farcical and boisterous level—a level resumed later on in *Love for Love*—and not at all after the truly characteristic manner of Congreve.

Perhaps Congreve did well to turn copyist, to stand in other men's shoes while trying out his wings. For by making no effort to create, he had the better chance to concentrate on language. One has only to hear the first few speeches of *The Old Bachelor* to feel the verbal talents of its author—talents that may bespeak a specific age, but that in the end belong to one particular man.

Take the very first speech in the play—Bellmour meeting and hailing Vainlove:

> *Vainlove, and abroad so early! Good morrow; I thought a contemplative lover could no more have parted his bed in a morning than he could have slept in it.*

It would be absurd to say that this must be Congreve. And yet in the elegant directness of the salute—"Vainlove, and abroad so early!"—and in the elegant artifice of the antithesis, it seems more like Congreve than like anybody else. The point, in any case, is that already in the first sentence of his first play, Congreve has both acquired style and struck out a style of his own. The sentence is very literary, to be sure, but in a good rather than bad, a deliberate rather than unconscious, sense. It is the work of a man whose métier, whose true mistress, is words— words as an end in themselves, as a projection of worldliness, an envelope of wit. The gift of words and of wit so stands out in Congreve that his other valuable qualities are what most need to be emphasized, but it is the preëminence of the words and the wit that must be emphasized at the outset. Consider, in a writer of twenty-one, this badinage between Bellmour and his Belinda:

> BELINDA: *O Gad, I hate your hideous fancy—you said that once before—if you must talk impertinently, for Heaven's sake let it be with variety: don't come always, like the devil, wrapt in flames. I'll not hear a sentence more, that begins with an 'I burn'—or an 'I beseech you, madam.'*
>
> BELLMOUR: *But tell me how you would be adored. I am very tractable.*
>
> BELINDA: *Then know, I would be adored in silence.*
>
> BELLMOUR: *Humph, I thought so, that you might have all the talk to yourself. You had better let me speak; for if my thoughts fly to any pitch, I shall make villainous signs.*
>
> BELINDA: *What will you get by that; to make such signs as I won't understand?*
>
> BELLMOUR: *Ay, but if I'm tongue-tied, I must have all my actions free to—quicken your apprehension; and I-gad let*

> *me tell you, my most prevailing argument is expressed in dumb show.*

And here is Belinda meeting Ariminta in the park and conscious of not looking well groomed:

> *O Gad, I hope nobody will come this way, till I have put myself a little in repair. Ah! my dear, I have seen such unhewn creatures since. Ha, ha, ha. I can't for my soul help thinking that I look just like one of 'em. Good dear, pin this, and I'll tell you—very well—so, thank you, my dear—but as I was telling you—pish, this is the untowardest lock—so, as I was telling you—how d'ye like me now? Hideous, ha? Frightful still? Or how?*

In those last ejaculations, we have a sample of the mature Congreve's elegant, frilly prattle.

The Old Bachelor is not at all hard to pass judgment on: we are pleased by its wit and its prose, bored by its plot and its people. Wherever Congreve is in some one else's debt, we are not in his. In his second play, *The Double Dealer*, there is in terms of talent a conspicuous advance: here, in any direct sense, Congreve borrows very little. Instead of copying he has begun to create; and his story, instead of mingling characters at will, is quite carefully charted. Yet the second play, like the first, is half a failure; and again in a sentence we can distinguish where it fails from where it succeeds. Where it fails is in everything that has to do with the machinery of the plot; where it succeeds is in almost everything that hasn't. In the indefatigably villainous Maskwell and the sex-driven vengeful Lady Touchwood, Congreve both went wrong and went too far. Purely as a villain, Maskwell is not without a certain fascination—but for his ingenuity alone, from our asking ourselves: What will he do next? He is too overt and explicit a villain to be interesting in any deeper sense: every villain of really great appeal must be still something of a man, or—failing that—constitute something of a mystery. However inhuman Richard III becomes, it is for a very human reason—he is a hunchback. However evil an Iago may seem, there is something impenetrable about his evil-doing: we see through his wiles, but not through what dictates them. There is perhaps one further type of villain with very real appeal—the heroic villain, the magnitude of whose designs, the scale of whose operations, imparts a grandeur to what he does. But in this case, he is either something more than a villain, or we are impressed by something more than his villainy. Milton's Satan is too great a rebel to seem villainous; Macbeth is too heartsick a man. There is yet Volpone, who boasts as little humanity as mystery. But is it Volpone himself who fascinates us?—is he not as simplified as he is large, has he not great symbolic but very slight psychological appeal? We see him clothed in poetry and thirsting after power; he is dazzling, appalling, astounding—but too abstract to be interesting. He is greed itself rather than a greedy man; malevolence itself rather than an evildoer; and where not an abstraction, an animal—with a beak for a nose, a claw for a hand, and a fox for a forebear.

Maskwell, in *The Double Dealer*, is in any case all villain and only villain: it is his nature and it is his trade. He concocts schemes against people as some one else sells furniture or builds fences; to call him a double-dealer is to indulge in understatement, for he adds lie to lie, piles stratagem on stratagem. His motives—sex, love, ambition—are just conventionally plausible enough to weaken belief in him, and his plotting is so incessant as to prevent any real interest in the plot. Moreover, he is neatly caught out in the end, as is required if *The Double Dealer* is to be a comedy, but as is required no less if *The Double Dealer* is to be melodrama.

And a melodrama is what it often seems to be, all the more for Maskwell's connection with Lady Touchwood, a woman with the hot blood and cold fury of Elizabethan drama, a woman whose desires are both violent and unsatisfied. These two characters seem doubly wrong to us—seem cast in the wrong play, seem living in the wrong period. For Congreve here has roused his moral sense at the cost of putting his esthetic sensibilities to sleep. He is in a mood to arraign and condemn, but the villainy he would arraign in Maskwell, the vengefulness he would condemn in Lady Touchwood, cannot be coupled with comedy. To revert to *Volpone* again—this time to the play—though much of it is pervaded by something too harsh and sinister for comedy, the main action *is* comic because Volpone and Mosca are tricking people as coldblooded and grasping as themselves; it is a case of cheating cheaters, of diamond cut diamond. But Maskwell and Lady Touchwood conspire against the good and decent people in the play, whose desires are reasonable and hardly selfish; so that if what they contrive is not to be melodrama, it must be something higher in degree—drama, or even tragedy; it cannot be something different in kind.

Yet the real trouble is not so much that the main action is melodrama as that it is bad melodrama. It requires, for example, that Melfonte shall be even more credulous than Maskwell is crafty; it allows Lady Touchwood to loathe the idea that Maskwell will marry Cynthia, though that means that Melfonte, whom she really loves, will not. The whole business is much too contrived, the whole effect too specious. It is worth noting that Congreve, who in his first play had discovered a way to make fun of the soliloquy in the very act of making use of it,* should in *The Double Dealer* backslide almost to Elizabethan lengths, and employ the soliloquy very often and awkwardly. In the presence of anything so stagy, and as we should say slick, one cannot be made to care, one cannot believe that this has to do with actual Restoration society, however depraved or vicious Restoration society may have been. Wycherley's *Plain Dealer* fails morally quite as Congreve's *Double Dealer* does, but for precisely the opposite reason. Wycherley is reacting too violently against what he has seen and known. Congreve, though wearing moral harness, is personally reacting against nothing; his indictment is all made to order. He is what might be called a hack moralist, as are many writers whose view of life is naturally skeptical. Time and again, in all forms of literature, comic writers seem mechanical and false so soon as they turn "serious." The trouble with most accomplished comedians

---

* He turns it against its users, suggesting that any one who talks to himself must be a little off his trolley.

who want to play Hamlet is that they play it as sententiously as though it were Polonius.

In the face of so much disparagement, it may seem odd to have termed the play a conspicuous advance over *The Old Bachelor*. But it is: for one thing, because the good qualities of *The Double Dealer* are remarkably good; for another, because here, along with virtues of style and wit, we find virtues of characterization and what might be called attitude. Maskwell and Lady Touchwood inhabit a region into which Congreve should never venture, and Cynthia and Melfonte exist on what might be termed neutral ground—they are a pair of attractive but scarcely distinctive lovers, the kind of people who impose their shape upon no play, hence fit into any. But the Pliants and the Froths and Mr. Brisk—these five are fully of Congreve's world. It is with these five, indeed, that his world is first created. They are delightful characters of comedy whom Congreve handles as does a juggler his colored balls, keeping them in the air for the same reason—because they are without interest if they touch the ground. All five of these characters are fools, or at any rate foolish, but they are high-comedy fools, people with enough finish or pertness or social aplomb as almost to seem superior when they do not seem absurd; people on ice-skates, as it were, who cut something of a figure when they don't happen to be falling on their faces. They are the *more* idiotic for so often being worldly and even witty; all the worse popinjays for having a genuine instinct for elegance; all the sillier flirts for knowing the true nature of flattery and yet swallowing it. They are at once totally unreal and rather disturbingly like ourselves. They are unreal because they have been made comic to the exclusion of being anything else; but they seem curiously familiar for believing what they want to believe or ignoring what they want to want to ignore.

They are, in fact, ideal figures for the comedy of manners, for a world that may come to seem entirely vapid and petty, but must never seem brutal or gross. We watch them and are amused by them much as Gulliver watched and was amused by the Lilliputians. Only in Etherege, and in Etherege only in

The Man of Mode, have we earlier met with anything very similar: with some one like Wycherley we have had rather more the sense of Gulliver in Brobdingnag. Doubtless Congreve's Pliants and Froths are coldhearted enough if we choose to examine them coldly; but we do better if, like Congreve, we all but caress them, for they have foibles rather than vices, and are made to be exhibited rather than exposed. It is sufficient to see Lord Froth hee-hawing in the very act of eschewing laughter, or Lady Pliant initiating an amour while denying she can even be made to succumb. Here she is "remonstrating" with Melfonte, after she has swallowed the information that he is marrying her stepdaughter in order to have greater access to her:

LADY PLIANT: *O fie, cousin Mellefont!*

MELFONTE [who of course hasn't the slightest interest in her]: *Nay, madam, hear me; I mean——*

LADY PLIANT: *Hear you? No, no; I'll deny you first and hear you afterwards. For one does not know how one's mind may change upon hearing. Hearing is one of the senses, and all the senses are fallible. I won't trust my honour, I assure you; my honour is infallible and un-come-at-able.*

MELFONTE: *For heaven's sake, madam——*

LADY PLIANT: *Oh, name it no more. Bless me, how can you talk of heaven, and have so much wickedness in your heart? Maybe you don't think it a sin—they say some of you gentlemen don't think it a sin. Maybe it is no sin to them that don't think so; indeed, if I did not think it a sin—. But still, my honour—if it were no sin. But then, to marry my daughter for the conveniency of frequent opportunities, I'll never consent to that; as sure as can be, I'll break the match.*

But Lady Pliant is but one in this group; Lady Froth, in her way, is just as successful, and Sir Paul Pliant perhaps even more so, though also more caricature than fool. The final excellence in all this springs from the touch of wildness it possesses, the darting anarchic wit that leaves cracks in the polished surface: a wildness that has none of the capering of an animal, but rather the unchartable leaping of quicksilver.

Congreve's ability to be amused by this pack of fools while being so insincerely aroused by his pair of villains is a little wild in itself. One wonders how any one capable of Lady Froth's chatter could yet have cranked out Maskwell's soliloquies. But perhaps one need not wonder: Congreve was still too young a man and too new a playwright to have recognized his own true self or his proper métier. Or rather, he had not yet grasped their importance. It was the Maskwells and Lady Touchwoods who would loom largest in the play, and galvinize the plot, and point the moral; the Pliants and Froths would seem trivial, minor, incidental. Congreve was at the stage of accepting his medium; not till later would he say the medium be damned, and accept himself. That is an always difficult and perilous decision to make; with Congreve, in fact, the thing that crowned his career in the theater also put an end to it.

The Double Dealer is, I suppose, a rather bad play with delightful things in it. Perhaps it can be best summed up by analogy, an analogy that at first blush will seem odd enough. *The Double Dealer*, for me, is like a number of Dickens novels, where we care little about the nominal hero and heroine, where the main plot seems lurid and the sentimentality distressing, but all of which we endure for the sake of those great comic creations that refuse to be sucked into the whirlpool of the story. Even in the best-constructed Dickens novels—say *Bleak House*—how much there is that has only the stagiest sort of appeal, or no appeal at all. Do we care very much more for Lady Dedlock than for Congreve's Lady Touchwood? And certainly the unrelieved villainy of Maskwell is more easily borne than the unrelieved virtue of Esther Summerson. Grant *Bleak House* its wonderful sketches of London and satire on Chancery, surely we read and re-read it chiefly for Chadband and Guppy and Mrs. Jellyby and the rest. I won't push the comparison any further; but Congreve here mingles good and bad much as Dickens, however much greater, does.

And it is interesting that in this play, where Congreve sought to be a correct playwright and observe the Unities, he should yet have denied the play all unity of tone—half of it having the dark heavy look of a traditional oil painting, half the light, bright airiness of a wash. In Dickens, to do him justice, the lurid and the ludicrous mingle much more acceptably because they are both rooted in grotesquerie.

Having tried to write a good play by following directions, Congreve next managed a very good one by being completely relaxed. *Love for Love* is far and away Congreve's best theater piece; along with Wycherley's *The Country Wife* it perhaps constitutes the most actable Restoration comedy for the present-day stage we have so far encountered. It plainly represents Congreve's conquest of his medium, though there is once again a certain sacrifice of himself. Here he has learned to do well what in *The Old Bachelor* he had scarcely learned how to do at all. Much of the plot and many of the people in *Love for Love* are the common coin of the Restoration theater. We are even carried backward from the comedy of manners to the comedy of humors, and downward from comedy of any kind to farce. But by now if Congreve is, consciously or unconsciously, writing within the framework of the popular theater, he has also fitted himself inside the frame. *The Old Bachelor* is like something in a child's drawing book, where the picture is printed beforehand and the child colors it as he sees fit. Congreve's coloring is that of a child of genius, but there his contribution stops. In *Love for Love* Congreve has done the designing and the coloring alike. The design is very competent but wholly conventional; the color is often wonderful and very much his own. *Love for Love* exhibits, in a sense Mr. Eliot never intended by the phrase, a blend of tradition and the individual talent. The two have met, as they never did in *The Old Bachelor*; have met and, in fact, have married; and the marriage is a success, but on the principle by which most marriages are a success—the principle of compromise. In *Love for Love*, Congreve and the Restoration theater are running in harness, running smoothly and briskly for every one's enjoyment. It is a good relationship, though there is of course a better one—where the movement is as harmonious and brisk, but the man sits in the saddle, on the theater's back.

But though we must look critically at *Love for Love*, we need not look down on it. Because it is a sign of taste—and it *is* a sign of taste—to recognize the far greater distinction of *The Way of the World*, it is sometimes thought proper to be dismissive of *Love for Love*. There are always people who, because they are either snobs by nature or connoisseurs by intent, must love one thing at the expense of another. Having, for example, discovered that *Emma* is more subtle and mature than *Pride and Prejudice*, they drop *Pride and Prejudice* not to a lower eminence but to limbo. There is a blend of the prig and the parvenu in all this that should be strongly condemned. One may wish many things about writers and writing, for their sakes as well as one's own, but one ought not to wish their good things away on the ground that they might have been better. And *Love for Love* is distinctly one of Congreve's good things. We can almost rejoice that the difference between it and *The Way of the World* is not, in the end, one of degree, but of kind, the sort of difference we note between *Tom Sawyer* and *Huckleberry Finn*. Essentially *Love for Love* is fun, and *The Way of the World* is art.

Essentially, also, *Love for Love* is of the theater. It opens well, develops well, shows a sense of form as well as of construction; it is only late in the play, when Valentine's feigned madness is exploited for more than it is worth, and the ruse of the disguised marriages is flung on top of it, that we get impatient and even bored. Congreve, in a sense—or is it his audience?—is reaping the whirlwind: easy is the descent into farce, pleasant the first stage of hocus-pocus. But till near the end, *Love for Love* has real vivacity.

A more pervasive weakness is that some aspects of the play are so inferior to others. Foresight the astrologer might have walked right out of *The Alchemist*—assuming he would ever have been allowed in. But Foresight is quite the poorest of the stock characters: if Sir Sampson Legend is hardly less of a type, he is something less of a bore. And though Ben the sailor is as glaringly out of place as a beer bottle on a formal dinner table, he is not bad fun. The fact remains, however, that Ben, and Foresight, and Sir Sampson, and even—amusing though she can be—Miss Prue, are all pretty stock figures in themselves, and collectively figures of farce rather than comedy. And taken in conjunction with the feigned madness and the faked marriages, they infuse a great deal that is merely popular into *Love for Love*. If even this part of the play is often far more tolerable than it sounds, that is because Congreve manages to write it far better than nearly all his predecessors. But this is no more the essential Congreve than the livelier scenes in *The Merry Wives of Windsor* are the essential Shakespeare. Still, they damage our opinion of Congreve rather more than they do the play itself—if only because the play never mounts so high that the drop becomes disastrous. The play holds together; the good things are able to absorb the not so good ones; the general effect is checkered rather than clashing.

And there are many good things. For one, in Valentine and Angelica, Congreve for the first time gives us a satisfying hero and heroine. Valentine, it is true, is not much more than a typical Restoration young man who is very steadfastly in love. He has nothing, really, to show for himself but his debts; he has no sense of responsibility toward his creditors, and has little conscience about his father; he's not unusually dashing, not overpoweringly witty. But he comes off—through what might be called glamour by association—quite well, for we sympathize with his predicament, take his side against his father, and enjoy the wit of his friends, the pertness of his servant, and the genuine attractiveness of his young lady. Jeremy, the servant, is also something of a type, but seems better than the traditional valet who amuses by his impudence—seems more a fellow whose wit and insight are not completely part of his calling. Jeremy is less the witty servant than witty by nature and a servant by sheer accident of birth.

Angelica is an engaging heroine, even if she is another of those girls who are a little victimized by the plot, and must be testing the motives and repulsing the advances of their lovers longer than would seem necessary. But the best fun springs from something truer to Congreve's genius, from those scenes and characters that have an assured and unshakeable worldliness. A good instance is the famous dialogue between Mrs. Foresight and Mrs. Frail:

> MRS. FORESIGHT: *You never were at the World's End?*
>
> MRS. FRAIL: *No.*
>
> MRS. FORESIGHT: *You deny it positively to my face?*
>
> MRS. FRAIL: *Your face, what's your face? . . . But I do deny it positively. . . .*
>
> MRS. FORESIGHT: *I'll allow you now to find fault with my face; for I'll swear your impudence has put me out of countenance. But look you here now, where did you lose this gold bodkin? Oh sister, sister!*
>
> MRS. FRAIL: *My bodkin!*
>
> MRS. FORESIGHT: *Nay, tis yours, look at it.*
>
> MRS. FRAIL: *Well, if you go to that, where did you find this bodkin? Oh sister, sister! Sister every way.*

But this is still *fun*, still broadly enough based for a popular audience to appreciate. The point is not just that Congreve is working at less than the highest level, but that he is doing what other playwrights, rather than what he alone, can do. It is only here and there, and briefly and almost by chance, that the essential Congreve breaks through, that there is at once more elegance and more undertow to the rhythm of his prose; and more reverberation also:

> *"I know you," says Valentine to Angelica, "for I loved a woman and loved her so long that I found out a strange thing: I found out what a woman was good for."*

This is one of those sentences which are like Congreve's very signature; amid so much in Restoration comedy that is indistinguishable, they are his, and only his. The finest of these sentences occurs in that last and finest of the plays, which may now engage us—in *The Way of the World*.

Here is the high-water mark of Restoration comedy. Congreve's total achievement is nothing like Ben Jonson's, or for that matter Bernard Shaw's; and simply as a play, *The Way of the World* is very much less effective than *The Alchemist*. But it remains the supreme example of high comedy in the English theater, and the supreme example of a certain species of prose in the English language. In a way, one does not know where to babble first—whether over the tone, or the wit, or the language, or the heroine. Perhaps one can get round that by resolving not to babble at all, and by seeking to be precise rather than excitable. I know few works of art that have inspired so much stringing together of adjectives, so much reverting to worn-out metaphor, as *The Way of the World*. Critics run on without pausing for breath about the exquisite wit and exquisite lightness of the play and its dazzling shower of epigrams and silvery tinkle of laughter and luminous prose and radiant heroine and all the rest of it. But somehow we don't get much more from their pearly sentences about *The Way of the World* than that they seem to like it.

Let *us* begin at the cold end of the poker, with the historical fact that *The Way of the World*, when first produced, was a failure; and with the esthetic admission that it is nothing very remarkable as a play. The two things are not, however, so closely related as we might infer: almost certainly it was not its shortcomings as a play that defeated *The Way of the World*, but its extraordinary qualities as literature. Had Congreve just held fast to his plot, and been merely playful and cynical about his characters, *The Way of the World* would doubtless have had a very pretty success. It would have been judged colder and more worldly, it would have appealed to a drier taste, than *Love for Love*; but it would not have been too disastrously unlike it. Our own reservations about *The Way of the World* as a play grow, I think, out of our finding the tricks and wiles, the plots and counterplots, rather too many and too familiar, and out of our finding the end conventional and even stagy. But the playwriting suffers, not from being loose and sloppy, but from being elaborate and contrived; so that had Congreve *otherwise* worked at a more obliging level, he would have probably been praised for a neat, well-ordered play.

But Congreve at last, and when we may suppose that his powers had quite matured, was setting out to please himself. Now unless one feels guilty about not having done so before, one does not *set out* to please oneself. One simply writes with a sense of creative freedom that comes from being nowhere in livery or harness. When a man has written a *Love for Love*, he has learned how to write a successful— that may yet be called a creditable—play. And when he next writes a *Way of the World*, it may be presumed that he is not interested in repeating that kind of success. He is, in fact, pouring into the new play everything that he consciously or unconsciously withheld or watered down in the previous one.

And a great deal had been withheld or watered down; which means that a great deal of sheer talent had been stifled. The first difference to be noted between *Love for Love* and *The Way of the World* involves the quality Congreve is most famous for —his wit. And the difference is very great—in amount, in degree, in effect. *Love for Love* is full of wit, whether scoffing or playful, whimsical or worldly. But it is not wit of so high and pervasive a kind as afterwards to dominate our whole recollection of the play. We grant how much manner the play had at times, but are conscious of something essentially high-spirited— of feigned madness and false marriage, a sailor named Ben, a hoyden named Miss Prue. If it is comedy of manners, it is also farce, and except here and there, we would dub it comic or amusing rather than witty.

The point about *The Way of the World* is not just that it boasts a great deal more wit or a great deal better; it is not a matter of keeping score. Wit, in *The Way of the World*, is not one of the ingredients of the play, but its essential nature. *The Way of the World* is not, so to speak, witty; it is wit. We can speak of it as "wit" as we can speak of an ode of Keats as poetry, or a speech of Pitt's as eloquence. The wit of *The Way of the World* is not a matter of how many brilliant remarks Congreve may have written, but is in itself a way of writing, even a way of thinking. If you tried to paraphrase a speech in *The Way of the World* you would have hardly more luck than if you tried to paraphrase a stanza of the *Ode to a Nightingale*. The idea is completely married to the words, and if you kill off the words, the idea—like a Hindu widow—will fling itself into the same grave.

I shan't try to define wit, for one thing because no definition can be completely adequate; for another, because no definition can be sufficiently alive. It is one of the great misfortunes where literature—or the transmitting of literature—is concerned, that we are so much oftener bidden to investigate what goes into something than what comes out of it; to find out, say, whether something is poetry by giving it an elaborate pedagogical lie-detector test rather than by smelling and tasting and spontaneously reacting to it. I don't want to be misunderstood: I don't say for a minute that most of us can tell whether something is poetry by smelling and tasting it; I only know that we can never tell whether it is poetry in any other way. After all, a thing is more likely to be poetry from having something about it that is not found in other poetry; though, conversely, it is also more likely to be poetry from having something about it that *is* found in other poetry. But surely wit (like poetry) both demands and provides a peculiar climate, a particular atmosphere. Like poetry, wit lives in a house without stairs, moving upwards in a rush, in dizzy leaps; though where poetry is a bright creature with wings, wit is more like a witch on a broomstick. And the lightning suddenness is part of the thing itself: for wit is like lightning in that sometimes it merely flashes, and sometimes flashes and hits something.

And wit must glitter exactly as poetry must glow; neither may show wear or tarnish, neither may plod. But quite as important as their having something bright about them is their having something concentrated. Compared with realism—or reality—wit and poetry alike are under much greater atmospheric pressure. We think of them as being more brilliantly clothed, but we must also see them as more essentially naked. About what they say or show or do there is something barer and more direct than about all other forms of expression. That, of course, is why they are so fatiguing: we have so much to absorb in so little space. A line like

A bracelet of bright hair about the bone

uses as much up in us as a whole paragraph of prose; and so, in a different way, does a line like "We refuse praise from a desire to be praised twice." One reason why—from a normal audience point of view—*The Way of the World* finds it hard to succeed on the stage is that theatrically it moves too slow, with talk where one would welcome action. But a perhaps deeper reason is that verbally it moves too fast: the wit has us panting and puffing to keep up with it. Such writing is too concise for the stage.

Of course wit, like poetry, is a matter of context; it has even been said, with much cogency, that the quintessential wit is that which arises spontaneously of the moment and which, being part of the flow of talk, briefly sparkles and is then borne downstream and out of sight. (And it is true that what gets remembered is usually in the form of a wisecrack, an epigram, or a specific description of a person or an event.) The wit of Congreve, the pervasive and carpeting wit of *The Way of the World* depends, I think, on context and even on character. Although a fair amount of it is in the form of epigram and antithesis and metaphor, it loses greatly if detached from the body of the play. Congreve's wit purrs so smoothly that one is not always aware how sharply it bites. It would rather be wellbred than emphatic, would rather chime like a clock than go off like a gun. If you turn to Bartlett's Quotations you may be surprised, as I was, to find there just one example from Congreve's *prose*, though you will find columns of quotations from Oscar Wilde. Wilde, I think, was in one way or another almost the wittiest man who ever lived; no one could write more brilliant nonsense, or better epigram or repartee. But one must still say that Wilde was witty and Congreve was wit; by which one means that in Wilde all the trimmings have glitter, but that in the Congreve of *The Way of the World* wit constitutes the texture itself. With Congreve, wit becomes an actual pair of spectacles for looking at life; with Congreve at his finest, it becomes a burning lens. Listen to Witwoud telling what trouble Petulant took to make himself seem sought after:

> *Why he would slip out of this chocolate-house, just when you had been talking to him. As soon as your back was turned— whip he was gone; then trip to his lodging, clap on a hood and scarf and a mask, slap into a hackney-coach, and drive hither to the door again in a trice; where he would send in for himself; that I mean, call for himself, wait for himself, nay, and what's more, not finding himself, sometimes leave a letter for himself.*

Listen, again, to Mrs. Marwood on the subject of getting married:

> MRS. MARWOOD: *If I could but find one that loved me very well, and would be thoroughly sensible of ill usage, I think I should do myself the violence of undergoing the ceremony.*
>
> MRS. FAINALL: *You would not make him a cuckold?*
>
> MRS. MARWOOD: *No; but I'd make him believe I did, and that's as bad.*
>
> MRS. FAINALL: *Why had you as good to do it?*
>
> MRS. MARWOOD: *Oh, if he should ever discover it, he would then know the worst, and be out of his pain; but I would have him ever to continue upon the wrack of fear and jealousy.*

Neither quotation ranks with the best things in *The Way of the World*; but taken in context, both serve to show how fundamental the *idea* of wit is to the play, and in how many ways; for they represent something in terms of style, and of tone, and of characterization. The hardness of Mrs. Marwood's remarks derives from the hardness of the woman herself; while Witwoud on the subject of Petulant is not only satirizing, but is being satirized.

We shall come back to the characters of the play; let us first, along with its wit, say something about such related qualities as its style and tone. The tone is as worldly and aristocratic and urbane as any play could be, and perhaps more than any effective stage-play can afford to be. It is not only that, barring Lady

Wishfort and Sir Wilful in two or three scenes, nobody raises his voice or cries out upon life in any natural way; it is that in capturing what might be called an ideal of drawing-room elegance, Congreve has exhibited its limitations as well as its lustre. So brilliant is his brushwork and coloring, so unified his tone, that this is a kind of fairyland of fine manners; this is how we may expect people to talk in Heaven. But these are people we must expect to find in Hell. These are people we must pass judgment on, and call as tarnished within as they are polished without. The play is well named; its concern is not with this person's folly or that one's vice, but with all leisure-class society, its incentives of pleasure, its temptations to betray or misbehave. But if what we are watching is in one sense the way of the great world, where courteous words hide treacherous hearts, there is something else to be observed: not simply how self-indulgent or inconstant these people are, but how foiled and frustrated. They cannot, many of them, have what they want in the way of a husband or lover; they dare not believe in friendship or hope for love. They are trapped by the baseness of their own view of life and by the very selfishness of their own desires. Even in suffering they cannot find salvation, for they do not know how to suffer; their reaction, on feeling pain, is to try to inflict it elsewhere. Having shaken our heads in disapproval of them, we must at the last shake our heads more sadly, in dismay. There is no need for others to moralize about them: they themselves point the moral all too vividly.

This is something apprehended in the midst of the spin and sparkle of language and wit, as we apprehend of a winter sun that it gives, for all its brightness, no warmth. It is a question of tone; the teaching of the play, so far as it does teach, is in the tone; Congreve is not only too good an artist to try to teach more overtly, he is perhaps too skeptical and baffled and—if you choose—superficial a philosopher to know how. He was, one supposes, the perfect worldling, with far too much taste and sensibility to acquiesce cynically in what he saw of life, and yet with too strong and pessimistic a sense of the way of the world—and too great an affinity for it—ever to protest very

much. It is a matter of his particular temperament: I think we
may fairly say that a Congreve who would have felt the need of
stronger measures, of raising his voice instead of his eyebrows,
would not have been Congreve. We must look elsewhere for
writers with more severe and positive values, for writers who
aspire beyond tone to something like vision; but *The Way of the
World* yet furnishes, in its own esthetic fashion, a sense of the
melancholy in life, the awful hell of life. No tone could be more
civilized than Congreve's, yet no story suggests how little being
civilized avails.

But how much it avails, how enormously it counts, in art. No
merely "natural" talent could conceive, let alone execute, a
Millamant or contrive, beyond even the verbal merits of the
play, its decisive sense of style. When, finally, well on in the
second act, Millamant appears and Mirabel salutes her with his
celebrated words—"Here she comes, i'faith, full sail, with her
fan spread and streamers out, and a shoal of fools for tender,"
with what a splash, with how great an air, she enters. Mirabel,
indeed, so glorifies Millamant, we are scarcely aware that he is
also making fun of her. She enters, and after a little give-and-
take comes the business of the letters:

> MILLA.: . . . *Mincing, what had I? Why was I so long?*
> MINC.: *O mem, your laship stayed to peruse a packet of letters.*
> MILLA.:*Oh, ay, letters—I had letters—I am persecuted with
> letters—I hate letters. Nobody knows how to write letters;
> and yet one has 'em, one does not know why. They serve
> one to pin up one's hair.*
> WIT.: *Is that the way? Pray, madam, do you pin up your hair
> with all your letters? I find I must keep copies.*
> MILLA.: *Only with those in verse, Mr. Witwoud. I never
> pin up my hair with prose. I think I tried once, Mincing.*
> MINC.: *O mem, I shall never forget it.*
> MILLA.: *Ay, poor Mincing tift and tift all the morning.*
> MINC.: *Till I had the cramp in my fingers, I'll vow, mem.
> And all to no purpose. But when your laship pins it up with*

*poetry, it fits so pleasant the next day as anything, and is so
pure and so crips.*
WIT.: *Indeed, so crips?*
MINC.: *You're such a critic, Mr. Witwoud.*

Here again it is not just the language, still less the fancifulness,
but a certain turn and heightening, a certain effect of style that
gives this trivial little scene distinction. It is the style that really
gives the play the exact pitch, the sure mark, of high comedy,
that adds a kind of breeding to the brilliance. It is, at any rate,
the decisive element in a prose of the finest sort—a kind of
prose, moreover, that in word-choice and rhythm and movement
is the equal of fine poetry, and yet not in any usual sense poetic.
We have simple prose masters like Swift and Defoe; we have
supple prose masters like Arnold and Newman, but with none
of these do we often linger over the turn of a phrase, the shape
of a sentence, the balancing of words or clauses against one
another, as we linger over corresponding things in distinguished
poets; while those prose writers whose phrasing and capacity
for style do triumph as things in themselves—Donne, Jeremy
Taylor, Sir Thomas Browne—are writers of insistently rhetorical or poetic prose. But Congreve's prose, however precise in
language or perfect in rhythm, never loses a certain low-pitched
dryness and coolness, a certain colloquial ease. It remains do-
mesticated. Sterne, in his own way, is the same kind of prose
writer, keeps the same kind of colloquial ease.

I have spoken at length about the literary qualities of *The
Way of the World;* I have said nothing, and mean to say nothing,
of the plot; and have still to speak of the characters. There is no
use going into *The Way of the World* as a play in the technical
sense, because whether or not it is rather better than is generally
supposed is wonderfully unimportant; and to try to work up
enthusiasm for *The Way of the World* in terms of its stagecraft
would be like trying to work up enthusiasm for Chartres cathe-
dral on the basis of its acoustics. It is so easy to admire the
briskly competent in literature or painting or drama; the second-

raters, the craftsmen, the conformists, the middlebrows have naturally the fewest faults. As playwrights and novelists they are tidy because they worship neatness; as critics and appreciators they are reliable because they spend their lives taking conducted tours rather than exploring for themselves. But very little first-rate work is flawless, and an artist who is great for one or two things, and great in a truly individual way, is to be cherished and set apart, no matter what his faults and limitations. There is a great deal wrong, very offensively wrong, with Macaulay: he is smug, he is philistine, he is brassy, he has no respect for the truth, and almost no understanding of human beings. But he happens to have a kind of genius for rhetoric and a great genius for narrative. Who cares whether, had he tried, Pope could have been the kind of poet Keats was? Who cares whether he was a poet at all, seeing that never in history has a man been born with such mastery over the heroic couplet or such genius for vilification? Who cares whether Jane Austen couldn't treat of passion—though actually she could—or whether Emily Brontë could treat of little else? Just so with how competent a play *The Way of the World* may be. As a matter of fact, whatever concessions it makes to the mere mechanics of playwriting only do it harm, only enforce on the play one or two inferior characters and an ending that is stock and even stagy.

Almost every talented writer who sets about writing plays must be often plagued by the dilemma of writing for the theater or writing for himself. There are times when he virtually cannot do both. This is not a matter of "integrity," but of working in a medium that to be effective must quite literally achieve *effects*—something vivid or startling, carefully planted or staged. Stage-craft, to an extent not found in the craft of other arts, is tricks. And the playwright is always menaced by dangers from both sides, by the Scylla of flatness, by the Charybdis of falsity. The artless method leads all too often to boredom, the artful method inspires disbelief.

Moreover, in the case of high comedy—of *The Misanthrope* or *The Way of the World*—we tend to deal (as mere realism does not) with the scarcely amendable faults and contradictions of human nature, with life as a process rather than as something that forges a plot. We are to understand that the conflict between an Alceste and a Célimène is unresolvable, and that the way of the world is no passing fashion, but an eternal fact. Action, in the realistic or dramatic sense, is not only a little too crude for high comedy; it is really a little irrelevant. There is too much awareness involved; and rather than the struggle against defeat that we find in drama, high comedy has a skepticism that is very nearly defeatism. Millamant holds Mirabel off throughout most of *The Way of the World*, but this is not simply a conventional plot device, or the tactics of a "romantic" heroine. Millamant is not simply choosing a man, or even choosing one man from many; she is deciding whether to marry. It is a donnée of the novel and the stage that everybody wishes to marry, and marriage is the only way an ordinary novelist or playwright has for conveying that certain characters lived happily ever after. But the issue is not so simple, and the idea of marriage, which is not the same thing as the idea of mating, must be particularly disquieting to a very clever, high-mettled, attractive, sought-after girl who is as much her own mistress as Millamant.

The marriage scene between Millamant and Mirabel is so supremely witty and delightful as mere banter that we almost fail to notice the quite realistic basis of the bargaining. We are so pleased with Millamant's remark about how she "may dwindle into a wife" that we may miss the point of her conditions—which are plainly made that their marriage may not stagnate into a farce or deteriorate into a failure. Congreve, like other masters of high comedy, employs a kind of paradox—suggests the tarnish of life through the glitter, the lees through the froth, the clouds and shadows through the moment—the all-too-passing moment—of sunshine. This marriage-contract scene is pure Mozart; this is the shimmer and gaiety that those people alone are capable of who know how fugitive is pleasure, how fraudulent are even the best-meant vows, how touched with melancholy is life. Reading the scene, we may of course ignore everything but its charm, and will still have been notably rewarded; but there is more to it than charm. Edward Fitzgerald said somewhere that we are so conscious of how beautiful Mozart is that we do not realize how powerful he is also; and though Congreve is no Mozart, he no more tinkles than Mozart does. All plodders, all earnest souls, all people who judge things by mere size and weight, distrust and dismiss gaiety as minor and even frivolous. But we ought not to be deceived; there is not only more health in the moment of joyousness, but very likely more depth. What could be gayer than Natasha at the ball in *War and Peace*—or more beautiful and memorable? What has more brilliance than the court scenes in *The Charterhouse of Parma*, and the relations between Mosca and the Duchess— and yet more, at bottom, of that hard truth, and even of the tragic *sense*, of life? And who in a way, for all his celebrated melancholy is gayer, brisker, more playful, more full of spring and wit, than Hamlet?

Millamant seems to me an extremely successful creation as much for what Congreve didn't make her as for what he did. Thus he didn't make her lovable: there is nothing warmhearted or self-effacing or innocently girlish about her; one cannot imagine her being terribly kind to people she cares nothing about, or staying home from a ball to sit at a sick aunt's bedside. She is not at all noble-minded or even, by our standards, very humane. She is spoiled, she is pert, she is given to airs and even to affectations, she is invincibly feminine, she is a complete coquette. She makes light of most things; she makes fun of many. She is a fine lady, and not to be put upon, a very superior girl who knows her own worth. And like any person who is honest about it, she loves being sought after and complimented and courted.

The point is that she is the very best product of a certain world, a certain kind of life: the point is, equally, that she does not rise above it. She is captivating rather than lovable, and much easier, I imagine, to find fault with than to resist. She has taste and sensibility and perceptiveness, and at moments that incomparable hoity-toityness wherewith women always have, if not the last word, the last laugh. Nowhere has she it more superbly than concerning the vanity and fatuousness of lovers:

> Lord [she asks] *what is a lover that it can give? Why, one makes lovers as fast as one pleases, and they live as long as one pleases, and they die as soon as one pleases: and then, if one pleases, one makes more.*

One particular virtue about Millamant is that, though a perfect character of artificial comedy—endowed with an air too completely perfect for real life—her actual behavior and motivations are realistic and convincing. That is to say, we shall probably never meet any girl who talks quite as well as she, but we shall meet a girl, now and then, who has something of the same gift, and says much the same things. It is her graces, not her virtues, that are incomparable. And it is a tribute to Congreve's honesty as well as to his talent that he has made Millamant so radiant a figure without making her a romantic or entirely girlish one.

After Millamant, the other characters—including Mirabel—rather tend to pale. But something special must be said for Witwoud, the type who must be always in the know and never caught napping, never lacking a clever answer or an up-to-date tidbit of gossip or slang; a good kind of second-rater, really, whom we almost admire till we see him come up against some one better. I do not share the usual opinion about how tragic Lady Wishfort is: pathetic, yes, and a very wretched figure, burning with sexual desire while grown old and ugly. But she is too much a fool, too shallow, too gullible, for us to care about *her*; what we feel for is her situation, is that of any one unloved and wanting love. She is also—and wisely—made quite farcical: otherwise, without becoming tragic, she might seem too uncomfortably realistic. We all but laugh out loud, hearing this hag wonder to her maid how "Sir Rowland" will behave on his first visit

> *Will he be importunate, Foible, and push?*

Congreve does better with certain other characters, even with his villains, Fainall and Mrs. Marwood. They have a remarkable scene together—I quote the end:

MRS. MAR.: *Truth and you are inconsistent.—I hate you, and shall forever.*

FAINALL: *For loving you?*

MRS. MAR.: *I loathe the name of love after such usage. . . . Farewell.*

FAINALL: *Nay, we must not part thus.*

MRS. MAR.: *Let me go.*

FAINALL: *Come, I'm sorry.*

MRS. MAR.: *I care not. Let me go. Break my hands, do—I'd leave 'em to get loose.*

FAINALL: *I would not hurt you for the world. . . . You know I love you.*

MRS. MAR.: *Poor dissembling! Oh, that—well, it is not yet—*

FAINALL: *What? What is it not? It is not yet too late—*

MRS. MAR.: *No, it is not yet too late—I have that comfort.*

FAINALL: *It is, to love another.*

MRS. MAR.: *But not to loathe, detest, abhor mankind, myself and the whole treacherous world.*

FAINALL: *Nay, this is extravagance. Come, I ask your pardon. No tears—I was to blame, I could not love you and be easy in my doubts. Pray forbear—I believe you; I'm convinced I've done you wrong; and any way, every way will make amends: I'll hate my wife yet more, damn her, I'll part with her, rob her of all she's worth, and we'll retire somewhere, anywhere, to another world; I'll marry thee—be pacified.—'Sdeath, they come: hide your face, your tears. You have a mask: wear it a moment. This way, this way: be persuaded.*

Now this is a scene which those people who always speak of how exquisite everything is in Congreve, as though he were as dainty as a coffee spoon, must have a little trouble over. For it seems to me, and I was glad to find that it seemed so to Mr. Dobrée, a scene of quite inexorable realism. Or rather, as realism is only a method, this scene is better called reality—a few speeches exchanged by two suddenly very believable people who have been in a very real relationship. It is not at all comic; and it is not *merely* worldly. It is the work, a little out of his usual run, of a man who had a cold heart but could understand what it was to feel, and who, though he might refuse to be tragic about love, had had some sense of what a tragedy it could be. One has so much to say about what is characteristic in Congreve, that it may be useful to take leave of him where he gives us something so unexpected as this, and so unexpectedly good.

CHAPTER IX

Cibber and Vanbrugh

CONGREVE is the high point of Restoration comedy, and is equally, in a sense, the end of it. His cold brilliance, his spotless worldliness represent something too special to be wholly at one with the general attitude of a period; yet they never collide with that attitude. *The Way of the World* is something more than Restoration comedy, rather than something different: the artist transcends his age as an artist, but participates in it as a man. Yet a sense of change was in the air, new attitudes were coming into being. Literature, for a generation, had been not only licentious but heartless, not just indecent but cynical. The prevailing note was not that dalliance was pleasant, but that wives were deceitful; not youth's natural advantage over age, but delight in making age wear horns. Clearly this could not last forever. It must change, on general grounds, because of the pendulum swing in taste and morals; but change, too, because people dislike taking a low view of human nature—it means taking an unflattering view of themselves. Now and then—after a long age of piety and repression—they will be so resentful of all the straitlacedness about them, and so emboldened by the example of King and Court, as to delight in saying, "Let us be bad together." And then it becomes fashionable to be bad; and next, it becomes priggish not to be. All the same, many people do not want to be bad. Drinking makes them sick; late hours make them irritable. And many other people are upset by being bad: they feel self-conscious at the time or guilty afterwards. There is furthermore the matter of satiety, which is presumably why rakes marry or rich people go in for the simple life. There is finally the matter of sensibility: the moment arrives when a certain kind of loose talk seems distasteful, when a drunken brawl no longer seems dashing. Both satiety and sensibility operate on us, just as *readers* of Restoration comedy: the time arrives when we, precisely like Restoration audiences before us, can enjoy no more of it.

I am not speaking, as you see, of repressive forces clamped on society from without—of the influence of religion or respectability—but of reactions generated from within; and together with that must be mentioned the psychological element, the appeal of forbidden fruit. In Restoration times, there was too much permission—even encouragement—to sin, for sin to seem at all glamorous. As for those who, despite all this, had no wish to be reformed, they came more and more to be restrained. They remained wicked, but no longer flaunted their wickedness: a token morality, a surface decorum began to prevail. Harlotry may not have declined, but hypocrisy increased; and as it became less permissible for flesh to be weak, it became less so, as well, for hearts to be hard. In literature and the theater, there came to be rather less of sex and rather more of sentiment. A new formula was waiting in the wings and was now to dash out upon the stage. The formula still exists, still flourishes wherever there are circulating libraries or movies. The formula decrees that virtue and morality shall triumph—at the very end: the rake is reformed; the bad woman sinks to her knees; the good woman, though fiercely tempted, is never quite seduced; the Devil has every laugh but the last one. Such sentimental comedy is often said to have been born in Colley Cibber's *Love's Last Shift*. Doubtless most elements in it had appeared much earlier, but here suddenly, though the voice seems still the voice of the Restoration, the hands are the hands of Respectability. Cibber has found a way to reconcile virtue with spice. At the end, his hero Loveless is indeed reformed and put into harness. But only at the end—as Cibber tells the audience, reassuringly, in the epilogue:

He's lewd for above four acts, gentlemen.

We may hope that Cibber had the grace to smile, if not blush, when he wrote those words, for in their conscienceless pandering they are surely among the most indecent ever written. And they are among the most permanently offensive—the very spirit of what is meretricious, and calculating, and mercenary, the epitome of all the crocodile tears and sanctimonious headshakes that crowd fast upon four acts of titillation and suggestiveness. After two or three such sentimental comedies, we sigh for the wholesome decency of Shadwell or Wycherley.

No single instance of sentimental comedy need quite so much offend us; nor is *Love's Last Shift* a particularly outrageous example of the breed. It is that line from the epilogue that is impossible to pardon. The play itself, besides being passably readable on its own score, enjoys the distinction of inspiring Vanbrugh's *The Relapse* as a kind of retort, as "proof" that Cibber's rake would not stay reformed. The story of *Love's Last Shift* is typically Restoration enough. In the center—though constantly shunted to one side—are Amanda and Loveless, he having married her and tired of her and hence deserted her and gone to the Continent to squander his fortune in high living. Now he has come home penniless to England, and is told by his friend Worthy, who hopes to reunite the pair, that Amanda is dead. Young Worthy's design (which is love's last shift) is to make the husband fall in love again with the wife by thinking himself in love with some one new. Hence Loveless is introduced into Amanda's household and Amanda's bed without realizing that she is Amanda; and he becomes so ardent a lover that he is only too glad—not least because she is now rich—to become once again her husband.

The particular ruse involved is surely not new with Cibber; but it gets sentimental comedy off to a spanking start. The lady and the audience can alike enjoy the sense of something illicit when it is all the time respectable; though the end is hardly satisfactory even on its own terms. Loveless has been not so much reformed as bought, Amanda regaining him only when he learns she is an heiress. But it is all very seemly: even Loveless' servant, who has seduced Amanda's waiting woman, is made to marry her.

The rest of the play sticks rather close to the more romantic and satiric side of Restoration comedy. There are two young ladies, along with two brothers who are in love with them; there is Sir William, who tries to trick one brother out of a fortune, only to be tricked back; and there is a fop, Sir Novelty Fashion, who has nuisance-value in the love affairs and amusement-value in the play. Historically the important thing is the ending, where the wedding march is played with a new and holier gusto, and constitutes the funeral march of pure Restoration comedy. The "reform" of Loveless means that henceforth it is not the maiden who will be debauched, but the stage itself. But the ending aside, the play is tolerable hackwork. Congreve's famous remark about it pretty well sums it up: there were a great many things in it, he said, that were *like* wit but were not wit. The first page or two bears this out. "What a fine pack of guineas have you had," Worthy tells the down-at-heel Loveless, "and yet you would make 'em run till you were quite spent." Or: "A man is as unfit to follow love with an empty stomach as business with an empty head." These have the rattle that goes with wit; they have what, in the one case, might be a pungent metaphor, in the other a bright antithesis. Only in both cases, there is nothing at all sharp or amusing. Wherever Cibber serves notice on you of being witty, he particularly fails; he comes nearest to being amusing when he least tries to be, as the play itself is most agreeable when least ambitious. Whenever it pretends to real emotion, it becomes mere rant. "Oh thou hast roused me," Loveless tells Amanda, "from my deep lethargy of vice! . . . Here will I fix, thus prostrate sigh my shame, and wash my crimes in never-ceasing tears of penitence."

The most diverting thing in the play is the character of Sir

Novelty, the fop whom Vanbrugh was to convert into Lord Foppington. Already here Sir Novelty keeps saying "stap my vitals"; already here he catalogues his services to costume and dress. His modesty can be delightful, as when he poohpoohs what he takes to be a compliment by saying "Stap my vitals, I don't believe there are five hundred women in town that ever took any notice of me." His best performance perhaps comes when he makes love and, as it were, proposes marriage to Narcissa not by speaking of her charms or his devotion, but by summarizing his services to fashion:

> *In short, madam, the cravat string, the garter, the sword knot, the centurine, the burdash, the steenkirk, the large button, the long sleeve, the plume and the full peruke were all created, cried down, or revived by me.*

He is an easy mark to shoot at, but here and there Cibber does bring him down.

The play also, here and there, catches out a Restoration attitude, such as that in courtship often the object was less to win the lady than to defeat a rival. It is not hard to see why *Love's Last Shift* succeeded. It was the same old drink, only with more sugar in it; it pointed a moral out of the same material it used to adorn a tale. In itself it was scarcely decisive—one Cibber doesn't make a sentimental drama. But he sniffed what was on the breeze, he read what was on the cards. In strict chronology, *Love's Last Shift* preceded *The Way of the World* by several years; and thus Restoration comedy was sinking into a swamp before it had gained its highest peak. But before sentimental comedy took over, though the old sharpness and brilliance might be gone, good nature and high spirits were to have their innings; while dusk gathered and darkness spread about, Vanbrugh and Farquhar were to hang up their colored lanterns and bid the musicians play a medley of brisk tunes.

The Relapse, the first of Vanbrugh's plays, was conceived as a sort of sequel to *Love's Last Shift*. The play had a considerable success, and for a first play exhibits uncommon merit. However much may be wrong with it, it is frequently entertaining—and in a slightly new way. The play itself may carry over from Cibber, but the playwright does more than merely echo Etherege or Shadwell or Congreve. Vanbrugh introduces something fresh —though less by way of talent than of tone. It is something a little breezier and brisker than we have so far met with—the sort of thing that can make a scene "go," though not necessarily make it live. No significant change has come about in the writing of comedy; we have reached no turn in the road. Yet already with a first play—and a sequel to another man's play at that— we are past mere imitation and conformity. We might say that the elegance of good Restoration comedy seems a little diminished and the exuberance a little enhanced. The going, in Restoration comedy, is rather slow because one either wants to linger over the wit or is bogged down by the plot. But with *The Relapse* one moves faster: the wit and the prose are not so special that one stops to linger over them, while the story-telling has a freer swing.

The first thing to be said about the play, in terms of content, is that it is actually two plays. And two plays, or plots, that again offer something different, for this is not, as with Dryden, the interleaving of a serious plot with a humorous one, nor again, as with half a dozen earlier playwrights, a matter of plot and subplot. The pundits tell us very complacently that the plot involving Tom Fashion, Lord Foppington, and Miss Hoyden is the *real* plot; but that may well be arguing after the fact, judging by results rather than intentions. There is no question that the plot involving Tom Fashion, Lord Foppington, and Miss Hoyden is the successful plot, the one that we enjoy. But Vanbrugh devotes almost as much space to the one action as to the other; the characters all belong to much the same social class; and certainly, of the two plots, that involving Tom Fashion, Lord Foppington, and Miss Hoyden is much the more farcical and old-fashioned. It is the sort of plot to be found anywhere, at any time; where the plot involving Loveless and Amanda, Berinthia and Worthy, would be labeled "Restoration comedy" at a glance.

No doubt Cibber saddled Vanbrugh with this double plot. But somehow Vanbrugh lacked judgment about it, and dramatic tact—if we are to have two sets of stories, clearly they must either come closer together or stand farther apart. There is a kind of pleasure—not the highest kind, but a very real one—in watching a good craftsman intertwine two separate strands of plot. There is also a certain liveliness to keeping two stories in motion that are operating at different levels, in different moods, to create different effects. We seldom, with such stories, feel *esthetically* comfortable: about them, instead of an eventual happy marriage, there is a strong sense of misalliance; and misalliances, in literature as in society, bring out the snob in us. But though it makes us esthetically unhappy, such a play can be the more fun for leading a wench-in-the-kitchen, wife-in-the-parlor double life.

The trouble with the two plots of *The Relapse* is that they are mere next-door neighbors, adjacent but unrelated. Indeed, they meet but twice—once when Lord Foppington literally comes from next door to call and remains to duel, and at the end, when the Loveless group are guests at what turns out *not* to be Lord Foppington's wedding party. Vanbrugh's scheme of things requires, to succeed, a larger canvas and less merely farcical movement; it should be social comedy on a scale to suggest a whole milieu, more like modern novels that are really concerned with London or New York itself.

But we do not get this in *The Relapse*. Instead, we get just two compact groups. The first group form around Amanda and Loveless, the faithful wife and would-be faithful husband. The pair go from their country place to London, where Loveless is smitten at the playhouse with a young woman who turns out to be his wife's cousin. Her former lover, Worthy, is smitten with his wife; and the cousin, Berinthia, while pursuing her amour with Loveless, tries to further Worthy's cause with Amanda. All this is in the unmistakable vein of the Restoration; all this involves deception, duplicity, adultery; on Loveless's part every trick and wile that can be practiced by a husband; and on Berinthia's, conduct equally shameful in a friend, a cousin, and a house guest. It involves colloquies—splashed with cynicism and sprin-kled with wit—about love and marriage, women and men; it frequently achieves that bland tone of discussing the most out-rageous betrayals as though they were mere pleasantries.

Yet something has crept in and something has been dropped out. What has crept in, I think, is a certain self-consciousness, a too-distinct awareness of the whole Restoration perspective. Vanbrugh seems quite at home with it, in terms of society and the stage alike; he does not have to bluff, or imitate, or pilfer. Nor is he intimidated or distressed or incensed by what he sees, or moved to examine and re-assess it. But neither does he quite instinctively respond to it: we do not feel that, had there been no Restoration comedy, Vanbrugh would have felt the need to invent it. Or that, even had it been ten years out of fashion, Van-brugh would have been the man to revive it. Vanbrugh, in this first play, isn't simply familiar with Restoration comedy, as with the house one lives in; he is over-aware of it, as with a house one is about to move out of.

At first sight, *The Relapse* is genuine Restoration comedy. And yet something has been left out; something that on Vanbrugh's part shows not incompetence but incompatibility. In the most characteristic Restoration comedy there is a kind of artifice that controls the entire action. One can like it or not, but no one can understand Restoration comedy without grasping that this is a world in which people wear dancing pumps, and not walking shoes, by intention, because this is something stylized, some-thing meant to be danced. The scene need not on that account be fairyland; on the contrary, the characters are often dancing on the edge of a volcano. They are almost always at a masked ball, almost always eager to change partners. Almost always they are not just people, but performers: wit with them is one kind of game, sex another. In a sense, the truth about them comes out in the lies they tell; artificial as Restoration comedy is, it is yet not emptily or fortuitously so. It mirrors a real, however loathsome, social ideal. On the stage all is artifice because in society all is hypocrisy.

The reality of every established society *is* artifice; good society is like a stage, and what goes on backstage is no part of its domains. One shuts one's eyes, in good society, to the source of money, even to the need of money. People must be told they look well, even if they are clearly dying; and people are to say they feel well, even if they crawl home ten minutes later to die. One chats in public with one's mistress as though she were one's music teacher; one tells one lie about coming late, another about leaving early. In time such pretense seems far more natural than the truth; as it seems, in time, far more natural to wear clothes than go naked.

In *The Relapse*, however, the artifice that ought to condition the whole ensuing activity never quite does so. We miss a certain tone, a certain traditional voice-level: Vanbrugh, like his Amanda, *wants* to take the worldly fashionable view, to treat love and sex as a game, to give a hard enameled surface to life. But he rarely does so. Or rather, he never does for long; he can contrive but not sustain the sort of hard frivolity he is after. He lacks the right mixture of urbanity and brutality; he cannot, as it were, delicately crisp and starch his characters with vice. Indeed, he cannot treat the situation of Amanda and Berinthia as either a confederacy of women against men or an alliance of reciprocal deception. Amanda not only remains virtuous, she becomes in time almost Victorian, first resisting the tempter's advances, then receiving his remorseful idolatry. (Nor is this because she is inherited from Cibber.) Berinthia, on the other hand, not only sins with Loveless, but proves utterly treacherous to Amanda, and serves as procuress for Worthy. She becomes one of the basest of Restoration characters—far *too* base for the situation Vanbrugh has contrived. The two women are set against each other like characters in sentimental drama, but the story they are part of is not sufficiently weighted for such a contrast. The whole thing is personal in tone where it should be social, and ends by substituting staginess for artifice. The whole thing misses, goes flat, turns a little dull, and, in Berinthia's case, offers a really hateful character whom we never care enough about to hate.

It is in the other plot, involving Tom Fashion, Lord Foppington, and Miss Hoyden, that Vanbrugh comes to life. Here, where the action is so largely farcical, the treatment can be brisk. Here we are in a world of mischievousness rather than malice; here deception has more the air of a prank than of a betrayal, here are no tender feelings to consider nor highbred sensibilities to display: the characters bear not names but labels —Miss Hoyden, Lord Foppington, Sir Tunbelly Clumsy. Only Tom Fashion, the younger brother who decides to make his fortune by courting Miss Hoyden in Lord Foppington's name, could fit equally well into either plot. He could remain a rakish man-about-town, part of Amanda's set, or go forth, as he does, an impostor into the country.

His imposture is high-spirited and amusing. Except for a few shots at Foppington's expense, the fun in *The Relapse* is reasonably primitive, with a smack of the eighteenth century about it —of that side of the eighteenth century that tends to be forgotten. No century could show more elegance and finesse, but none either, had a beerier or rowdier sense of fun. There is a childlikeness—a needed emotional escape from reality—about the English that equally makes poets or pranksters of them. And perhaps the strong materialistic streak in the English—the streak that makes them supreme philistines no less than supreme poets—is a compensating *approach* to reality for a race that, emotionally, is always in flight from it. Emotionally the English are such lurid romantics, such arrant sentimentalists, so given to wallowing in heroisms and gallantries, that they had to create the stiff upper lip on the same principle that the Dutch had to invent the dike. The Restoration—at least on its higher social levels—probably reveals the English at their most foreign (in this case, their most French). But they were perhaps most like themselves—their essential selves—during parts of the eighteenth century, when they were sexually still not repressed, when they were socially still very privileged. In the eighteenth century the typical aristocrat lived in a sort of Garden of Eden; he had shed all his ancestors' gloomy fear of God and the Devil, and had not yet acquired his descendants' panicky dread of bad form and public opinion. He lived in a halcyon age that had escaped from Thou Shalt Not and not yet been enslaved by It's Not Done. The eighteenth century had, in any case, a rather boyish and often quite boorish sense of fun, and it is this sense of fun that we begin to encounter in the better half of *The Relapse*.

The new quality lies, much less in the fortune-hunting, brother-impersonating plot than in the breezy, good-natured tone. Good nature is something we rarely encounter in Restoration comedy. Etherege is even-tempered; Dryden is large-natured; but perhaps only Aphra Behn impresses us as bringing an easy, benign acceptance to life. With Vanbrugh, good nature has in a way been substituted for grace. Even the wit is turning to humor, the satire is shaded with whimsy:

> "*Pray, which church*" [Berinthia asks Lord Fopping-ton] "*does your lordship most oblige with your presence?*"
> FOP.: *Oh, St. James's, madam—. There's much the best company.*
> AMANDA: *Is there good preaching too?*
> FOP.: *Faith, madam—I can't tell. A man must have very little to do there that can give an account of the sermon.*

Again, Foppington objects to reading books on the ground that it is "to entertain oneself with the forc'd product of another man's brain." This is too ingenious for mere satire. So is Foppington's insistence that pockets can never be placed too low—"the pocket," he says, "becomes no part of the body but the knee." The difference between Foppington and Etherege's Sir Fopling is that Sir Fopling's remarks always have some bearing on his own vanity and egotism—Cordovan gloves nauseate *him*, etc. Sir Fopling is more ridiculous and unreal because he is more than a mere coxcomb, because he is the quintessence of coxcombry. And coxcombry, at bottom, is not only mania but megalomania, not only a love of dress and fine airs, but a love of self. And Lord Foppington is no such megalomaniac as Sir Fopling; is not even so megalomaniac as his Cibber-self, Sir Novelty Fashion. He is almost more poseur than fop, and is very much more the slave of public opinion than a seeker after public acclaim. "Come, Mr. Foretop," he tells the periwig-maker, after the tailor and bootmaker have been and gone, "Come, Mr. Foretop, let me see what you have done, and then the fatigue of the morning will be over." Sir Fopling would never make us smile that way. Lord Foppington is indeed—as others have observed—in many respects practical and rational, with a hard head for business and a pretty hard heart for other people. We see him, in fact, in all sorts of relationships —as a suitor, a neighbor, a brother, a climber, a snob, as a man who bought his title because it was good business. His foppishness gives him a comic-character halo, it makes him entertaining where he might otherwise seem unpleasant.

In the way his brother Tom outwits him, and in the whole sequence of countryhouse scenes, we have the kind of good-humored farce that is simply written to be enjoyed. In these scenes most of it is enjoyable, or has at any rate an old-fashioned liveliness; as has Sir Tunbelly Clumsy himself.

> *"Here," he says to his servant when Tom arrives impersonating Foppington, "run in-a-doors quickly: Get a Scotch-coal fire in the great parlour: set all the Turkey-work chairs in their places: get the great brass candlesticks out, and be sure to stick the sockets full of laurel: run."*

And to his other servants:

> *"And do you hear, run away to Nurse, bid her let Miss Hoyden loose again, and if it was not shifting day, let her put on a clean tucker—quick."*

We are suddenly thrust into an eighteenth-century world of fox-hunts and draughty country houses, where men may be brutes but aren't villains, and ways will be gross but never venomous. There is a quite new sort of bustle and joviality. And yet there is something a little wrong about the way in which *The Relapse* winds up: in proper farce, when a Tom Fashion bests a Lord Foppington, when brother outwits brother, there must be a real contrast of character or a sufficient rough justice or wild luck to the outcome to make it all go down. Here there is too much the suggestion of a swindle; here, though Foppington has given Tom cause enough—by refusing him help—to attempt his prank, he hasn't given him quite cause enough to succeed at it. We feel a moral scruple, as we do more strongly about Berinthia's baseness. It may be that Tom seems the worse swindler and Berinthia the greater villainess just because the tone is otherwise so good-natured; but whatever the reason, we do feel a little jarred. Even though he attacked the play chiefly on other grounds, we can understand how Jeremy Collier should have chosen *The Relapse* as a chief target. In one way, it is among the least offensive or, at any rate least heartless, of Restoration comedies; but for just that reason, where it does seem immoral it seems glaringly so. And if we are to be blunt, we must find something wonderful in Collier's—and virtually every one else's—silence concerning the quite pointless homosexual fooling between Tom and Old Coupler. It, too, mars the tone of the play. Two traditions, the one dying, the one coming to birth, meet here but fail to harmonize; even in the matter of whether to use prose or a kind of verse, Vanbrugh still shilly-shallies. But for all that, *The Relapse* is a decidedly promising first play.

Perhaps the chief superiority of Vanbrugh's second play, *The Provoked Wife*, is that, unlike *The Relapse*, it is just one play rather than two. It is better ordered, indeed very compactly ordered. The situation is made clear at once, with an opening soliloquy by the husband, a passage-at-arms between husband and wife, and a soliloquy by the wife; and it is in the speed with which it communicates that the soliloquy finds its best defense. The soliloquy that corresponds on the stage to stream-of-consciousness in book form has gone out of fashion, and is not worth having back; but is really no worse—and is sometimes better—than certain other methods that have replaced it. For myself, I'd as soon have Sir John Brute go bang into soliloquizing at the start of *The Provoked Wife* as have some butler or brother-in-law announce how brutally he treats his wife.

The rest of the play can be pretty well foreseen when we add that Lady Brute has a devoted admirer, Constant; a marriageable niece who loves Constant's friend Heartfree; and an affected, conceited neighbor, Lady Fanciful, also in love with Heartfree; while Heartfree himself is not of a mind to marry. The story follows out of prevailing Restoration attitudes, but is actually given a more farcical and at the same time more realistic turn. The realism—which is merely relative—lies in the characters' reasonably "normal" behavior. We feel that Constant is really in love with Lady Brute, that he is also a typical young man-about-town, neither heartless nor sentimental. We feel that Lady Brute is a slightly—but only slightly—better-than-average young society woman, who got a worse husband than might be expected by marrying for position, but who did marry for position. And so on. Even Sir John Brute himself, however uncivil at home or obstreperous abroad, is no coldhearted Restoration villain; is, in fact, less brute than surly boor. The characters, in other words, are such as then or now could be found in any street without causing a scandal. At the same time, we would never find them in any actual street, because they are all distinctly stage characters.

The situations, on the other hand, the general swing and movement, smack of the farcical. One reason for this is their having a typical Vanbrugh breeziness; but another is that the situations matter more than the characters in them; we care more about the plot for the fun it brings than for the light it sheds. From inhabiting London during a particular age, Vanbrugh wrote a certain kind of play, just as he must have worn a certain kind of coat. If he was not very original, there was yet much that he could report at first hand, much that came out of personal experience or observation. And yet if one were pinned down to say what point of view Vanbrugh expresses here, in terms of Restoration life or of all life, one would find it very hard to answer. Perhaps the nearest to a sound answer is to say that Vanbrugh wrote from the point of view of the *playwright*—with the desire, that is, to be more than anything else theatrically effective. His is simply the psychology of the entertainer; even where we feel the touch of the satirist, it is not the nature of his target that seems to interest Vanbrugh, but only the accuracy of his marksmanship. This raises, though it does not quite resolve, the question whether Vanbrugh was a hack. We should need to know whether he was, at bottom, stage-minded or audience-minded, whether what interested him was the stage itself, or the box office.

Either way, he has a good enough plot in *The Provoked Wife*, but little by way of theme—only a moral dilemma as to whether, because her boorish husband *is* her husband, Lady Brute shall remain faithful to him. Moreover, this dilemma is never really resolved. The story fades out with nothing really resolved, with Sir John and Lady Brute hardly even reunited; they are merely still married and in the same room. But intentional or not, that perhaps is the most lifelike touch of all; we are back, as we might be in life, exactly where we began, with nothing accomplished. But in a play where nothing of the sort has been accomplished, we may wonder how much has been essayed.

The moral dilemma not only fails to add significance: it actually takes off from the fun. Once Lady Brute begins to have scruples, once she becomes a conscious judge of her own behavior, she forces us to become conscious judges of it too. She intrudes a sense of guilt and a sense of honor into a situation where, if they are not to carry real weight, they are better off ignored. Moreover, her compunctions seem in part the result of a growing propriety in the theater and in part the result of Vanbrugh's being above all a playwright—in other words, they seem a stage device, of a will-she, won't-she? sort. We have so far, in Restoration comedy, been little concerned with scruples, only with tactics. Just *how* will the rake make the lady succumb—through what gay arguments, on what persuasive terms?

It is worth noticing that no one sins in the play—and that we have reached the stage where it is referred to as sinning. And neither here nor in *The Relapse* is any husband cuckolded; nor are the gallants either so heartless or so rakish as they once were. The language, to be sure, is still so free that one might easily infer that the morals still are loose, but free language is from this time on pretty much a thing in itself, which persists throughout most of the ever more moral eighteenth century. Already here, whether by accident or design, the coarsest scene is allotted to the servants.

The play contains its snatches of agreeable enough wit. "You know," says Belinda to Lady Brute, "we must return good for evil." "Oh," Lady Brute replies "that may be a mistake in the translation." But Vanbrugh is seldom witty for long: indeed the instinctive playwright in him is better at ideas than is the writer of comedy at execution. When Lady Brute and Belinda agree to be frank with each other about what they want and like, the scene (Act III, Scene 3) is ready-made for the stage. No doubt it rattles along, but consider what Congreve or Etherege would have made of it. Consider, again, Lady Fanciful. Mr. Dobrée compares her—for her affectations—to Melantha in Dryden's *Marriage à la Mode;* but the women are otherwise so unlike that the comparison seems pointless. It seems more to the point to compare her—for her conceit over her non-existent charms— with Lady Pliant in Congreve's *Double Dealer.* Here, at any rate, we need not speculate on how Congreve would have gone at such a woman; we know how he did. Congreve's is a special talent, but in Restoration comedy generally we find a more precise treatment of character, a more specific delineation of manners than we do here. Everything seems a little brisker now, and a little more blurred.

All this does not leave us with a great deal to say about Vanbrugh's *The Confederacy,* though it seems to me Vanbrugh's best piece of work. Despite how much of it is borrowed, *The Confederacy* reflects credit on Vanbrugh the playwright. It makes plain, once more, in how great a degree he just *was* a playwright rather than a social critic or student of manners. *The Confederacy* strikes me as easier to read—and perhaps easier to act—than any other of Vanbrugh's plays. It is well formed and well knit, having a plot that happily embraces two separate intrigues and that concisely involves *all* the characters. We are very far from the plotting of *The Relapse,* with its two intrigues that never really meet at all.

Also the play is as satisfactory in one sense as it may be

limited in another. In terms of sexual morality, we have moved still farther away from the Restoration. Dick Amlet, posing as Colonel Sprightly, ventures on nothing even faintly illicit in his courtship of young Corinna: he is all scamp and no rake. And though Gripe and Moneytrap are infatuated with each other's wives and doubtless would sin if they could, the wives themselves have no thoughts of sinning with them or with any one else. Even Brass, posing as Dick Amlet's valet, has no sexual designs on Clarissa Gripe's pert maid, Flippanta. We are out of the tunnel at last: this is a play in which sex plays only the most perfunctory part. And what is so satisfactory about *The Confederacy* is that sex has simply been put to one side—it has not been discarded in favor of sentiment. Hearts that used to be made of stone are not turning into hearts made of pudding; we have not exchanged the betrayed husband for the repentant rake. And Vanbrugh has come far closer than in his earlier plays to creating a classic comedy pattern. Here he was helped, of course, by the particular French play he was borrowing from, a play that regards deception as a conscious *game*. The two wives, with the help of Brass and Flippanta, deliberately form a conspiracy, and one that is based on a good comic point: namely, that men will give to other men's wives what they refuse to give to their own. We are back again in a world of fraud, where the young gallant is an impostor, with designs on rather the young lady's fortune than her virtue, and where wives seek to make, not cuckolds of their husbands, but benefactors of their swains. We are closer to the Jacobean stage, and not simply because the economic motive is more pronounced, but because the social milieu is less exalted. Gripe and Moneytrap are mere scriveners, and Dick Amlet's mother (though she has amassed ten thousand pounds) is hardly better than a pedlar, and in most of her dealings much worse. As there is a more general comic formulation, there is a less particularized point of view. The plot and characters could be moved back and forth in space and time at will; the whole thing is classic, but only to the extent that it is also cut-and-dried.

Hazlitt complains of a "heartless want in principle" in the

(*163*)

play, and of its showing "no anger or severity against vice."
He is, strictly speaking, right, for Vanbrugh is quite as easy-
going about morality here as he is about everything else. He
lets the wives bilk each other's husbands; he lets Dick Amlet
turn impostor with impunity. Nor are the ladies otherwise very
charming; nor is Amlet very much of a friend, or even a son.
But as no one is particularly virtuous, so no one is particularly
vile, while those who are wronged are themselves up to mischief. There is nothing comparable here to Tom Fashion's successful cheat or Berinthia's genuine baseness in *The Relapse*,
and the whole thing is saved by being treated as a game. "We
have been more lucky than wise," says Flippanta at the end—a
phrase that doesn't so much sum up this comedy as it does all
light comedy, for the characters cannot be wise, or they will
never get into trouble, and they must be lucky, or they will
never get out. Hazlitt's objection seems dubious in terms of the
play, but rather valid in terms of the playwright. Through car-
ing very little about morals, Vanbrugh fails to calculate certain
of his effects; that is why a Berinthia emerges as so much worse
than she was probably meant to be. In his rather flabby good-
naturedness, Vanbrugh stands at the opposite pole from a moral
extremist like Wycherley.

For that matter, much that might be thought morally ques-
tionable in *The Confederacy* has actually the smack of mere fashionable cynicism; much of it is as wholly of the theater as stage
money. "There's no sin," says Flippanta, "in plundering the
husband, so his wife has a share in the booty": what could be
more pat, what would surprise us less if it turned up in this
week's new comedy? Or hear the wives discussing how each
must show a little interest in the other's husband if they are
to plunder them:

BRASS.: *A civil look only.*
ARAM.: *There's no great harm in that.*

. . . . .

FLIP.: *Receive a little letter, perhaps.*
CLAR.: *Women of quality do that from fifty odious fellows.*

BRASS.: *Suffer (may be) a squeeze by the hand.*
ARAM.: *One's so used to that, one does not feel it.*

We regard this as mere verbal give-and-take, and never for a moment as anything given and taken. To find it immoral we would have to think of it as in some sense personal, not as the set talk of a hundred plays written over a period of several centuries. To be sure, *The Confederacy* is in places very much of the year 1705—as, for example, with Clarissa's peculiar regrets that she is not a real lady of quality. But barring such moments, the play seems very traditional. Gripe and Moneytrap are called scriveners in one age, butter-and-egg men in another, but the breed does not change, the Flippantas do not change, the Mrs. Amlets do not change; and amid all the conniving and confederating, stands forth the changeless ingénue, Corinna.

At a distance of two centuries and a half, Vanbrugh may be allowed to have used a story well. The plot is neat, the talk lively, the telling smooth. It is a wine of a good year, only not in itself a very notable wine. That special bouquet which those bores who chatter about wine call "breeding" is what the play most lacks. It could not but lack it. A man whose dominant characteristic is good nature cannot have any very dominant characteristic; he is, at least for stage purposes, too extroverted and amiable. He may not conform, but he will certainly not protest. The Vanbrugh type runs through the centuries, in one sense always the same, in another sense never the same—because every age is different, and a Vanbrugh will acquiesce in too many of his own age's attitudes.* Because Vanbrugh flourished when his own age was breaking up, he conveys a certain feeling of flux and change, and seems at moments to be making stage comedy turn a corner. But it is the times that are actually turning it.

---

* Vanbrugh as an architect was far less a conformist.

CHAPTER X

Farquhar

GEORGE FARQUHAR brings us to the last of the Restoration playwrights; and it is quickly evident that he *is* the last. It is less,
with Farquhar, that the tradition has thinned out than that it has
been mingled—we cannot call it blended—with something new.
He is not a wine made from elderly or withered grapes; he is
not a wine at all, but a mixed drink; and not just one that mixes
two elements, but one that mixes two flavors. He is—to be
modern about it—not scotch and soda, but something as misguided as rye and ginger ale. And the pity is that the rye itself
is quite excellent.

Right off, in *The Constant Couple*, we feel something new,
something individual; a release of air, a certain brightening of
the theatrical landscape. Taking each man at his characteristic
best, we are inclined to call Etherege airy, Wycherley lusty,
Congreve witty, Vanbrugh lively. Farquhar might well be
called exuberant, but is perhaps best called gay. Gaiety is, in
either case, something one does not merely possess, but communicates; something that creates an atmosphere, that evokes a
contrast: we know that life is ordinarily not like this, and that
this is too enchanting to last. Gaiety is a quality that cannot be
too much prized; it is something that solemn people confuse

with frivolity, or attribute (not always incorrectly) to alcohol. But Stendhal was wise, indeed, in insisting that gaiety is a prime characteristic of healthy art. It is personal in origin and yet social in effect, so much so, that it not only creates a social atmosphere but re-creates it. A gay Mozart minuet, a gay Strauss waltz are equally atmospheric, and tinged, at times, with melancholy, with the knowledge that this is what life should be rather than what life is.

We must pull back a little: the Farquhar of *The Constant Couple* is not Mozart or even Strauss, is indeed not very good. But already he has gaiety, already he can make a scene a little better or brighter than the thing itself strictly is, a character rather less typical or trite than his behavior stamps him. *The Constant Couple*, on the whole, is a pretty perfunctory and mechanical job: Farquhar has plainly gone to the Restoration for his material and his methods. And yet he has come back with something that the Restoration does not have; he offers, certainly, a bad play, yet not too bad an evening in the theater. Or we might better compare it to a party—a party where the guests were commonplace, and the games were silly, and the food was rather bad, but the hosts had a knack for making it all seem rather pleasant.

Some of the characters in *The Constant Couple* are sheer stereotypes. Vizard is the outwardly pious, well-behaved young man with an incessant eye to the main chance and a black unscrupulous nature. Who knows today in what primitive piece of fiction he first appeared, or in what work of interstellar television he will expire? The Restoration knew him; the eighteenth century will know him best as Blifil in *Tom Jones*, as Joseph Surface in *The School for Scandal*. His uncle, Smuggler, equally pious and sanctimonious on the surface, equally grasping and heartless underneath, though even more familiar in Restoration and later comedy, has been less so since Victorian times: he gradually passed out of comedy into melodrama, and was repudiated even there when, after Victorian times, melodrama cleaned house. There is nothing new, either, about Farquhar's Colonel Standard or his Clincher brothers.

Lady Lurewell, however, is more convincing because a cross-breed. As a woman whose lover betrayed her and who thereupon vowed revenge upon all his sex, she is a rather tiresome type. But as a woman whose methods of revenge have a certain cruel ingenuity, a touch of Volpone, about them, Lady Lurewell is not without interest. Our enjoyment springs from the number of aspirants to her favors and her fortune, and from her ability to disappoint them one and all. The ending, to be sure—where her betrayer-beau doesn't so much turn up again as prove to have been there all the time—is in the silliest traditions of romantic comedy. But we have now reached that point in the theater's history where the characters will more and more wind up in each other's arms, having been less and less in each other's arms at earlier and more illicit stages of the play.

It is Sir Henry Wildair who fans *The Constant Couple* into life and gives it, fitfully, its exhilaration. He is in no sense an exceptional character: he does nothing very new, says nothing very witty, suggests nothing very piquant. But that is in some sense what is good about him: he is a young rake who, though his principal adventure is farcical, is in all his motivations and reactions perfectly realistic. His point of view and his philosophy of life are completely convincing. He indulges in neither hypocrisies nor heroics; he has no need to. When Colonel Standard challenges him to a duel, and he refuses, Standard cries, "I hope you're no coward, sir." And Sir Harry answers: "Coward, sir? —I have eight thousand pounds a year, sir." This is as profoundly honest and sensible as can be: why should a young man with everything in the world to make him happy, duel with a man he doesn't dislike over a woman he isn't deceived by? "Coward, sir?—I have eight thousand pounds a year." It clears the air. It has the force and thrust of "Dost thou think because thou art virtuous there shall be no more cakes and ale?" And everywhere we have the sense of a young man who does what he pleases as politely as he can but as forcibly as he has to, without embarrassment or concealment, of a young man who can enjoy every luxury, even that of being honest. And on no one can Farquhar better bestow his own gift of gaiety than on a

Sir Harry, for whom life is indeed a charming thing, and living an uncomplicated business.

Sir Harry's relations with Lady Lurewell have a good seventeenth-century comedy-of-manners air about them; his encounters with Angelica are merely in the vein of farce, half romantic and half rowdy. His being led to understand that Angelica is a courtesan full of genteel pretensions, and that her mother is a procuress with the manner of a grande dame, opens one of those classic situations in which, once the situation is sprung, the rest is up to the individual author. It is the author's resourcefulness, imaginativeness, humor that will count. Farquhar, on the whole, does an entertaining job, and Sir Harry helps him. For Sir Harry, with presumably better knowledge of demi-mondaines than of great ladies, takes all this fine talk for a way of commanding the highest price from him; and Farquhar, too, has the sense to make Sir Harry arrive at the climactic interview all befuddled with burgundy. And, befuddled with burgundy, he is free of tongue and of purse alike; and when, after he offers Angelica a hundred guineas for a single night's hospitality, she draws herself up in outraged virtue, he himself becomes a little irritated:

> SIR HAR.: [Aside.] *This is the first whore in heroics that I have met with.*—[Aloud.] *Look ye, madam, as to that slender particular of your virtue, we sha'n't quarrel about it; you may be as virtuous as any woman in England, if you please; you may say your prayers all the time.*—*But pray, madam, be pleased to consider what is this same virtue that you make such a mighty noise about? Can your virtue bespeak you a front row in the boxes? No; for the players can't live upon virtue. Can your virtue keep you a coach and six? No, no, your virtuous women walk a-foot. Can your virtue hire you a pew in a church? Why, the very sexton will tell you, no. Can your virtue stake for you at picquet? No. Then what business has a woman with virtue? Come, come, madam, I offered you fifty guineas: there's a hundred.*—*The devil!*

Virtuous still! Why, 'tis a hundred, five score, a hundred guineas.

·   ·   ·   ·

SIR HAR.: *Affront! 'Sdeath, madam! a hundred guineas will set you up at basset, a hundred guineas will furnish out your lodgings with china; a hundred guineas will give you an air of quality; a hundred guineas will buy you a rich escritoir for your billets-doux, or a fine Common-Prayerbook for your virtue. A hundred guineas will buy a hundred fine things, and fine things are for fine ladies; and fine ladies are for fine gentlemen; and fine gentlemen are—egad, this burgundy, makes a man speak like an angel.—Come, come, madam, take it and put it to what use you please.*

This final speech is what is characteristic of Farquhar, and pleasant about him: what it has is not sparkle, but spin. It is also, in its way, very much to the point. In Farquhar a certain sense of reality is always conjoined or contrasted with the romantic plots and trappings; there is always something down to earth as well as up in the air. And Farquhar can not only challenge the increasingly fashionable trappings with a pinch of the old realism, he can enliven them with a pinch of the old raciness. Farquhar can have Sir Harry mistake a private house for a bordello; seventy years later Goldsmith will only have his young men mistake a private house for an inn. It is to Goldsmith's credit that he makes a far better play of it, partly because he *does* make a play of it, where Farquhar merely exploits it for two or three scenes. Indeed, Farquhar's whole play is jumbled: a halfway house between the seventeenth and eighteenth century that is a rooming-house to boot, where a variety of people lead aimless and unrelated lives. The author himself still lives in lodgings, has not yet found his artistic home.

What comes out in Farquhar's next play, *The Twin-Rivals*, is how naturally gifted a man of the theater he was. Here, again, is a kind of gaiety or exuberance; and here, in the treatment of scenes and the handling of stories, is a kind of flow. This, however, is to emphasize something in the author rather than praise very much in the play, for what Farquhar possesses here he has also very sadly misused. He was bound to misuse it perhaps, he was bound to burst the mold of Restoration comedy; it was all too dry for him, and foppish, and enameled. Congreve gives us, as no one else, the sense of drinking very dry champagne, but it is already poured and in the glass, we never hear the cork pop. Farquhar makes us hear the cork pop—his is precisely that sort of exhilaration, not the elegant and civilized side of champagne-drinking, but the festive and slightly tipsy side. And unhappily, though the cork pops to perfection, what pours out of the bottle isn't champagne at all. It's a wine of another color and, in *The Twin-Rivals*, with an increasingly unsatisfying taste.

For an act or two *The Twin-Rivals* might well be a Restoration vintage, because the plot is nondescript enough to fit any age and because all the evil characters engross the action. Benjamin Wouldbe, besides being hunchbacked, is the younger twin, the one who will not inherit either the title or the estate; and he is disgruntled enough to stop at nothing in his efforts to beat out his brother. Although touched with Elizabethan vigor, he has sufficient Restoration coldheartedness to fit the familiar Restoration frame. And Richmore, callous about all obligations —he will abandon a mistress, trap a nephew, walk out on a friend—fits the Restoration pattern to a *t*. So, too, does Mrs. Mandrake, who having presumably started as a midwife and moved on to become a procuress and go-between, literally knows about everybody from birth, and can put what she knows to excellent use. And so long as these villains hold the limelight, the play moves forward with real dash and go, only stopping now and then for a cynical delineation of the way of the world. A scene like that between Ben Wouldbe and the tavern-keeper Balderdash, in which Balderdash forsakes the man who has been his most liberal patron because he can no longer give him patronage, has a truly brutal frankness about it, all the directness of a glass of water thrown in one's face. And when Ben has installed himself in his father's house and has assumed his brother's title, the crowd of hangers-on have the old Restoration

smack. And every so often there is something in the writing—
of sheer humor or curiously modern irony—that without being
in the familiar Restoration manner perfectly consorts with it.
Consider Richmore refusing to do anything about the girl he
has got with child:

MRS. MAN.: *And won't you marry her, Mr. Richmore?*
RICH.: *My conscience won't allow it; for I have sworn since
to marry another.*
MRS. MAN.: *And will you break your vows to Clelia?*
RICH.: *Why not, when she has broke hers to me?*
MRS. MAN.: *How's that, sir?*
RICH.: *Why, she swore a hundred times never to grant me the
favour; and yet you know she broke her word.*
MRS. MAN.: *But she loved, Mr. Richmore, and that was the
reason she forgot her oath.*
RICH.: *And I love Mr. Richmore, and that is the reason I for-
got mine. Why should she be angry that I follow her own
example, by doing the very same thing from the very same
motive?*

.   .   .   .   .

MRS. MAN.: *But won't you provide for poor Clelia?*
RICH.: *Provide! why, ha'n't I taught her a trade? Let her set
up when she will, I'll engage her customers enough, because
I can answer for the goodness of the ware.*

The reaction is familiar Restoration, but there is an odd, almost
whimsical, touch of humor involved in the callousness. Much of
the time, too, there is a decided recognition of the way of the
world—though this, in Farquhar, smacks of one who has rubbed
elbows with hardship and even felt the whip of insolence, where
in Wycherley or Congreve there is rather the sense of drawing-
room hypocrisies and the cold treachery of one's own friends.
Not that Farquhar scamps the treachery: Ben can dispose of
whatever qualms he has for cheating his brother by remarking,
with a shrug, that even the first two brothers were enemies.
Up to the second scene of the third act we can, I think, enjoy

ourselves. In many ways it is the same old Restoration story, only without the brittleness. If there is not so much wit, there is a good deal more humor. And though sex plays its part in the proceedings, the main part is allotted to money. Mrs. Mandrake, we feel, is not just an old bawd, but a very accomplished businesswoman; Ben Wouldbe's grudge against life may have started, we feel, with his hump, but the hump, like Richard III's, is as much a pretext for being a villain as it is a cause; and after so much amorous thieving, it is enjoyable to see some one set about cheating his brother out of a fortune. In all this, we have a vague sense of heading all the way back to Jacobean times, but there is a good, spanking breeze to carry us backward.

Still, we cannot but feel that the sky is clouding over. We cannot help knowing that with so many things amiss—usurpers in power, damsels in distress, betrayers at large—the forces of Virtue and Vengeance must be marshalling themselves backstage. When clouds form in circumstances like these, we can be sure that every cloud has a silver lining. Act III, Scene 1, closes with Benjamin Wouldbe uttering words of fashionable cynicism about a rogue. Act III, Scene 2, opens with the return of his brother, the true heir and the virtuous one, mouthing blank verse. The fact that the blank verse is intolerably bad, and that the sentiment it clothes is moth-eaten and stagy, is hardly the worst of it; the worst is what a portent these things are. And not of a return to bloodstained, highbooted Elizabethan times, but of that long trek forward, through mile after mile of painted cardboard scenery, into the Victorian future. With that one blank-verse speech we have crossed a frontier; we are in the realms of tiresome romantic comedy, even in the foothills of tawdry melodrama; and Mrs. Mandrake at her worst—as when she descants on which twin was born first—carries us clean across the mountain range, past melodrama to burlesque: she sounds like practically any nurse in any opera by Gilbert & Sullivan.

Simply as playwriting, *The Twin-Rivals* does not collapse; Farquhar keeps it going with this device or that; the plot thickens along with the language; the villains are still far from undone, the damsels remain in distress; and now and then, there is even a return to form, a certain humor and briskness, even sharpness. This humor never quite deserts Farquhar, any more than the romantic conventions of the story ever quite destroy his realistic sense of values. But there is no use pleading this or that small extenuation; it would be like summoning character witnesses who, with the defendant on trial for murder, would depose that he always brushed his teeth before going to bed. The plain fact is that in the last half of *The Twin-Rivals* Morality so brazenly triumphs that Comedy is pushed clean over the precipice.

The triumph is pervasive. That the good brother should oust the bad brother is not the crux of it; commonsense almost insists that he should, and comedy never balks at seeing justice done. The trouble goes far deeper, in the way virtue everywhere wins out, in the way that vice itself bolts to virtue's side. The rake is reformed: Richmore takes Clelia in matrimony. Romantic comedy sits enthroned, with Restoration comedy dead at its feet. The pity is that comedy should be rushing from one undesirable extreme to another; that something too brutal should give way to something so bogus.

In *The Recruiting Officer*, we find Farquhar even further removed from the traditional atmosphere of Restoration comedy. The scene is not simply Shrewsbury rather than London; there is a sense of the countryside and the out-of-doors, of military stir and almost plebeian bustle. This may suggest anything from the Mermaid dramatists to outright musical comedy, but in climate or coloration at any rate, it does not suggest Etherege or Congreve. A little later we may question whether Farquhar harmonized all these new and undomiciled elements, but we can certainly say right off that he had broken the Restoration mold, that by now something had quite vanished in terms of manners as well as morality. Tucker Brooke has said that, compared with Wycherley, Etherege, and Congreve, Farquhar seems more a man of the world and less a man about town, and the distinction is weightier than at first may appear, for it distinguishes not simply Farquhar's performance from the others', but his potentialities. Although Farquhar died at twenty-nine, we already are conscious of some one who lived a more varied and, so to speak, more absorbent life than his predecessors. It's not just that he is putting his own military adventures to use in *The Recruiting Officer*, but that he was moving in all kinds of directions at once —and not just backward into the bucolic byways of the Elizabethans, not just forward into the taradiddles of romantic comedy, but directly outward, to provide touches and glimpses of early eighteenth-century *country* manners, of recruits and bumpkins side by side with rakish captains and pretty heiresses. Farquhar was, finally, moving inward, into the wistful, humorous gaiety of his own nature, and the *sense of the truth* of his mind. Here and there we shall find a scene we have nowhere found earlier, one that instead of having a Restoration cynicism or a Wycherley-like violence, has a harsh satirical humor—a humor that is harsh because it is humane. Farquhar, whose own personal life was full of struggle and whose own social life was not spent among the highborn, knew something about what life itself, the world rather than the great world, was made of.

It cannot be said, however, that in his playwriting the world was too much with him. It was often far too little. If in *The Recruiting Officer* we escape from the town into the country, we shift equally from an artificial world of masks to a romantic one of disguises. We pass from a milieu where friends cannot be sure of each other's hearts to where a father does not recognize his daughter's voice, from a world where people are deceived by character to one where they are misled by plot. Silvia, in *The Recruiting Officer*, dresses up like a man; Kite dresses up like a fortune-teller; Worthy is led to believe that Melinda cares about Brazen; Brazen, for that matter, is led to believe it too. Palpably, the play might have been written a hundred years earlier.

In its own day, and for generations after, *The Recruiting Officer* was a great success—thanks, no doubt, to the variety of its scenes and characters, to its facile mingling of realism and romance, thanks also to its humor and verve. But if such a mélange was refreshing to Farquhar's contemporaries, it is not at all satisfying to us. The plot, as it proceeds, grows rather tiresome and exceedingly cut-and-dried. What one finds dullest about romantic comedy isn't the idea that people will live together happily ever after, but that for so very long they aren't allowed to live together at all, that we must watch the author inventing or appropriating ruses that will keep them apart—the letter that doesn't arrive, the message that isn't delivered, the words that are overheard and can be taken two ways, the lover who is carried off to a tavern when he has promised to call on the girl—not to speak of those sudden quarrels that blow up over nothing at all, in which the hero stomps and the heroine flounces out of the room. And in the next scene, he sullenly watches her trip arm-in-arm across the stage with Lord Poodle; or she bites her lip—or tosses her head—as he exits laughing like mad with Miss Wick. In *The Recruiting Officer*, the complications that separate both romantic couples are at once too pat and too protracted. With one of the pairs it is no great matter, but the relations between Silvia and Plume could prove much more rewarding, as they are people of spirit: and the idea of an attractive girl who is also not so much tomboy as a forthright, no-foolishness toughie, is fairly novel. But once Silvia dresses up like a man, all individuality vanishes. Nor does Farquhar provide any great fun by way of compensation.

Storywise, the play is loose and ungartered, and lacking, too, in tone and point of view. Farquhar is groping for something that will channel his talents in the very act of liberating them, that will be expressive as well as creative. But beyond the fact that he is still young and a little green and living sorely from hand to mouth, clearly the voice of Jeremy Collier has been heard in the land. There is finally the fact that this is an Irishman with the quick bright humor of his race, but also with its sense of hurry and want of control. He is facile: he writes with a pen that need never slow down, and that frequently ought to. When we think of his next achievement, of *The Beaux Stratagem*, as the work of a dying man, we can even better grasp how gifted Farquhar was. But it is hardly a blessing to be thus gifted; some one has said that good writing consists of natural facility and acquired difficulty.

So here, too, in *The Recruiting Officer*, there is much less to be said of its achievement as a play than of the incidental accomplishments of the author. He has only to speak—the play has only to open—for us to feel what swing and freshness he has:

> KITE: [Making a speech.] *If any gentlemen soldiers, or others, have a mind to serve her Majesty, and pull down the French king: if any prentices have severe masters, any children have undutiful parents: if any servants have too little wages, or any husband too much wife: let them repair to the noble Serjeant Kite, at the sign of the Raven in this good town of Shrewsbury, and they shall receive present relief and entertainment.—Gentlemen, I don't beat my drums here to ensnare or inveigle any man; for you must know, gentlemen, that I am a man of honour. Besides, I don't beat up for common soldiers; no, I list only grenadiers—grenadiers, gentlemen. Pray, gentlemen, observe this cap. This is the cap of honour, it dubs a man a gentleman in the drawing of a trigger; and he that has the good fortune to be born six foot high, was born to be a great man.*

There is little of the elegance of earlier Restoration comedy: but there is a new sort of verve.

> SILVIA: *What do you expect from this captain, child?*
> ROSE: *I expect, sir—I expect—but he ordered me to tell nobody. But suppose that he should promise to marry me?*
> SILVIA: *Have a care, my dear, men will promise anything beforehand.*
> ROSE: *I know: but he promised to marry me afterwards.*

Even here, where the dialogue follows a charted enough course, there is something a trifle gayer, a trifle more humorous, than we find in Etherege or even Vanbrugh. And it is sheer humor when Melinda tells Lucy that the fortune-teller informed her she should die a maid. "Die a maid!" Lucy answers—"Dear madam, if you should believe him it might come to pass, for the bare thought of it might kill one." It is his humor, not his wit, that distinguishes Farquhar from his predecessors. He is greater in germ, because richer in humanity and sheer creative fancy, than they are. But it is true that, as John Palmer says, he killed Restoration comedy as it had existed. And he killed it without creating anything better or even counter-balancing.

Certainly his wit is not up to his predecessors': but like his humor his satire introduces something new. In the trial scene, the judges are indignant that a man with a wife and five children should have been impressed into the army. It is not so much that Farquhar, here, shows feeling for the poor as that in a sense he shows feeling at all. The very words, during the scene, that carry us to a humane level of writing carry us, almost for the first time, to a human one. This is the harshness of a writer capable of indignation, and when, a moment later, the next culprit is brought to trial, Farquhar achieves more irony with a single play on words than did any other Restoration playwright with his finest epigram:

BALANCE: *What are you, friend?*
MOB: *A collier; I work in the coal-pits.*
SCRUPLE: *Look'ee, gentlemen, this fellow has a trade, and the act of parliament here expresses, that we are to impress no man that has any visible means of a livelihood.*
KITE: *May it please your worships, this man has no visible means of livelihood, for he works underground.*

One is reminded not of Farquhar's fellow-countryman Congreve but of his fellow-countryman Swift, or one jumps a couple of centuries to the domains of Farquhar's fellow-countryman Shaw.

Farquhar's last play, *The Beaux Stratagem*, is almost certainly his best; but only for reaching a more brightly sustained level of entertainment than his earlier works do. It fails to resolve the discord sounding through all his works. No more than his first play does it achieve a settled point of view. Or rather, just at the very end, after retreating to the frontier of Restoration comedy without crossing it, and after plunging off the

cliffs of romantic tutti-frutti, it does sound—in the dissolving
of the marriage of the Sullens—a refrain that seems to clarify
Farquhar's feeling toward sex and society. This marital break-up
is singularly sane and down-to-earth and modern; it simply
argues that incompatible marriages shall not be made bearable
—and also farcical—by outside attachments; or very hard to
bear, and as we should say full of frustration and neurosis, by
the parties resigning themselves to an unhappy life together.
It suggests—at least where there are no children involved—
that husband and wife amicably part. Thus it retorts equally
upon Restoration sin and romantic suffering; thus it makes an
end of marriage as a mere game, but equally of marriage as a
form of servitude. And the scene between Mrs. Sullen and her
countryfied toper of a husband is managed with a proper lightness and banter, driving in no moral spike with heavy blows,
only, as it were, throwing up a window-blind to let in the light
of day upon the dim seduction chambers and garish romantic
corridors of the rest of *The Beaux Stratagem.*

The rest of the play, in terms of attitudes and ingredients, is
the merest gallimaufry. There are familiar elements in it of
Elizabethan comedy, of Restoration comedy, of the horseplay of
the Goldsmith school, of romantic comedy tinged with melodrama, of romantic comedy garnished with music, of mild swash-
buckle and of momentary realism. There is also the matter of
setting—the fact that so much of the play is laid at an inn, as so
much of eighteenth-century fiction rides in and out of innyards;
the fact that the plot thickens through the presence of highwaymen, as so much of eighteenth-century fiction lumbers along till
accosted by the gentlemen of the road. The inn here is by no
means the first one to play a great role in stage comedy—even
the inns where Falstaff roistered were not the first—but Farquhar enjoys the honor of having, in the character of Boniface,
given to common speech a generic name for an innkeeper—or
is it for an innkeeper who is also a robber? Of course an inn as
the setting for a play is an extraordinarily good one: nowhere
can people meet and mingle so quickly and easily, nowhere
come from such differing worlds or be of such different kinds.

Despite the stratagem advertised in the play's title, the plot offers nothing very vivid or new. That two gallants should make a last try at marrying a fortune by alternatively posing as master and servant, is not startling; that one of them should be rather dashing and worldly, the other more romantic and susceptible, is not startling either; Dorinda and her sister-in-law Mrs. Sullen are both continuators of a type; the presence of highwaymen may have then seemed less pat, but seems all too routine now. The story fails to be enriched by either outlaws or in-laws. And though Lady Bountiful, even more than Boniface, has given a name to the language, her chief importance is perhaps historical, marking the arrival of a truly benevolent character on the comedy stage—for which only brief congratulations are in order, as Lady Bountiful's successors will tend to drive comedy off it. Virtue, clearly, is mounting her steed, and Romance is already in the saddle. In the culminating episodes of the romance between Dorinda and Aimwell, we are witnessing —incident by incident—the finale of every piece of twaddle that is said to be loved by servant girls and known to be by finer folk. First Aimwell, having won Dorinda's love and being about to succeed in marrying her, must break down and confess that he has been an impostor. And Dorinda can but answer:

Matchless honesty!—Once I was proud, sir, of your wealth and title, but now am prouder that you want it.

She then exits, to create a little suspense; when she returns, she too—after flying to his arms—must make confession. And what a pleasing confession it is: she has learned that Aimwell's brother is dead, and that Aimwell is now a viscount with a fine estate.

Doubtless this element of highflown tosh—brightened with Farquhar's gaiety of spirit and rather lusty use of sex—doubtless this blend of the romantic, the comic and the spicy, has kept *The Beaux Stratagem* alive all these two centuries. The play does have variety, and variety, at no matter what expense of tone or style or lifelikeness, is welcome to most playgoers. What makes *The Beaux Stratagem* an artistic muddle makes it equally a popular success. We, at least, can prize the small special things that are evidence of how good Farquhar might have become. He cannot touch the level of Congreve (though he scarcely tries to), but at a reasonably high level, where the writing is starched with at least a pinch of style, he can be perhaps the most satisfying, or at any rate enjoyable, of all the Restoration writers. The gaiety that benefits from the Queen Anne prose is more welcome than more-wit-with-less-spirit would be. But the satiric, the ironic note is fitfully present also. "How can you be merry," Lady Bountiful asks her daughter-in-law, "with the misfortunes of other people?" "Because," the girl answers, "my own make me sad." And there is that excellent retort that Mr. Dobrée noted ahead of me. When Archer has caught one of the highwaymen and, on the point of killing him, says: "Come, rogue, if you have a short prayer say it." "I have no prayer," the man answers: "the government has provided a chaplain to say prayers *for* us on these occasions."

Farquhar is rather hard to sum up. None of his plays is really satisfactory. He used too much of the old to be regarded as having produced anything truly new—used, and in many cases, misused it. It is hard to see how, twenty years after the death of Charles II, Farquhar or any one else could have written in the old spirit; and once Jeremy Collier mounted the moral barricades and Queen Anne sat stolidly on the throne, it was impossible. Farquhar had, besides, the soul of an Irishman and the spirit of a humorist, and they soon drove him out-of-doors and to provincial towns for his settings. Unfortunately, he was also —as it were—driven out-of-doors for his plots, and the romantic, the bucolic, one must almost say the archaic, insisted on being part of the proceedings. Farquhar is perhaps not so individually culpable as he at first may seem: the novel during the century just beginning was to be stuffed with scraps and bits of the same sort. Moreover, a man dead at twenty-nine, working —if not indeed potboiling—in a medium that is not only the most rigid in form but perhaps the least truly adventurous in spirit, and at just the moment when social and sexual morality were under indictment and changing course—how could he be expected to shake the heavy seaweed of convention and popular taste from him, and to strike out, with clean strokes, toward what his talents really craved? Unless, to be sure, he was altogether an artist.

Instead, he was the child (and the rather lost child) of a transition, and all the more lost because it was a transition from something artistically better than himself to something artistically worse. He gains by contrast with what went before, but he also, and very heavily, loses by comparison. Whatever the reputation, or popularity, or fitful merit of *The Beaux Stratagem*, it simply cannot find a place in the company of Etherege's best, or Wycherley's, or Congreve's, or even Vanbrugh's. Farquhar's place is really with Shelley's inheritors of unfulfilled renown. But amid so much that is uninteresting and unabsorbed and meretricious in his work, so much that the best comic tradition must deprecate and even find hateful, there are an exuberance and a flow of spirits that are very engaging, and a sharp sense of life and a sudden ability to blow the gaff clean off it that are very impressive. That, out of deference to conventional morality, he often blew it right back on, and sometimes blew back even more than had been there before, is what we must most regret. As the child of a transition, he was caught between two sets of antagonistic values; he necessarily formulated no harmonious values of his own.

CHAPTER XI

Goldsmith

Just sixty years after Farquhar's *Beaux Stratagem*, appeared Goldsmith's *The Good Natur'd Man*. Although the interval between is not quite without interest in the theater, it is never comedy that makes it interesting. The interval between saw, rather, the development of prose drama, the rise of the panto- mime, the popularity of ballad opera, notably *The Beggars'*, and of burlesque, notably *Tom Thumb*. Artistically all this meant something, as it meant historically a good deal; yet it leaves us seeking an enjoyable comedy during all sixty years that separate *The Beaux Stratagem* from *The Good Natur'd Man*; nor is it, indeed, with *The Good Natur'd Man* that we can honestly claim to find one. For enjoyment we must wait a few years longer, for *She Stoops to Conquer*; the merits of *The Good Natur'd Man* are rather that it lacks the faults of the other stage comedies of its period: it is low in sugar-content rather than rich in salt.

With Cibber, and in part with Farquhar, we noted stage com- edy going under a cloud; we even felt the first warm drops of sentiment. Of the downpour that came afterwards, in which au- diences were drenched and comedy itself was drowned, we need not say much. Comedy had not disappeared, but it had changed its address. It took leave of the stage to re-emerge in the novel. By the time of *The Good Natur'd Man*, fiction was the richer for

Joseph Andrews and *Tom Jones*, for *Peregrine Pickle* and *Tristram Shandy*. But it was quite otherwise in the theater: the stage, after the Restoration, had got itself so bad a name that to exist at all it had to make a fetish of respectability. The novel was still a young girl, but the stage was a woman with a past, making the most strenuous and sanctimonious efforts to live it down. Often the prompt-book might as well have been a prayer book; while the stage itself, which had once boldly mirrored the vices of society, now made every effort to screen them. As an eighteenth-century commentator more or less put it, the worse people were in real life, the more fervently they applauded morality on the stage. It is not clear whether any of the old vices diminished, but it is certain that a new one—the vice of hypocrisy—arose. And as low morals were condemned on the stage, so—very soon—low manners were also. That great plague of middle-class life, gentility, now pervaded the theater.

The genteel comedy of the eighteenth century came merely, in time, to travesty human nature, to be mawkish as well as preachy, to simper as well as shed tears. The moment was a critical one for the stage, and dealt it a blow from which in a sense it has never recovered. Such a loss of freedom ensued from this onset of gentility that for a hundred and fifty years the theater was crippled in terms of content. In any such arid theater world, a Goldsmith could only bloom the brighter. And he was warrior as well as comedian: whatever his own virtues, he attacked the reigning vices of sentimental comedy. *The Good Natur'd Man*, as I said, is not really an enjoyable comedy. It has some good dialogue and good scenes and good characters, but taken as a whole, it is ambling and tiresome and, even at its best, a little tame. But, though itself genteel in spots, it did on the whole open fire on the age's prevailing gentility, and though scarcely proof that Goldsmith was much of a playwright, it offers considerable evidence that he was a genuine humorist.

And if—for humor still enjoyable today—we must turn to minor characters and largely farcical scenes, there is yet in Goldsmith's handling of young Honeywood, his good-natured man, a satiric rather than a sentimental approach to a type of person as easy to praise in theory as he is hard to pardon in practice. Honeywood's benevolence is mere weakness, his good nature mere flabbiness; he agrees with everybody and must sooner or later let everybody down; he is generosity itself, but unhappily with other people's money. If no one could be less subject to vice, no one could be a worse salesman for virtue. The plot so stretches credulity as to carry young Honeywood beyond the limits of rational satire into those of romantic farce, but his character is in essence of a kind oftener met with in life than in literature. Literature abounds in people who arouse our hatred or indignation or pity, but offers reasonably few who merely exasperate us, and exasperate us only the more because they *are* well-meaning.

Goldsmith makes very little of Honeywood, but he does, at any rate, make fun of him. Yet while banishing sentimentality, Goldsmith retains sententiousness; if he shows no respect for the good-natured weakling, he is all deference toward the beneficent, worthy man of affairs. To Honeywood's uncle Sir William himself we can have no real objection, either as character or comedy, but we might wish for a man who had blood in his veins and talked less the way Dr. Johnson often wrote. Doubtless his edifying harangues were by long custom as acceptable to theater audiences as the "low" scene between young Honeywood and the bailiffs was not. Today, however, they, like the plot intrigues and the behavior of the chief characters, decidedly weary us: for diversion, we must turn to the broad but sprightly doings of Croaker and Lofty. Even these two rather keep to an agreeable level than have any notable scenes. *The Good Natur'd Man* is, in truth, no more than good 'prentice work whose virtue is much less that it is amusing than that it is not sentimental.

She Stoops to Conquer is a play that most people are forced to read at school, at an age when far finer literature seems a bore and a burden. As if that were not handicap enough, it is a kind of schoolmaster's delight, a textbook darling, hallowed by time and haloed by respectability. Yet it is really good fun. It is the only play of its kind—or classic of its kind—that is; the only farce-comedy of situation, in other words, that while never brilliant, never bawdy, never greatly concerned with manners, yet does have life to it and does hold up, not just here or there, but as a play. Perhaps it remains entertaining in modern times because it was from the very outset old-fashioned. It was the work of a humorist; and humorists, in a sense, are all of one race and one age—and never necessarily of their own. Wit is subject to fashion—sparkling heavily, in one age, in the form of a conceit; in another displaying itself in polished prose; in another, in glittering talk; now being condensed into aphorism or counterfeited into gags. But humor, which is too human to be preeminently social, too elemental to be at all sophisticated, is essentially too out-of-fashion to be subject to fashion. And in *She Stoops to Conquer*, not only was Goldsmith himself a humorist, achieving a nice old-fashioned flavor, but the point on which the play turned was more old-fashioned still. So old-fashioned— even in Goldsmith's day—was the Hardcastle house that it could be taken for an inn; so rustic were the Hardcastles that they could be mistaken for innkeepers; and so arrant a booby was Tony Lumpkin that he could make practical joking his trade. The country antics of the play must have seemed as remote from fashionable eighteenth-century London as they do from us; indeed, after 175 years *She Stoops to Conquer* has perhaps come up in the world: where it once seemed dowdy, it now seems only quaint; what was a country cousin is today a rather picturesque forebear.

The play itself is founded, at any rate, on one of the most indestructible methods of providing entertainment: on a mistake that creates not merely a personal, but a *social* contretemps. When Tony sends Marlowe and Hastings to his stepfather's house with the information that it is an inn, he sets going comic possibilities not just begotten of ignorance, but constituting violations of etiquette; he brings into play all the difference between man's behavior toward those he considers his equals and those he considers his inferiors, all the differences between man commanding his pleasures and man attempting to please, all the difference, in the case of sex, between seeing a woman as a wench and contemplating her for a wife. Mistaking a private house for an inn is genuinely entertaining in germ because the same man is *not* the same man in both places. Mistaking one man's house for another's may lead to considerable personal confusion, but will provide nothing like so much fundamentally social comedy.

And to the extent that Marlowe and Hastings misjudge the social status of the Hardcastles, *She Stoops to Conquer is* social comedy, is, indeed, in the most accented fashion, an instance of that misunderstanding on which comedy is pre-eminently founded. We enjoy Hardcastle's being appalled at the monstrous liberties his guests are taking—calling for drink, bidding their servants get drunk, at best interrupting and at worst ignoring what he says. We get some enjoyment, too, out of Marlowe's mistaking Miss Hardcastle for a barmaid, though our enjoyment, here, is more moderate because Goldsmith's approach is so genteel. As social comedy, *She Stoops to Conquer* has, in the end, only a limited amusement value. It is essentially farce, a play where *many* misapprehensions flourish, where many deceptions are practiced. Miss Hardcastle goes on with Tony's joke about the inn; Tony later comes up with his joke about being forty miles from home; Tony and Miss Neville pretend to be in love; Hastings and Miss Neville pretend to be strangers; Mrs. Hardcastle imagines she has lost the jewels that her son has stolen; and Marlowe's servant returns them to her, thinking she is the innkeeper's wife. So much commotion as all this has ceased to be social comedy and become farcical chaos.

And though that reduces the play to a level of the merest entertainment, we can be glad that it keeps to that one level so pleasantly; that it crystallizes as farce from the outset, rather than dwindles into farce as it proceeds—that, granted it is all contrived, very little of it seems forced or dragged out. The humor, if very broad, is no more broad than bright. Tony, if no more than a prankish booby—which is to say, much less than a Fopling Flutter or a Monsieur Jourdain—is the best kind of booby: good-natured, but not so good-natured that he can be talked out of having his joke, nor yet so great a booby that he hasn't a very shrewd sense of what he can get away with. It is, indeed, Tony's tastes that are loutish, not his understanding. The two pairs of lovers are none of them especially interesting: Miss Hardcastle has spirit and a sense of fun, but of a conventional kind, and Marlowe's split personality—of being at ease among wenches and painfully shy with young ladies—seems no better employed by Goldsmith than to further the plot.

There is little wit, but a good deal of humor, most of it pleasant, some of it a shade too whimsical. But the dialogue is in general agreeable and easy to follow, the play getting tiresome only when romance pushes farce to the wall. This it does very little, in the face of the reigning sentimental comedy that *She Stoops to Conquer* was seeking to combat, and did combat very effectively. It is genuinely unsentimental comedy, where no one strikes attitudes for long, and few attitudes are struck at all, and none perhaps that is not a little tongue-in-cheek. We may never mount very high, but we are on dry land all the way; we may never be among real people, but they are at least not Noble Abstractions or Horrible Examples. Goldsmith is to be praised for breaking with a mawkish tradition, but he is to be praised for more than that, too—for being so consistently entertaining. No doubt there is a slightly excessive element of good clean fun about the play; the adulterous bed and the unlawful sheets have given way to a rousingly prankish pillow fight. But one cannot honestly assail *She Stoops to Conquer* for anything it is; only for something it isn't.

CHAPTER XII

Sheridan

SHERIDAN appeared on the heels of Goldsmith—like Goldsmith, like almost every good writer of English stage comedy after Farquhar, an Irishman. But Goldsmith and Sheridan, Irish though they both were, and coupled though their names have been, are not really much alike. They are two lamp posts set very close together on a long and otherwise unlighted road, but it is much more nearness in time that unites them than any nearness in temperament. Goldsmith, as we have noted, was a humorist of an old-fashioned or at any rate timeless sort: he looks at life with some of the innocence of his own pranksters. From *She Stoops to Conquer* alone, we could hardly know much more about Goldsmith than his sense of fun and gift for farce, than his belonging—as a commentator on human folly—to the tribe of Puck rather than to that of worldlier cynics and satirists. He much less makes fun of people than shows them as funny in themselves. Mrs. Hardcastle's doting attitude toward her booby son is at the expense less of the woman herself than of undiscriminating motherhood in general. Tony is funny because he is so much brighter than he seems; it is his cleverness, not his clumsiness, that makes the plot thicken; the imp in him, not the oaf, that gets everybody into trouble. The humorist, planting himself at the center of things, draws us next to him and says:

Let us laugh at people. The satirist, the student of manners, stand off to one side and beckon us, saying: Let us laugh at other people. With the humorist, there is a link between himself and the subject of his joke—the link, at least, of the ventriloquist to his dummy. But the satirist dissociates himself to the extent of having not a subject for his joke, but an object; not a ventriloquist's dummy but a duck in a shooting gallery.

Sheridan was a born satirist and student of manners: he had a sharp eye, especially for detail; a skeptical mind, and a witty tongue. He, like Congreve before him, was a thorough worldling, the difference being that Congreve was an incorruptible one, whose worldliness nothing outward could shake, whose attitude nothing *else* could discolor. Congreve must always, in a sense, portray and never participate. He shows us the way of the world with no more illusion than anger. He quite lacks idealism; he does not fight—he does not even protest—for virtue's sake, but he does have a sort of hard integrity; he does recognize the obligation to tell the truth. Thus though in his worldling's way he scarcely so much as lays a finger on vice, he gives fraud a merciless thrashing.

Sheridan is the successor, the inheritor of Congreve, but he fails to achieve the same success. The reason is not one of talent only, is rather perhaps one of temperament and of the different ages into which the two men were born. There was something more romantic and quixotic about Sheridan, and something more ambitious. Sheridan has quite as much the sense of society, quite as many of a worldling's tastes, as Congreve, but he had much less of a worldling's mind. Sheridan made a romantic elopement; Congreve never married at all. Sheridan, while still young, abandoned the theater for politics; Congreve, while still young, went frostily into retirement. Sheridan made what was considered the most brilliant parliamentary speech of England's most brilliant age of oratory; it is difficult to imagine Congreve making any public speech at all.

But the seventy-five years that separate the two men in time possibly create a wider gulf than the qualities that divide them in temperament. Where Congreve's chief concern was to attack appearances, Sheridan had himself some to keep up. Sheridan writes for a considerably more genteel age, and accepts a more genteel tradition. There are some things one can no longer talk about at all; there are many that one cannot talk about with the old frankness and freedom. Immorality may not go unpunished, and indecency must go veiled. The difference between the two ages is most clearly discerned by comparing Vanbrugh's *The Relapse* with Sheridan's cleaned-up version of it, *A Trip to Scarborough*. Not all the disadvantages are on Sheridan's side; his world is often tidier than Congreve's or Vanbrugh's. But it is in every way tamer, at least where truth or revelation is concerned; for sheer superficial glitter it has almost never been equaled.

The glitter hardly flashes out upon us at the start: no one would be likely to use the word to describe *The Rivals*. It would be rather difficult, indeed, to find any one word to describe it: though it satirizes a number of types, the prevailing tone is not really satirical; nor is it quite farcical; nor is it exactly romantic. Nor, though it tells us something about life at Bath in the 1770's, and of fashions and foibles among people generally, is it a comedy of manners. Actually it is a hodgepodge, a pastiche; or we may simply term it a stage piece. To be sure, Sheridan sets out to make fun of sentimental comedy in the person of Lydia Languish, a romantical young lady who sighs for everything out-of-the-ordinary. She would rather elope than be married at church. Captain Absolute in his own person would be too prosaic a choice, but Captain Absolute posing as Ensign Beverley, and conducting a secret and unlicensed courtship, is ideal. There is still some fun in Lydia Languish, but it would be absurd to call such broad spoofing by the name of satire. Bob Acres, again, belongs to so long a line of boastful cowards as to have become, long before Sheridan's day, a mere stage type; Sir Lucius O'Trigger and Sir Anthony Absolute are the merest stage types, too; while Mrs. Malaprop, though no stage type when she first appeared—though no prototype, either: we need only think of Dogberry—is simply a made-to-order character part. Indeed, *The Rivals* is a perfect paradise of character parts, and as such, has about it much more of the comedy of humors than of manners, and all the paraphernalia—practical joking, mistaken identity, huffing and bluffing—of stock farce.

Amusing though parts of it are, *The Rivals* is on the whole not only a relative failure, but a relative bore. There is too much of everything and everybody, and much too much that is tame and even ladylike. It seems to me completely Victorian, and its great reputation has been made by the Victorian-minded, by people who are as easily amused as they are shocked, and who much prefer the whimsical to the truly witty. But if the whole thing, for a grown-up taste, is all too vanilla-flavored, *The Rivals*, for a first play, is undeniably talented. The writing may verge on the cute, but one at once gets the sense of a writer, the feel of a playwright. Lydia languishes with a certain verbal adroitness:

> *I had projected one of the most sentimental elopements—so becoming a disguise!—so amiable a ladder of ropes—conscious moon—four horses—Scotch parson—with such surprise to Mrs. Malaprop—and such paragraphs in the newspapers.*

Sir Lucius, warning Bob Acres that the duel may be the death of him, speculates with a certain verbal adroitness:

> *Would you choose to be pickled and sent home?—or would it be the same to you to lie here in the Abbey?—I am told there is very snug lying in the Abbey.*

As for Mrs. Malaprop, all her good things long ago passed into the language, and it is hard to have an unhackneyed sense of them: still, there remains something to savor in things like "the very pineapple of politeness" or "a nice derangement of epithets" nor has all the point vanished from "Tis safest in matrimony to begin with a little aversion."

The greatest bore in *The Rivals* is the romance between Falkland and Julia, which is often cited as sounding a note of straight sentimental comedy in a play that sought generally to discountenance it. But Sheridan, I feel sure, knew perfectly well how milksoppish Falkland was, and how excessive and humorless were the pleas and denials on both sides. The truth, I suspect, is that Sheridan was having his joke and concealing it too —making sly fun of Falkland for those who would relish the slyness and giving other people the fodder they liked. But Falkland, whether or not he is made fun of, is yet no fun. Sheridan failed here through playing safe; the whole play, in fact, suffers from playing safe. The targets are of a kind no one could object to, the jokes of a kind no one would blush at; the plot is confected of the most familiar ingredients, and the play no part of Sheridan's true claims to celebrity and brilliance.

They lie pre-eminently, of course, in *The School for Scandal*, which remains the most famous comedy of manners in the language. As a work for the theater, in which plot, characterization, social background, and a kind of characterizing theme are mingled and blended, it can hardly be held unworthy of its fame. As a work, moreover, that constantly flashes with witty thought and polished diction, that has a true drawing-room air and eighteenth-century London lustre, it deserves its fame no less.

The play's characterizing theme is set forth in its title: we are allowed to watch, as it were, the preparation and distribution of scandal all the way from manufacturer to consumer. We are shown scandalmongers who make great oaks from exceedingly little acorns, who make scandal from what they hear, from what they overhear, from what they hear wrong. We are offered scandal for scandal's sake—where the motive is artistic and virtually disinterested; we are shown it equally for the scandalmonger's sake, where the object is to draw suspicion to the wrong person. And such scandalmongers as Lady Sneerwell and Mr. Snake are, we must allow, true artists in their line. It is part of the fun that when they and Mrs. Candour get together, they indulge in the same sort of shop talk and trade secrets that so many booksellers or pastrycooks might go in for. The tone is set right at the start, and scenes like the opening one recur all through the play. They constitute its thematic whalebone; equally they are an illustration of manners and a commentary on society. They give the play spice; they also give it glitter. And it is worth noting that the scandalmongers are Sheridan's only way of providing the play with that sense of naughtiness which is the very atmosphere of Restoration comedy. The play is concerned with the *imputation* of sinning; of sin itself there is absolutely nothing. The famous screen scene is one of circumstantial evidence only, not at all of guilt. Not only is Joseph Surface a villain without being demonstrably a rake, but Sir Peter Teazle is an aging knight without being a cuckold. Even Charles Surface, though the most imprudent of spendthrifts is nowhere shown to be even the mildest of libertines.

There is perhaps good reason why, whenever we find much sin or much scandal, we should find little of the other. In communities that are habitually sinful, there cannot be anything very newsworthy about sin; moreover, in a community of glass houses every one thinks twice about throwing stones. Scandal is a kind of amusement tax that virtue exacts of indecorum. For it really to thrive, there must, in other words, be people who behave no less than people who misbehave. Gossip has a certain fellow-feeling about it, an equalitarian basis of talking about others but realizing that one is also talked about oneself. But scandal constitutes a sort of revenue in self-esteem: scandal concerns people who are not just (like oneself) humanly fallible, but who are socially culpable as well. And scandal, I think, is always predicated of people who have a certain amount of relative position, who are the equals or the superiors of those whom the scandal delights. When a society woman's housemaid gets herself into trouble, it may seem to her employer an outrage or a misfortune or both, but it is not a scandal. I mention all this, not from wishing to elevate scandal to the level of philosophy or impose upon it the rules and laws of science, but because it *is*, on the other hand, a permanent and important social phenomenon that, like snobbery, is often slurred over as not worth serious thought. But it *is* worth serious thought, certainly in any study of the comedy of manners; and here, as the very theme of the most famous social comedy in the English language it is worth a good deal of serious thought, the more so as, in English comedy, a devout interest in scandal has by Sheridan's time superseded the old Restoration absorption in sin.

Sheridan is writing for a straiter-laced, a more squeamishly refined audience than Etherege or Congreve did; he is writing in an age when "taste" is not a matter of how you deal with things, but of what things you may deal with. In *The School for Scandal*, quite as in *The Rivals*, no one sexually sins. But as a result, sin now seems far more wicked and important than it used to. Restoration comedy is an almost tedious succession of ladies and gentlemen thrust behind screens, pushed into closets, hidden under beds, flung down back stairways; nothing, after a while, could seem more routine. And now here we have Lady Teazle hiding behind a screen—in what is certainly the most famous scene in all English social comedy, just as the moment when that screen is knocked over represents the most climactic moment in all English social comedy. Some of this is doubtless due to Sheridan's great gifts as a playwright, to his building up the scene to get the utmost from it. But some of it is surely due to its being, as similar scenes a century earlier never were, so zestfully scandalous. We are back in an age when sex has become glamorous through being illicit.

Scandal also, at least superficially, harmonizes with the study of manners: for it is not only something that people talk about in drawing-rooms, it is something that taxes all their ability to be clever and insinuating in talk. Scandal is, indeed, most an art in that it seeks to suggest far more than it actually can say. And scandal concocted by artists for the enjoyment of audiences, scandal that not only causes loss of reputation but is leveled at people who have reputation to lose, is one of the worldliest of recreations. Though nothing improper happens in the whole course of *The School for Scandal*, impropriety is yet the very essence of what goes on.

All this bright scurrility and malice is the framework for a story that of itself is almost obstreperously fictional and by no means at the highest level of comedy. It is a good story, to the extent that we regard it as nothing more than one, and it is worked out by somebody who has clearly mastered his medium. The key point about Sheridan—or at least Sheridan's great success—is not his comic but his dramatic sense, the way he can give, even to his scandalmongers, not just the sheen of wit, but the deviousness of spiders; the way he can raise a colloquy into a scene; the general way that he can plot; the specific way that he can unravel or expose. *The School for Scandal* tells, just so, of a well-knit *group:* of Sir Peter and Lady Teazle, and Joseph, Charles, and Sir Oliver Surface; while even Lady Sneerwell and Mr. Snake have their places in the plot, and perhaps only Maria takes less of the limelight than we should expect. The whole thing has the conciseness of good artificial comedy: Maria is Sir Peter's ward; Sir Peter and Sir Oliver are old friends; Maria wants Charles for a husband; Lady Sneerwell wants Charles for a lover; Joseph wants Maria for a wife; Joseph wants Lady Teazle for a mistress. Thus the story is both concentrated and complicated. The plot thickens, as a good plot should. The hero's future darkens, as a proper hero's must. With but two acts to go, Sheridan leaves himself an enormous lot to work out and clear up.

Sheridan solved everything in the fourth act—including the perennial success of the play. And he solved it not just with the ingenuity of some one with a knack for plot, but with the visual magic of some one who has a sense of the footlights. First, Charles Surface's fortune is made in the picture scene, when he refuses to put his uncle's portrait up for auction. Then Joseph's goose is cooked in the screen scene, when Lady Teazle exposes and denounces him. One such scene immediately following and, as it were, capping the other, the two constitute between them a triumph of stagecraft. They also provide an exhilarating contrast, one scene showing how essentially good is the bad boy, the other, how essentially bad is the good one.

They are not quite the same *kind* of scene, however. The screen scene, descending straightforwardly from the Restoration, belongs wholly to the comedy of manners. In altogether classic style, it involves the husband, imperils the heroine, and unmasks the villain; in equally classic style, it maintains the tone of artificial comedy. The picture scene—at least on Sheridan's terms—would be very unusual, would be hardly possible, in Restoration comedy. Its appeal, to the audience quite as much as to Charles's uncle, is unabashedly sentimental; and though audiences in Sheridan's age and forever since have found the appeal irresistible, one may doubt whether audiences would have done so in the age of Charles II. The theme of the good and bad brother is literally the oldest in the world, for it turns up first—and perhaps most forcefully—with Cain and Abel. But the Restoration, which much modified conventional ideas of virtue and vice, rather transformed good and bad brother into better and worse one, and preferred to contrast the two, less in terms of good and bad than of naïveté and sophistication, of gaucherie and grace. Perhaps what I am now going to say argues a Restoration cynicism on my part; but I suspect that had any Restoration playwright thought up the picture scene, *his* Charles would have refused to part with the portrait through being shrewd rather than warmhearted. The effect would have been the same on the story, but not on the audience, who instead of dabbing at their eyes would have knowingly nodded their heads, and—it may be—would less have condemned Charles for his wiliness than Uncle Oliver for his vanity. But more to the point, any young man who would have behaved in an Etherege comedy as Charles Surface does in Sheridan's, would have seemed a very singular fellow. A hundred years later—as well as two hundred years later—and he is simply a conventional hero. In other words, it is the Restoration, not Sheridan, that is anomalous; the Restoration, not Sheridan, that runs counter to popular taste and "normal" sentiment. And though the Restoration stage is as extreme in offering such scanty virtue and decency, as other ages are suspect for offering such an abundance, it is just because the Restoration provides such an offset that we feel a certain gratitude toward it. Lack of feeling is at least superior to fraudulent feeling.

Charles and Joseph Surface are not, indeed, really in descent from characters like Shadwell's Belfond senior and junior; they descend much more plainly and immediately from Tom and

Blifil in *Tom Jones*. Fielding, a really humane and not really a sentimental man, with his deep hate of hypocrisy and warm sympathy for heedless youth, felt a strong compulsion to contrast a Tom with a Blifil, to insist that goodness was a thing of the heart, that decorum was not virtue, nor animality vice. But for all that, his contrast is too pat, and his dénouement a little too pleasant. Yet though Fielding may be voted over-generous, he was not, like Sheridan, too genteel. Tom's heart might be made of gold, but his will power was made of tinfoil and his moral scruples were scarcely sawdust. For almost two centuries, and in certain quarters perhaps even now, the character and the book alike were attacked because Tom allowed himself to be kept by Lady Bellaston. Charles Surface, so far as we know, isn't even the lover of any fine lady. There is only enough wrong with him to make him endearing. He drinks—but presumably like a gentleman. He is careless of money and always in debt—but as much from being goodhearted as extravagant. Although he needs money, he won't sell his uncle's picture; though he needs money, he gives much of what he obtains to a struggling kinsman.

One tends to make fun of Charles not because he is particularly implausible, but because he is so exceedingly calculated—and for the light he throws on Sheridan, who begot him, and on the theater, that boasts of him. The theater *may* boast, but art, in the finest sense, must blush. And blush the more for having also something to be proud of. The neatness of the plotting in *The School for Scandal*, the vividness of the scene-writing, the brightness of the dialogue, the brilliance of the scandalmongers, above all the perfect understanding of the tone of artificial comedy—all this is admirable. Call it adroit and scintillating theater, and—with due allowance for the ravages of time—it would be hard to find anything better on the English stage. But that is the most that you *can* call it: it offers neither a genuine point of view, as does all the best Restoration comedy, nor a serious criticism of life, as does all important literature. The trouble is not that it is artificial, but that it is superficial, and not, again, that it snaps its fingers at realistic truth, but that it clicks its heels before conventional morality. A man who acquiesces in the common morality of his age may just escape with his life—by rejecting the usual trickery of his profession. He may escape rather better if, while using the tricks of technique, he preserves his independence of mind. But a man who succumbs to both temptations, who gives in to stage effect and audience effect alike, cannot get off scotfree. What Sheridan wrote here was, I think, the most brilliant box-office comedy in the English language.

His sense of the theater wins out, in the end, over his knowledge of the world. *The School for Scandal* has more motion than Restoration comedy, which is to the good, but it posits more characters whose fortunes are at stake and fewer who express a point of view; it offers more situations that interest us for their story value than that interest us in themselves. And Sheridan, far more than the Restoration playwrights, deals at the end in outright rewards and punishments. And all this is to be sharp and emphatic in the way the theater loves to be and life does not; which, because it harmonizes with the genius of the theater, isn't necessarily a fault. What *does* seem a fault is to combine such sharp and emphatic dramaturgy with such mild and sanctified subject-matter; to indulge only in what is generally acceptable, to inveigh only against what is demonstrably safe. Sheridan satirizes scarcely anything that the world does not condemn; nowhere does he challenge fashionable opinion or shock fashionable complacence. Wycherley may not have shocked his own generation, but he still shocks us. Shaw may not shock us, but he did shock his own generation. So effervescent a writer as Etherege at least touches on much that is true and even tragic about human nature; so ambiguous a dramatist as Oscar Wilde will time and again, if only in an epigram, explode against his trashy plots social criticism that is challenging and even subversive. But Sheridan, though sometimes delightfully impudent, is *never* challenging or subversive. His scandalmongers are a kind of Greek chorus in a play that Sheridan never got round to writing. Their air of iniquity is a false-front for the play's intrinsic innocence. The most brilliant thing about it, perhaps—in terms of Sheridan's mastery of his trade—is not the actual brilliance of its dialogue, but the seeming wickedness of its plot.

CHAPTER XIII

A Note on
Gilbert & Sullivan

For something like a century after Sheridan brought forth *The Critic*, Comedy in any sense worthy of the name took leave of the English stage. The very best of what it produced was still too broad for civilized laughter, while the great bulk of it simply fell flat. Even after granting all the obvious reasons for a decline in comedy, this utter dearth, this utter death of it, is unaccountable. True, an embargo came to be laid on sex, and an age that made the most earnest treatment of sex no excuse for frankness, would have been outraged by frankness combined with frivolity. True too, that as hypocrisy more and more took over, Comedy, which cannot flourish without a keen eye and sharp tongue, found no way to depict how selfish even the best of men can be, or how grasping are the great run of them; or how completely the social world depends on money, and how frequently money is got by the most vicious means. We can suppose that *Volpone* would be much too acrid for the England we are speaking of, as *The Country Wife* would be much too shocking. Above all, we can suppose that the almost boastful lack of pretense and display of villainy that characterizes Restoration comedy would, from being itself unnatural, become everywhere taboo. No one, during the century that is the Dark Ages of English comedy, looks for another *Love for Love*. But surely one might look for another *She Stoops to Conquer*, and for something as playable if not quite as polished as *The School for Scandal*. It is not, after all, that talent has disappeared from the English scene—only from the English stage.

Nor had Comedy deserted England, either. On the literary side, during the same hundred years that constitute a theatrical Dark Ages, comedy flourished royally. Those hundred years contain all the works of Jane Austen, all the works of Dickens. They include everything written by so brilliant a small-scale satirist as Peacock, by so larger-scaled a one as Thackeray. They witnessed the work of a novelist as sane and gifted as Trollope. They saw Meredith approaching his heyday; they saw such humorists and writers of humorous verse as Sydney Smith and Hood and Lear, of witty verse as Praed and Calverley; they saw, finally, *Alice in Wonderland*.

Hence what we must explain is why a light went out in one place while burning on so brilliantly in another. We must explain why the comedy-of-manners tradition continued to flourish —only off the stage, not on. The great achievement of English fiction is indeed in the field of manners: at neither the dramatic novel nor the psychological novel can England match the Continent. Fielding and Jane Austen, Thackeray and Trollope, portrayed society; manners bulk immensely large in Dickens and Meredith. Assuredly, then, the comedy of manners had not failed of interest in England; it had simply failed of vitality on the stage. What had happened in particular to English comedy is much what had happened to the theater generally since the rise of the novel. By its richer opportunities, the novel everywhere tended to supplant the stage as a medium for men of talent and artistic scruple. Since the eighteenth century there has been only one incontestable genius who had also an incontestable genius for the stage—Ibsen. Not only could a Shaw or a Chekhov have written brilliantly in other fields; they actually did.

Moreover, Shaw and Chekhov, though both of them were in many ways brilliantly stage-minded, broke with the laws, and in some cases with the essential genius, of the theater, often to the disadvantage of their plays. But where there is only Ibsen who was clearly born to write for the theater and did, we cannot guess how many writers might have written well for the theater and didn't—but wrote novels instead.

What also happened, and most of all in England, was that in supplanting the stage as a creative form, the novel somehow in the artistic sense discredited it. Between novel and play there was not a mere division of labor, or differentiation of function. The two did not simply bifurcate and go different ways: they equally trod different levels, moved at different tempos, breathed different air. It was not just that whatever was most lifelike and realistic became the property of the novel: that was all to the good, as what befit the novel and hampered the stage. Not reality but intensity is the core of drama; and not reality but what might be called expressive artifice is the core of comedy. But essential truth became as alien to the stage as surface realism. Or rather, surface realism of a kind grew all-important. Thus Charles Kean's productions of Shakespeare became the rage because they were such elaborate spectacles, full of the most authentic historical detail in costumes and scenery.

But in general the theater lost caste, the theater—compared with literature—lagged sadly behind, from having no greater relationship to art than it had to life. The stage, in the worst possible sense, became stagy. On the serious side, it ran to either theatrical penny-dreadfuls or highbusted melodrama. On the comedy side, not much could be called comedy: most of it was farce or burlesque, and increasingly a sort of music-hall entertainment. Being an age of spectacle, it was also an age of historical drama, hence of turgid sentiment and highflown rhetoric. One very good reason for the death of civilized comedy was the debased language of stage-writing—its losing, for comedy purposes, first the speed and saltiness of good spoken language, and eventually even the sense of it. It was no longer talk, but prose; and no longer easy or elegant, but ornate and pompous, prose.

If you would see how inferior the writing for the stage was to that for the novel, examine a play called *The Noble Jilt* which Trollope wrote in verse; and then compare it with the well-known novel, *Can You Forgive Her?*, which it later became. Allowing for the intervening years during which Trollope matured, you will see, not how far behind fiction lagged the theater, but what a different road it trod.

Precisely as the eighteenth-century sun set, with *The Critic*, upon travesty, so it rose again upon travesty a century later, with Gilbert & Sullivan. Or rather, upon travesty embroidered with tunes. And it is perhaps a final indication of the desiccated state of the theater that it could only triumph by making fun of itself. The victory of satire in the theater accentuated the collapse of sense. But—with Gilbert & Sullivan—this triumph of satire opened the way for the restoration of comedy itself. For in the end it is not as satire that we value the Savoy Operas, but as extravaganza: and what in the end they exemplify is nothing outstanding in the way of criticism, but rather the English gift, the English genius, for nonsense. They did not take a sane view of too mad a world: they took a mad view of too sane a one. They did not set British misconceptions aright; they set the British comic imagination free. There is nothing, as a matter of fact, just like Gilbert & Sullivan, for inciting certain people to laughter. The peculiar whimsicality of the operas, their emphatic topsy-turviness, their almost glaring drollery— things that nobody can miss—have been a great blessing to people with a rather stunted sense of humor, people who on their own initiative are never quite sure of what to laugh at. Of the Savoyards, as such, I need not speak. They are the great blot on Gilbert & Sullivan, and hence on a certain insistent drollery in the Gilbert & Sullivan operas, and on a certain inhumanity in Gilbert's own character, which is part of his appeal among these persons, who seldom seem notable for humanity themselves.

But there can be, I think, no possible doubt whatever that the Savoy operas owe their length of life ultimately to Sullivan, both because they can only go on living *as* operas, and because *his* satire, his parodies—as of Italian opera in *The Gondoliers*—

manage to be lovely in the very act of being critical. Despite all the talk that rages over who is the better of the two, or how well they worked in harness, the real secret of their success is that Gilbert was inspired in the one place where he needed to be—in the writing of lyrics that should go with Sullivan's tunes.

As a librettist he is very far from inspired, very far, much of the time, from being really satisfactory. We may excuse him in part on the ground that a libretto *is* a libretto, a kind of writing that can have little continuity or momentum. But it remains true, I think, that Gilbert, in the very act of satirizing Victorian ideas, pretty much succumbed to Victorian ideas of writing. He is capable of a pleasantly dry remark, or an effective understatement; but his style generally is in the worst vein of polysyllabic and periphrastic humor, and not the less flowery because the flowers quite lack perfume. Gilbert's genius was for verse, and it is interesting that virtually all the phrases that have become household phrases should derive from the songs. "What, never! . . ."; "a policeman's lot"; "his sisters and his cousins and his aunts"; "the flowers that bloom in the spring"; "to let the punishment fit the crime"; "when everyone is somebody, then no one's anybody"; "a source of innocent merriment": no doubt this is often owing to the much more pronounced rhythm of verse, as with "No probable, possible shadow of doubt, no possible doubt whatever"; on the other hand, it has nothing to do with such phrases as "I've got a little list."

Gilbert's comparative failure at prose seems due to something more deep-seated than a fondness for circumlocution or a certain sluggishness that is the bane of librettos. Gilbert's librettos suffer from something unattractive and even repellent in his own personality. They have the really bad taste that comes from a lack of heart; they suggest the kind of man who was not simply cruel in order to be funny, but who was almost funny in order to be cruel. Writing so unhuman, so inhuman, as Gilbert's *should* be artificial, but his seems not merely that, it seems—to use a word that Shaw even ventured to apply to Gilbert's lyrics —arid. It is as unwatered by charm as it is unwarmed by feeling.

At its worst, Gilbert's want of feeling smacks less of satire than of sadism; and most notoriously in the case of the unattractive women—Ruth, Katisha, Lady Jane, and how many others—who are one of the mainstays of his writing. Their existence is depressing enough, but Gilbert's worst jibes at them seem, not only what the Victorians would have called caddish, but what later generations might suspect of being faintly pathological. I submit just one example:

> *Oh, is there not one maiden here*
> *Whose homely face and bad complexion*
> *Have caused all hopes to disappear*
> *Of ever winning man's affection?*

What seems to me more defensible is that Gilbert's satire, for all its sharpness of treatment, is seldom aimed at anything very central or dangerous. Light opera is hardly the place where satire should bring up its heavy artillery; and though one need not pander to the philistines, as in one sense Gilbert was doing in *Patience*, one can hardly be expected to pelt them with really big stones, or to challenge Victorian morality beyond the point where one could amusingly mock it. Besides, Gilbert's most individual gift was not for satire proper, but for extravaganza or satirical nonsense; not for making sin and folly bleed, but for making logic turn handsprings. His value as a satirist—which is to say as a critic—of society lies rather in his opening of a door than in what it opened on; in his being consistently irreverent, rather than in what he was irreverent about. Without Gilbert, moreover, we would not only not have had precisely the Wilde of *The Importance of Being Earnest;* we would not have had Shaw himself in quite the form we have him.

CHAPTER XIV

Oscar Wilde

THE brilliant stage comedy that glittered briefly in Sheridan and then remained dormant, if not dead, for over a hundred years is in some measure brought back to life with Oscar Wilde. Or rather, what Wilde wrote is often brilliant, though not often true stage comedy. His last and overwhelmingly best play, *The Importance of Being Earnest*, is a shining example of what we might call high farce; his previous three—*Lady Windermere's Fan*, *An Ideal Husband* and *A Woman of No Importance*—are no more comedies than they are problem plays or society melodramas, and probably a good deal less. They provided Wilde with an outlet for any number of things: the chance to indulge the insistent streak of theatricalism in him; the chance to find a home for all the wandering witticisms, the impromptu epigrams and paradoxes, that he made up in haste and repeated at leisure; the chance to share his own parvenu love of high society with those thousands of theater-goers whose love of it was equally snobbish; the chance, above all and dominating all, and in the end vitiating and adulterating all, to make good, to achieve great box-office successes. Wilde, we might say, found English comedy a corpse and left it a harlot. This is not quite true, because at the very end, in *The Importance of Being Earnest*, he more or less found himself. But *The Importance*, being farce, being nonsense, being partly descended from Gilbert, is not only an exception in terms of Wilde, but a side-trip, an excursion, in terms of English stage comedy. The three earlier plays, on the other hand, have all the earmarks of the merely fashionable dramaturgy of their day—and all the blemishes. Moreover, the trouble with them artistically, is not just how they are made but what they are made of; not the mere carpentry, but the incongruous materials; not that they creak but that they clash. They are a little like centaurs, or Strephon in *Iolanthe:* their upper half is frivolous, mocking, fin-de-siècle; their lower half highflown, hypocritical, heavily swathed in Victorian petticoats. You still recognize the dreary Victorian parlor even though Wilde has installed a glittering crystal chandelier; you still spot Mrs. Grundy, even though she has taken to sipping champagne and to smoking cigarettes.

These remarks are chiefly meant to characterize Wilde's plays, though it is impossible that they should not criticize them also. But, postponing general criticism till later, it should be stressed that Wilde was performing a delightful and not unimportant service, that, even if he raised comedy from the dead as a harlot, he did raise it from the dead. In the midst of giving a sensitive and sophisticated playgoer much to shudder at and shake his head over, he gave him much also to smile at and be charmed and dazzled by. He may not, in those first three plays, have brought comedy back into the theater, but he did bring wit. The curtain might clatter down, following some particularly turgid speech, on the sobs of the virtuous or the gloatings of the wicked, but while the curtain was up, there would be scenes in which Wilde's great gift for writing prattle, for writing gay and mischievous nothings—a gift that had not only hardly existed for a century, but that is far less common than it would seem to be—brought real lightness and exhilaration into the theater. And though there was very little to shock any one in these plays, there was always the expectation of being shocked, the sense of their being shocking. Nobody does anything very wicked: the plot, indeed, is all about people desperately trying to live down the one wicked thing they had done twenty years before. Sin, in Wilde, can boast of a past, but it has no future whatever; and so far from the sins of the parents being visited on the children, the parents themselves are seldom allowed to visit them. Yet what with the characters who had really been wicked in the past, and the characters who, with their audacious prattle, try to suggest that they are being wicked in the present, there must—in those still rather tight-lipped days of the Nineties—have been a real sheen of the scandalous, a real aura of the shocking, about these plays. If it was all a step down for Wilde in terms of his own potentialities, it was a big step up for the English stage compared with what had gone before.

Moreover—and this is meant as no defense of Wilde, but simply as a description of the society and the stage of his time—it was not a moment when it would have been easy to infuse any great amount of new blood into stage comedy. Comedy—much like the erstwhile sinners in Wilde's plays—is itself always trying to seem respectable, to be judged a worthy citizen, a useful member of society. Although comedy—far more than any other single form of true literature—is criticism, far from seeming so to the average person, it seems utterly frivolous, completely trivial. The average person prefers a comedy precisely because he feels it will take him out of himself, will offer escape, will make him laugh—and *won't* make him think. It thus exists in his mind as a holiday from the serious business of life; and just as it affords relief from being serious, so it affords relief from being dignified. And by that very token, he sees comedy itself as quite lacking in seriousness, quite lacking in dignity.

Hence Comedy, where the general public is concerned, must always mind its manners. Not having a very good reputation to begin with, it simply cannot afford to acquire a bad one. It usually must pay for any liberties it takes: people won't defend it, reformers won't crusade for it. Freedom of smile has not the same sanctity as freedom of speech. At the time Wilde began writing comedies, the dramas of Ibsen were still fighting for their life on the English stage. Their subject-matter appalled the timid, the genteel, the sanctimonious. But their seriousness found champions in all who were modern and enlightened, who were concerned with the facts of life, however distasteful those facts might be. And so voices were raised for Ibsen in England —powerful and persuasive voices—at the same time that powerful and persuasive pressures were exerted against him. But the very fact that Ibsen, in spite of his passionate and manifest seriousness, should have to fight for a hearing, or that Pinero's *Second Mrs. Tanqueray* had created a theatrical *cause célèbre*, will suggest what short shrift, what an outraged thwacking, any comedy that took a frivolous view of social or sexual turpitude, would have received. Ibsen was an issue; any one who should have mingled bohemian principles with broad jokes, would have been an outrage.

Thus it seems only fair to insist that in London, during the early Nineties, no playwright could have easily got any "subversive" comedy produced. Comedies in the Restoration style, comedies with the Restoration outspokenness, would have brought in the police. Comedies that took a hard, cold, realistic view of the money-motive would have alienated the carriage trade. Comedies that were essentially comedies of ideas—as Shaw's were not many years later—would have had so strong a meeting-house or classroom flavor that they would probably not have seemed comedies; for many people, in fact, they do not to this day.

This will not absolve Wilde from the kind of thing he went in for, but it will help explain his difficulties. If a man craves worldly success, as Wilde did, and has in him a strong streak of the garish, as Wilde had, and is overdazzled by the tosh and titles of the great world, which Wilde was—if, in other words, there is almost a predisposition on his part to write drawing-room melodrama, while it will be wellnigh impossible to make good at a higher level—we can at least understand, I think, why Wilde wrote *Lady Windermere's Fan* and its two successors. The only way he could write about sex was to call it sin. The only way he could make English society a subject of satire was to make it first an object of glamour.

Lady Windermere's Fan is the first of Wilde's four comedies, and, everything considered, is better than any of them except the last. Reading it today, we cannot but see of how mixed a composition it is, cannot but take a severe and impatient view of its faults. We actually take its wit and cleverness so much for granted that its melodrama seems only the more glaring. In the early Nineties, however, the play must have seemed a delight. It is the melodrama that audiences would then have taken for granted, while the wit and cleverness would have had an exciting glitter. Audiences would have expected Lady Windermere to be prim as well as pretty; they would have expected her fan, or something like it, to become the pivot of the plot. But they would not have expected such pleasantly frivolous remarks as: "If a woman really repents, she has to go to a bad dressmaker, otherwise no one believes her." And they would not have expected such golden if by now tarnished epigrams as "I can resist everything except temptation" and "Experience is the name Tuppy gives to his mistakes."

Lady Windermere's Fan is a sort of immortal play—it has, at any rate, an immortal plot: something like it, against something like its background, must, if it does not continuously persist in the theater, at least constantly recur. There will be a certain shift in emphasis: one age will play it chiefly for shocks, another chiefly for sobs, still another chiefly for laughter. Never again so much as in this first of his society plays was Wilde to establish such efficient communication between his writing table and the box office. In *An Ideal Husband* and *A Woman of No Importance* he was also to write about people with a past and about other people, quite close to them, who are ignorant of it. In the two later plays, however, the secret comes out. Here the secret is kept; Lady Windermere never learns that Mrs. Erlynne is her mother. Nor, in the other plays, can the person with a past prove capable of Mrs. Erlynne's heroic gesture of putting her daughter's honor before her own. *Lady Windermere* seems in many respects creakingly old-fashioned today, but at bottom, for what it is, it still has everything.

And what it is, plainly, is the most fashionable possible trash.

To begin with, it is all fearfully social: London, Mayfair, morning rooms, drawing rooms, duchesses, butlers, grand staircases, late parties, bachelor apartments, flowers in tall vases, jeweled fans. All this made the fortune of nineteenth-century fiction before it made the fortune of 20th Century Fox. But it is not only frightfully social, it is also frightfully sophisticated. The audience may swoon over high society, but the characters themselves must sneer at it. They must be equipped, not only with coronets, but with long exotic cigarette-holders. There must be spice along with glitter, but there must be something more as well. There must be a good woman and a bad woman—Amelia and Becky Sharp, Melanie and Scarlett O'Hara. And what better than for the good woman to be the bad one's daughter—who, best of all, doesn't know who the bad one is, and spurns and despises her. For now the bad woman may have her great moment; may, at one stroke, atone for her own past sins, save her daughter from ruin, and teach her daughter charity. It is, of course, the essence of the mother's gallantry that the daughter shall never know the truth, for in the very best high-society trash, gallantry is not enough, there must be renunciation as well. Sometimes one renounces a lover, sometimes a daughter, sometimes a fortune, sometimes the stage, sometimes the world, but one must renounce something—one must take the veil, or take the rap, or take the train. One may request a memento or two—a photograph or a fan—and plant a gentle final kiss, and take one long last lingering look, and turn quickly at the door, just before the butler or the plainclothesman follows one out. One may even, though it would seem to be cheating a little, marry Lord Augustus—provided one goes into exile.

If we must have trash, surely it is this way we should have it. Trash does no great harm when it is flagrantly so, when it stick to its own rules, when it is all *geste* and gallantry, all titles and tears. Most of us accumulate scraps and pieces of the romantic and sentimental, most of us need an outlet for getting rid of our day-dreams and our harp-twangings at dusk. If tragedy is a catharsis of pity and terror, trash might be defined as a catharsis of piffle and rot. The trash that is dangerous is the kind that has been mated with truth, the realistic kind, the superficially convincing kind; not the kind that dines off lobster and champagne, but the kind that breakfasts off eggs and bacon. The trash that is dangerous seems like fact; trash is harmless when it plainly seems like fiction.

Whether such trash is amusing is another story: there are certainly aspects of *Lady Windermere's Fan* that no longer amuse. Some of the talk has lost its sheen, while some of the speeches, and—worse yet—of the soliloquies, smack of the stagiest Victorian melodrama. Lady Windermere, with her straitlacedness toward women with a past, is very definitely a period figure, a woman from the past. It is hard to believe that even in Wilde's day women of the great world took so stern, so inwardly severe, a view of virtue as Lady Windermere. Women, no doubt, were conventional enough, or timid enough, or snobbish enough to be relentless toward women of unknown background or shady reputations. But Wilde, I think, had a special feeling about happy, high-placed women with rigid moral standards; Lady Windermere is repeated in *An Ideal Husband* as Lady Chiltern, in *A Woman of No Importance* as Hester Worstley. Indeed, among so much that is merely artificial and insincere in these plays, one feels something close to a compulsion on Wilde's part in his repeating this type, in his desire to chronicle the taming of a prig. It is partly, perhaps, that with a premonition of his own approaching downfall, his own eventual fate, he wished to chide the holier-than-thouness, the lack of charity, in those who constituted the backbone of English society. But it is partly, too, that Wilde—and as much when he was the toast of society as when he was the anathema—had a real gift of charity and understanding. From all one reads, he seems to have been even more good-natured than he was gross. The next most extraordinary thing about Wilde's wit, after its brilliance, is its almost total lack of malice. It is full of outrageous paradoxes, and it very often makes a monkey of morality, but it is almost completely lacking in personal spite. His plays have no real point of view, no true vision of life, partly from there being so much that is shoddy and made-to-order about them; but partly also, because they manifest so little concern for life. Wilde's forte was a kind of high and self-governing nonsense. He had always to be writing nonsense of one kind or another: *Lady Windermere*, in many ways, is quite as absurd and impossible as *The Importance of Being Earnest.* So soon as Wilde, in the theater, dealt with anything the least bit real, the tone was bound to seem almost utterly false. As a playwright he had just two talents: for brilliant nonsense and for bad movies. *Lady Windermere* has some very real wit, several amusing characters, rather much agreeable dialogue; in addition to which, on the score of plot, it is the best of the three bad movies.

In *An Ideal Husband*, it is the man's turn to have a shady past: in *An Ideal Husband*, we have Sir Robert Chiltern, the most brilliant, the most upright, the most up-and-coming of youngish public figures—a man destined to go far, save that he has gone too far already. Coming from a good but not prosperous family, ambitious for place, thirsting for power, he had once listened to temptation in the form of a wily, soft-spoken Continental baron: he had sold the Baron a government secret that had come under his eye. For this Sir Robert—plain Robert then—received one hundred and ten thousand pounds, which, grown larger with the years, enabled him to live fashionably and enter Parliament. It enabled him to marry an aristocratic woman who particularly admired him for the unassailable integrity that, once he got the one hundred and ten thousand pounds, he always displayed. As a man who had done a crooked thing, Sir Robert seems to have carefully chosen a mate who never would; Lady Chiltern, as no doubt she has to be for the purposes of the plot, is one of the worst prigs whose remarks have ever been committed to paper. I say for the purposes of the plot, since she is one of those people who cannot understand wrongdoing, and hence cannot forgive it, and hence cannot have it confessed to them.

For twenty years Sir Robert has lived with his secret without any one so much as suspecting it; and then one night his wife gives a crush to which Lady Markby brings a certain Mrs. Cheveley. Mrs. Cheveley possesses Sir Robert's secret. Much worse, she possesses Sir Robert's letter to the Baron, and she threatens to expose Sir Robert unless he supports in Parliament an infamous scheme which he has already denounced there. Worst of all, Mrs. Cheveley was a schoolmate of Lady Chiltern's, whom Lady Chiltern greatly disliked, not least because already then Mrs. Cheveley was doing shady things.

What can Sir Robert do? Exposure means the end of both public fame and private happiness: once his secret leaks out, Lady Chiltern will care as little as the House of Commons for his company. Greatly fearing, he accedes to Mrs. Cheveley's nefarious demands. Exit Mrs. Cheveley; enter Lady Chiltern. What! he has changed his mind about that outrageous bill before the House? Nonsense; and so, at his wife's direction, Sir Robert writes Mrs. Cheveley a note saying that he has once more changed his mind.

Things get much worse than this; things get ridiculous. Sir Robert has a friend, Lord Goring, in whom he confides; and all of Act III takes place at Lord Goring's bachelor establishment. Thither, having learned the truth, Lady Chiltern rashly proposes to come for advice and consolation; there Sir Robert in due course arrives; there Mrs. Cheveley turns up unexpectedly, to have Goring turn the tables on her by exposing her as a thief and then demand Sir Robert's incriminating letter as the price of silence; only for Mrs. Cheveley to grab Lady Chiltern's ambiguously-worded note about coming to Goring for consolation, and to swagger off, her face "illumined with evil triumph." This résumé does not, I trust, make too much sense, for if it does it misrepresents the play.

There is another, equally nonsensical, act to go, in which All Is Forgiven and everything made shipshape. Lady Chiltern temporarily turns human; she and Sir Robert look forward to many happy, devoted years together; Lord Goring marries Sir Robert's sister, whom until then he had always addressed as Miss Mabel; and Sir Robert, after denouncing that infamous bill in a thundering oration, is made Prime Minister, or almost. Let us put two bits of text in evidence—first, Lady Chiltern to Sir Robert when she learns the truth about his past:

> *Don't come near me. Don't touch me. I feel as if you had soiled me forever. Oh! what a mask you have been wearing all these years! A horrible, painted mask! You sold yourself for money. Oh! a common thief were better. You put yourself up to sale to the highest bidder! You were bought in the market. You lied to the whole world. And yet you will not lie to me.*

And Sir Robert in reply:

> *There was your mistake. There was your error. The error all women commit. Why can't you women love us, faults and all? Why do you place us on monstrous pedestals? We have all feet of clay, women as well as men; but when we men love women, we love them knowing their weaknesses, their follies, their imperfections, love them all the more, it may be, for that reason. It is not the perfect, but the imperfect, who have need of love. It is when we are wounded by our own hands, or by the hands of others, that love should come to cure us—else what use is love at all? All sins, except a sin against itself, Love should forgive. All lives, save loveless lives, true Love should pardon.*

Consider, beyond the incredible prose here, the odd psychology: if there is any distinction, surely men are more severe on women's transgressions than women are on men's. But the psychology of *An Ideal Husband* is frequently odd, as is demanded by such melodrama. Why, for instance, if Sir Robert had information to sell, should he have done it by mail? And why, if Lady Chiltern was coming to Lord Goring for advice, need her letter suggest she was coming for an assignation? Such letters! There may be a specific reason why the worst of this species of playwriting went out round the turn of the century. What a real blow to melodrama must have been the coming of the telephone! (On the other hand, *before* the coming of the telephone, how did farce keep going?)

One great trouble with taking on the *Ideal Husband* brand of plot is that you must take on the corresponding moral attitudes, the corresponding verbal altitudes. "Whom did I wrong by what I did?" Sir Robert asks; and answers, "No one." "Except," adds Lord Goring, "yourself." As for Lady Chiltern's conversation, you would imagine that Wilde had to drug himself to write such stuff—except that he had rather a love for it; his love of brummagem was anterior, really, to his desire for box-office. Often not just his taste, which was always shaky, but his sense of humor too, ran out on him. "That great inheritance throw not away—that tower of ivory do not destroy": yet a few pages further on, he could write: "When the gods wish to punish us, they answer our prayers."

The play contains other brilliant paradox, and a measure of wit and epigram; but surprisingly small wit on the whole, seeing that Wilde, whatever he was not, was a tremendously witty man. There is, however, a certain amount of good chatter. The ability to let characters rattle on, entertaining not so much by the quality as by the abundance of their remarks, less by single hits than by a continual barrage, is one of immense usefulness on the stage. Very witty writing, as Congreve bears out, not only slows down the tempo—one needs time to savor it—but eventually tires the audience. Good chatter, on the other hand, can afford to move fast, achieves further exhilaration just by moving fast, and has also a sort of ability to sketch in character as it dashes along. With Wilde, chatter had above all the merit of bringing out his nonsensical side. His chatter seems to me the thing that wears the best in his plays, if only because the best of the epigrams are so famous that we seldom, today, react to them, but also because epigrams, generally, stop conversation rather than keep it gaily in motion.

All in all, however, the amusing things in *An Ideal Husband* do not begin to compensate for the stagy melodrama and the hollow moralizings. Moreover, though the two sides have little to do with each other, whenever they do meet they seem rather to collide. We can perhaps accept Lord Goring in his double role of decorative dandy (who fires off epigrams) and of confidant and friend (who attempts to give advice). But a moment comes when Sir Robert opposes his sister Mabel's marrying Lord Goring from imagining that, because Mrs. Cheveley has been in Goring's rooms, she must be Goring's mistress! And at another moment, when Sir Robert is unburdening himself to Goring, and Goring tries hard to help, Wilde can't resist letting Goring suddenly blaze forth with conversational fireworks. The mixture—here and elsewhere—of problem and persiflage is so glaring that at moments Wilde might be credited with having invented a new form for the stage—the problem farce.

Wilde's crimes as a playwright culminate in *A Woman of No Importance* which, even if viewed in the light of the 1890's, seems one of the most improbable and unpardonable works ever turned out by a man of talent. This somehow goes beyond piffle, beyond parody. Wilde could have exploited the theme, however worn, and retained the plot, however shoddy, and even done what he did with the characters; and though he would have forfeited all our respect, it would have yet been comprehensible. But we just cannot grasp how a gifted man of the world—even tongue in cheek, or neck in noose—could write the kind of speeches in which *A Woman of No Importance* abounds.

There is only one thing more extraordinary about the play than how execrable is the worst of its writing, and that is, how truly brilliant is the best of it. Some of the finest things Wilde ever said will be found here, though perhaps that is it—they *are* things he had said, and now proceeded to say over again. But though that would account for the epigrams, it would hardly explain the prattle, the best of which is equally excellent. As for the story, in one sense it is only a few steps down from *Lady Windermere's Fan*. We are once again in the company of the fallen woman. We are once again on the subject of The Woman Pays. But at least *Lady Windermere* is somewhat worldly melodrama, in which a mother is concerned—for material as well as maternal reasons—with preventing her daughter from falling. In *A Woman of No Importance* we have a mother who is concerned—for moral as well as maternal reasons—with preventing her son from rising. As Wilde might have said, Lady Win-

dermere's mother is a good mother, Gerald Arbuthnot's mother
a good woman. Mrs. Arbuthnot has both sinned and been
sinned against—and such a character cannot just be put to use
by a writer; cannot be, artistically, a woman of no importance to
him. If she is not a woman of very real importance to him, if
she is not something of a tragic figure, she can only emerge as
a trashy one. Indeed, Wilde himself plays even more fast and
loose with Mrs. Arbuthnot, "betrays" her even more callously,
than the wicked Lord Illingworth did. There are not only moments, amid all that is pasteboard, when she herself seems suddenly serious; there are moments when Wilde seems serious
about her. But moments only—a sentence later, and he is once
more highflown and insincere. One can't help sympathizing
with Mrs. Arbuthnot, who suffers almost as much from coinci-
dences in the plot as from caddishness in the villain. That a
selfish, wicked peer should meet a provincial, uneducated young
bank clerk and decide to make him his private secretary is quite
as hard to accept as the fact that the young man should also be
his illegitimate son. There is no need to summarize the story;
it is enough to quote part of Mrs. Arbuthnot's speech, just after
Gerald has learned the truth:

> . . . *And you thought I spent too much of my time in going
> to church, and in church duties. But where else could I turn?
> God's house is the only house where sinners are made welcome,
> and you were always in my heart, Gerald, too much in my
> heart. For, though day after day, at morn or evensong, I have
> knelt in God's house, I have never repented of my sin. How
> could I repent of my sin when you, my love, were its fruit.*

There are many similar speeches in this child of *Wilde's*
shame, though few that are worse. Fortunately, the good—
which is to say the witty—side of the play is not entirely
negligible. If *An Ideal Husband* never sinks so low as *A Woman
of No Importance*, it never reaches its higher levels, either.
There are stretches of really amusing chit-chat; there is so
amusing an offstage character as the Archdeacon's wife. The wit
extends from those rather obvious paradoxes that Wilde over-

did, through bright remarks like "The youth of America is its oldest tradition; it has been going on now for 300 years" to such classic epigrams as "The Book of Life begins with a man and a woman in a garden; it ends with Revelations." And once or twice we have Wilde saying something that is truly searching, like his remark that the greatest tyranny in the world is the tyranny of the weak over the strong . . . "it is the only tyranny that endures."

There was never, perhaps, a sadder misalliance of tosh and wit than in this play, and it is understandable that the parties to so hopeless a marriage should eventually have separated. The worse half lies moldering in the graveyard of nineteenth-century problem drama; the better half has taken up residence in Bartlett's Quotations.

To speak of *The Importance of Being Earnest* as Wilde's masterpiece is true enough, but not very illuminating. The real point is not how much better it is than the other plays, but how much different. Here and here alone, by writing farce, did he truly write comedy. Here and here alone did he exhibit his great gift for phrase without also displaying his vile love of rhetoric. Here and here alone, by altogether escaping from life, did he not altogether travesty and misrepresent it. Here for the first time Wilde himself managed to scoff at the importance of being earnest—which, with him, meant always the necessity of being insincere, the need of being stagy. Here, in Miss Prism, he writes also of a woman with a past, and, in Jack Worthing, of a young man quite without one. Here, too, the plot turns on parentage; here a handbag becomes as vital to the story as earlier a fan was, or a diamond brooch; here the hero, like him of *An Ideal Husband*, for years has lived a lie. The only difference is that here nothing can seem bogus because nothing pretends-to-be-real; nothing can offend our feelings because nothing can affect them.

The Importance of Being Earnest stands very nearly by itself on the English stage through combining sheer nonsense with drawing-room comedy. The play can almost be summed up as Gilbert and Sheridan. The only other play that I think can fairly be classed with it is Noel Coward's *Blithe Spirit*, where, generally too, an element of fantasy and an atmosphere of elegance produce an effect of controlled high farce. In both cases, there is a complete sense of the joke for the joke's sake, a scrupulous avoidance of meaning. *The Importance* is all surface, even in its satire; all prankishness, even in its fantasy. Dr. Chasuble is not a caricature of a clergyman; Miss Prism is not a caricature of a governess; Lady Bracknell is not a caricature of a *grande dame*. Caricature goes to reality for a model; caricature is connected by an umbilical cord to life. But these people are devoutly unreal; are parthenogenetic in origin; and hence, on however mad or minor a basis, are not caricatures but originals or, at the very least, quite literally reductiones ad absurdum. Compare Lady Bracknell with even so outrageous a *grande dame* as Jane Austen's Lady Catherine de Burgh; it is poetry to prose.

In each case, to be sure, Wilde is in some sense caricaturing a manner, operating creatively on a social type. But the final effect of these people, for all that, is that they just are, not that they represent something. Similarly, the play just *is*. It is outwardly a most self-sufficient play: well-constructed, rich in "significant detail," in development, in cause and effect, in lies that create entanglements, in further lies that further entangle. And that partly explains its success: one thing arises out of another, comes on the heels of another, quite as things do in *Othello* or *Oedipus Rex*. Only here, while every detail counts just as much, nothing whatever matters. The only things that seem real in the play are the cucumber sandwiches that Lady Bracknell craves and can't get, the muffins that Algernon craves and can't get enough of. People have stomachs but not hearts, desires but no emotions; which is a way of giving fantasy feet without depriving it of wings.

It is all trivial; but because it is *all* trivial, it is also art. It is sternly true to itself, it makes a stubborn fetish, an absolute ideal, of triviality and artifice. And that, of course, is the only way of envisaging or enjoying it, or of producing it in the theater. It must never come close to reality, but it must never

(223)

be *played* as a joke; the madder the business of the moment, the
more suave, the more sovereign, must be the drawing-room approach. I need not enlarge much on the plot, I need not describe
what comes out of one young man's inventing a wicked brother
so that he can come up from the country to London whenever
he chooses, and of another young man's inventing an invalid
friend so as to go from London down to the country. This situation Wilde combines with something even more Gilbertian—
the fact that the one young man was found, as a baby, inside a
handbag in the cloakroom of Victoria Station. The most succinct
evidence of how beautifully Wilde blends his nonsensical story
with his enameled style is the most celebrated evidence as well
—the famous interview scene between Lady Bracknell, "a monster without being a myth," and Jack Worthing, who is seeking
her daughter's hand in marriage. It remains, throughout, tri-
umphantly in the drawing room, it occupies itself with something *socially* impossible as well as humanly absurd. But the
whole play moves at much this level; and though it is all nonsense, it has its roots in the same soil that nourishes so much
other comedy: its situations, its enjoyments, spring out of misunderstanding, out of deception, delusion, cross-purposes. Jack
invents a wicked brother; Algernon impersonates him; the two
ladies quarrel because they think that Jack and Algernon *both*
are Ernest, though at that point neither is. But the plot itself
is far less remarkable than is Wilde's refusal to let it run away
with him, Wilde's insistence, in fact, that it shall never stir
out of the drawing room. Nor is the plot allowed to do all the
leaping; the audience's imagination must leap madly, too; the
jokes are not the broad jokes of farce but the wild jokes of
fantasy. When Algernon says, "The doctors found out that Bunbury could not live—so Bunbury died," Lady Bracknell remarks: "He seems to have had great confidence in the opinion
of his physicians." And when she is preparing to sweep out
of the country house and return to town, Lady Bracknell says
to her daughter, "Come, dear, we have already missed five, if
not six, trains. To miss any more might expose us to comment
on the platform."

Wilde had, I must say once more, wonderful gifts for persiflage and nonsense, and it is a pity that he did not escape oftener through them from the world of reality that never interested him as an artist—that he chose, instead, to escape through melodrama. Lady Bracknell is not real, but she is alive, where Lady Chiltern is neither. Lady Bracknell is endowed with much of Wilde's genius; Lady Chiltern is stuffed with most of Queen Victoria's prejudices. Wilde had an ability to handle a plot that—as *The Importance* proves—could have been as effectively exploited for farce as for melodrama. Doubtless there is enough that is just bad—just hopelessly stock and lurid and flashy—about the first three comedies to make us overrate, or at least over-value, the final one. Some of the dialogue in *The Importance* is no more than smart and clever, and some is much less—is patently quite labored. And I have made clear, I hope, that the play is proudly, unconquerably trivial. But, on those terms, there is little more to be said against it. There are things and people that have the charm of not being easily compared to other things and people; and about which the question, "Has this importance?" is quite irrelevant. The proper question is simply, "Has this distinction?" *The Importance* quite lacks importance, but it has distinction. In the end, it must come off rather as a triumph of manner than of wit; otherwise it becomes mere farce-comedy, mere sandpapered Gilbert, which is how Shaw reviewed it when it was first produced, and which, to judge by his review, is what Shaw gathered from the production. But then, it is not Shaw's kind of trifling: carving cherry-stones is no sport for a man whose métier is smashing idols. And that the point of a play should be its utter lack of point is the one point that no Shaw could ever grasp.

CHAPTER XV

Shaw

GEORGE BERNARD SHAW was a kind of continent. That is meant
for very high praise, but not for unmixed praise. For he represents a continent both by reason of his stature and by reason of
his unevenness. A continent has mountain peaks, broad rivers,
great waterfalls, large cities, and the like; it has also deserts,
badlands, ghost towns, ruins, great stretches of flat country.
Much of Shaw was always worth very little; much else seems
worth very little now. He wrote too much; he sometimes wrote
too cleverly; sometimes he too obviously wrote to startle or
take the other side; he mercilessly repeated himself; he very
often ran on too long. Few people are beguiled by his novels or
his final plays. But those are things he wrote when very young
or very old; most things he wrote during some forty years in
between have distinct merit of one kind or another, and some
of the things have very great merit indeed. More than half a
century after he threw up the job, Shaw remains by all odds the
greatest of journalistic drama critics, as he remains the greatest
of journalistic music critics. It does not matter that many of the
plays and much of the music he wrote about are quite forgotten
today, or that virtually all the actors and actresses, the pianists
and violinists are dead: he can still be engrossing on subjects we

don't know anything about—and more engrossing still, on subjects we do.

But we are concerned with the playwright—with strictly speaking, the writer of comedies; and though Shaw also wrote criticism and fiction, treatises and tracts, pamphlets and prefaces, squibs and skits, and wonderful letters and on occasion wonderful postcards and wonderful cables, the playwright is quite enough. We are concerned with a man who put forth a vast body of theatrical writing, and who is to be judged, in the end, not just by the best work but by the whole work. Only so can we judge writers whose pre-eminence rests on a kind of inexhaustible energy and vitality: a Shakespeare, a Balzac, a Dickens, a Shaw. *King Lear* is perhaps the greatest single artistic production of all time; but who would identify Shakespeare as merely the author of *King Lear*—or even of *Lear* and *Hamlet* and *Othello* and *Macbeth?* As only that, he would be immensely great, but he would not be Shakespearean. In the case of Shaw, on the other hand, I am not sure that we can confidently pronounce a single one of his plays to be great; but whether or not he wrote a single great play, Shaw was unquestionably a great playwright. That body of work stretching roughly from *Mrs. Warren's Profession* to *The Apple Cart* stands unchallenged by any other body of dramatic work since Ibsen's.

The problem of how best to approach this continent is necessarily complicated, for in addition to how much Shaw wrote, there is how much he wrote about. Most of his comedies, in one way or another, are comedies of ideas: whenever he was writing something, he was apt to be fighting something as well. He tried to make people think, whether through making them laugh or making them gasp or making them splutter; in shocking people, he had almost always a purpose, as almost never a peer. He gave the early twentieth-century theater a shaking-up the like of which it has never known since, and in enjoying and even in assessing him as a writer, it hardly matters how much we agree with him now, any more than how much our parents agreed with him then. He may have written the plays for the sake of the ideas; we may read them, at times, in spite of the ideas. I much doubt that Shaw was ever a great thinker, but that isn't the point: his job, at most, was to make other people think. He was simply the most stimulating man of his age, and what he carried was perhaps not a lantern at all, but simply a whip.

Hence—and if only because our concern is with Comedy— we shall not approach this continent as anthropologists prepared to observe its native customs, or as scientists who shall study its rocks and examine its terrain, or as moralists seeking in Shaw a credo for the good life, or as enthusiasts, intent on extracting from him a religion, or as political thinkers, prepared to find in him a program for action. We shall simply approach the continent—or rather the largest country on the continent— as civilized and fairly worldly tourists. We shall go a tour of inspection of a dozen of the principal points of interest, noticing and enjoying as much as we can, comparing and summarizing as we feel we must.

Candida is a very early play. That hasn't prevented its being in some respects Shaw's most popular play of all. Some of its popularity, in the United States, is clearly due to Katharine Cornell's periodic revivals of it. It is perhaps her best role: it enables her to diffuse her gracious personality; it encourages her to be humorous; it does not allow her to be dramatic. But there is much more to it than Miss Cornell. In view of the old theory that Shaw was no playwright, it is interesting that this very early work should be so very clever, one might almost add so very slick, a play. As early as 1894, together with writing and wrinkles that are all his own, Shaw had mastered all the tricks of the trade. Along with a sprinkling of Christian Socialism, he contrived to give the essence of secretarial infatuation. Burgess, again, is not only petty capitalism but orthodox low comedy; and most of all Shaw has contrived a triangle story with all the interest of a real triangle but few characteristics of the usual one. Neither of Candida's men, for example, is at all worthy of her: she is presented as much too good for both. Again, Candida's final choice between them makes such a sharp and telling point as theater as to make most people overlook the fact that the whole point is beside the point. When her husband and March-banks force her to choose between them, Candida chooses "the weaker of the two"; and then goes on to explain that the weaker is the stronger, is her husband, not Marchbanks. It is thus as-sumed—and all the more because Candida is so warm and un-derstanding a woman—that it is for being weaker, for needing her more, that Candida chooses him. But of course she chooses him for no such reason at all; she chooses him because she loves him.* For Candida, we may suppose, there actually *was* no choice or thought of choosing; nor, until the two men threw an ultimatum at her, was there any triangle story, at least of the ordinary kind. Of an out-of-the-ordinary kind, there might al-ways be a triangle story where Candida was concerned. Flirta-tion, with her, partakes of motherliness: she thrives on having in her life an additional man whom she regards as an additional child.

Perhaps that is one reason why it is easy to portray Candida as choosing her husband from weakness rather than love for him: for here, as almost everywhere in Shaw, love has little passion or sexuality about it. Even Morell and Marchbanks seem rather to be fighting over a woman than for one. We may often be grateful to Shaw for not dragging us through tedious scenes of conventional love-making; but we must sometimes be a little disturbed by his communicating no sense of physical love whatever.

But—here too as elsewhere—Shaw really has Morell and Marchbanks open their hearts as a way of opening their eyes. Candida is not meant to be a *femme fatale;* where men are con-cerned she is quite the opposite, she is distinctly a constructive force. Understanding is her forte, not emotion, and her job here is to make Morell and Marchbanks understand themselves.

---

* Whether this ever occurred to Shaw is something else. Shaw cannot por-tray women in love: when he tries, as with the Lady Mayoress in *Getting Mar-ried,* he comes up with a monster. But audiences instinctively respond to *Candida* as a romantic comedy, even though—particularly in view of the dénouement—it is *presented* as a comedy of ideas.

Marchbanks shall be made to see that from being scorned and despised, he has come to rely on himself; Morell shall be made to see that from being spoiled and deferred to, he has come to take advantage of others. On that basis, Candida's true reason for choosing Morell hardly matters; in terms of sheer theater, Candida is much less making a choice than making a point.

In a certain sense, the play isn't represented by a triangle at all, but by the most obvious kind of circle—the family circle, the wedding ring. If *Candida* is nothing much in terms of love, it is —as Chesterton remarked—decidedly something in terms of marriage. For Candida understands so thoroughly, so success- fully, what it means to be a wife that Morell has never even reflected on what it might mean to be a husband. And the sense of the home is very strong in *Candida*, even though Morell's home is chiefly his office; even though Marchbanks would break up this home if he could, or Prossy perhaps if she had any chance or dared; even though the children are away from it and Candida has just come back. In a way, it seems remarkably much like a home—perhaps because it is so completely built around Morell.

Morell is an excellent character for comedy, because while his virtues are not at all belittled, the defects of his virtues are cleverly magnified. He quite fervently labors for humanity; only meanwhile humanity labors for him. He is too large-minded to be petty, but also too smug. He is a very good man but not a very good husband. He talks extremely well; in fact he possesses, as Marchbanks notes, a gift of the gab. Morell would be more interesting if he had in him just a touch of the woman and a touch less of the boy. But he might not then be nearly so mag- netic or masterful, and so on. Everything wrong with Morell springs in a sense from what is right with him; as in a sense, everything right with Marchbanks springs from what is wrong. Marchbanks is one of those characters, those devil's advocates of a sort, whom Shaw—without much admiring—finds useful for pulling other people down. Marchbanks, being something of a monster, can pass special judgment on ordinary human beings. Being a pre-eminent misfit, he can call down a certain amount of censure on society. A cast-off young aristocrat, he

can indict the aristocracy; a bohemian, he can cast aspersions on
the bourgeoisie; a poet, he can hurl taunts at the philistine. He
is a kind of modern-day young Shelley—shy, ethereal, effeminate, capable of that hardheartedness that often goes with delicate sensibility, of that coldness that often goes with romantic
idealism: he is, in other words, half ineffectual angel, and half
keen, perceptive, intuitive little toad. He has the courage of his
desperations; he makes a weapon of his cowardice, a war-cry
of his intolerances; even his love for Candida makes it easier
for him to despise everything else. He is not in any conventional
sense a sympathetic figure; indeed, he is an insufferable one, and
Shaw is brilliantly right in seeing that everything about Marchbanks—his youth, his high birth, his feminine nature, his romantic adoration of Candida, his ability to escape out of life
through poetry—should make him odious as a human being. For
youth is uncompromising, high birth is arrogant, feminine natures are cruel, adoration of one woman means concentrating
all one's selflessness on a single object; while if you can escape
at will into a world of poetry, you can snap your fingers at the
world of fact. The one enormous drawback to Marchbanks is
that he never seems a poet, never, at any rate, a good one. He
is fine when he tells Morell off in the manner of Shaw himself;
he is quite hopelessly bad when he tries to talk after the manner
of Shelley.

There remains Candida: and she too has rather the defects
of her virtues. Admirable she is indeed, and also radiant; attractive as well as good; wise and not without humor; motherly,
wifely, womanly, kindly, friendly; capable of being stern on
occasion, and even of flaring up in momentary anger. And yet,
though very likely an actress's dream, she is not quite an audience's. There is something faintly smug about her; there is
just a touch of the bright lady judge, of a Portia with the warmth
to utter "The quality of mercy . . ." and the wiliness to bring
up the matter of blood in a pound of flesh. No doubt she is perfect for Marchbanks, because she won't hurt him—and for Morell, because she won't let him down. But she lacks something—
if only a fault. She needs, I think, to be more feminine, and she

needs to be more frivolous. There is no mischief in her eye; she has that charm without any come-hitherness to it that every husband wants his wife to have for other men, but hardly for himself. Morell, perhaps, would have thought more about her if he'd had to worry more about her.

Shaw's *Devil's Disciple* can be treated quite briefly—and brusquely—as a comparative failure. My reason for treating it here is that it is also an instructive failure. It reveals Shaw with an obvious desire to make a joke at the expense of all kinds of theater nonsense, but the joke comes off rather at the expense of Shaw. For though his intentions were to spoof romantic melodrama, he came very close to merely reproducing it. He took the usual plot, supplied several of the usual characters, contrived the usual last-minute happy ending. His way of being different was to repudiate the usual motives; his mistake lay in his failure to supply any new ones. Dick Dudgeon's willingness to go to the gallows as Anthony Anderson makes neither good sense nor good nonsense. It is a kind of merely capricious resolve, and it is forced to be motiveless because Shaw, writing tongue-in-cheek, must frown on any highminded or romantic motive and cannot find any sane or realistic one. But melodrama that lacks motive is not better but worse than melodrama that has one; nor does melodrama without a motive constitute a valid joke about melodrama. Shaw's procedure isn't satirical or critical; it's merely cantankerous.

What *The Devil's Disciple* comes down to is a kind of general desire to be satiric bereft of any specific compulsion. It is like trying to be funny with nothing to be funny about; Shaw put the cart before the horse, the attitude before what should give rise to it, and therefore fell back, as he proceeded, on mere formula, on the most obvious of theatrical targets. Or, at any rate, of Shavian targets. It would be second nature to have a go at the amenities of family life, to take a few whacks at religion, at patriotism, at the army, at England itself. But in general he clung to the staples of romantic melodrama—from the reading of the will at the beginning to the striking of the church clock at the end; and exploited the plot of the black sheep with the heart of gold, who will mount the scaffold in another man's place, and only be set down from it at the last moment with a noose around his neck. A plot so threadbare requires almost as much hardihood to treat in jest as in earnest—and perhaps requires more, for while it might still make a pretty good story, it can hardly make good satire (our unsophisticated self is easier to please than our sophisticated).

Nor in Shaw's hands did it make a good satire; it merely turned up with a very good last act. As is often true, one shortcoming produced another. Shaw not only put the cart before the horse; the horse he put it in front of was not a very good one. For two acts the Shavianism is as mechanical as the melodrama is pat; Shaw dots so many *i*'s that we rub ours in amazement. It might still, however, be mechanical without being meaningless. But Dick Dudgeon can neither be explained nor be explained away. He makes clear that he did not impersonate Anderson out of any particular admiration for Anderson, out of romantic emotions over Anderson's wife, out of patriotic or idealistic feelings. The fact is equally clear that he is not simply cynical about life or fed up with living; not some one with the temperament of a swashbuckler or the cheap vanity of an actor —some one for whom the playing of a part might compensate for the price it is played at. Actually, Dudgeon is as commonsensical and unemotional as Shaw himself. He not only lacks a sound motive for his role, he even lacks the right manner.

And his mother, and his brother, and Essie, and Anderson, and Judith are so much part of the routine framework that they never manage to turn into fun. It is the failure of a method because it is nothing but method: for two acts Shaw keeps beating a dead horse without so much as producing a live donkey. The third act is very much better—and it is instructive to see why. With the trial scene, Shaw brings on something extra, brings on Burgoyne. Now Burgoyne is no part of the formula. In terms of the trial scene, he fits no role sacred to melodrama; indeed, far from being any one to satirize, he is himself satirical. Major Swindon is the perfect "spoof" figure; for Burgoyne to be, he would have to turn from a worldling with a cynical wit into an over-civilized villain who sadistically relishes trial scenes that end with the gallows. Burgoyne comes to life, and the play with him, through being extraneous to the formula, through making fun of others rather than being made fun of himself. Burgoyne's jokes, moreover, are drawn from a larger and better bin than Shaw has been dipping into. Dick Dudgeon is too much part of the melodrama to comment on it with success. Burgoyne is no part of the melodrama; he can only deprecate its existence, and so he is all comment, nothing but comment—and so, unlike the others, he is all Shaw, nothing but Shaw. In the very act of saving the play, he mercilessly shows it up.

The plays we have so far discussed Shaw wrote in the Nineties; and he was to write one more. *Caesar and Cleopatra*, though lumped with *The Devil's Disciple* and *Captain Brassbound's Conversion* in Three Plays for Puritans, must yet stand apart and might be labeled Shaw's first play for posterity. It is one of his best plays, one of his major works. And it is noteworthy that Shaw achieved his first big success while taking his first great leap. Nothing written earlier attempts anything like the same stature; and only *The Man of Destiny*, a mere playlet about Napoleon, attempts anything historical. Theoretically, *Caesar and Cleopatra* should have the peculiar interest and the mixture of faults and merits that characterize most transition plays. But Shaw proved not only more mature, more prepared for large-scale writing; he was also quite astute. At first blush, he seems —in glancing back through history for a subject—to have chosen the most obvious one possible, or to have chosen the most obvious two, and combined them. Shakespeare, moreover, had written major plays about both persons, and that might seem to clinch it. Here was Shaw ready to challenge Shakespeare while reinterpreting tradition, and prepared to give Cleopatra a master where Shakespeare had given her a slave.

In truth, however, Shaw wasn't being capricious or flippant or concerned with going Shakespeare one better. He was just being remarkably perceptive—or instinctive, for in Caesar he found some one entirely right for him. Caesar was truly great; Caesar—as a Shavian character must be—was also full of contraditions. There were the contradictions in the man: his being humane without being very human; his showing mercy almost because he was unable to show love; his belief in reason; his equal belief in the impotence of reason. "Caesar is superior to other men," Chesterton has said, "not because he loves more but because he hates less"; and the sentence might be applied to Shaw as well. We do not go to Shaw for warmth, but for lack of heat; we do not go to Shaw for humanity, but for hatred of inhumanity. Thus Shaw and the Caesar of history have enough in common for Shaw and the Caesar of Shaw's play to be understandably much alike. It would be going too far to say that Shaw re-created Caesar in his own image, but certainly he made him something very different from the image on a Roman coin. Although possibly he *was* very different from the image on a Roman coin, for that was the symbol of Caesarism. And that is what would principally have interested Shaw; the resemblances between Caesar and himself would have meant less than the disparity between Caesar and Caesarism. It is what principally interests us as well: this man who cried out against war and became one of the greatest of generals, who deprecated power and became the prototype of dictators.

Shaw does not go at Caesar psychologically. He doesn't portray him as schizophrenic, doesn't make him out a debased idealist, doesn't show him more and more the victim of his position. He goes at Caesar philosophically—as some one who, whether or not he understands his own nature, clearly understands his own position. His Caesar sees himself as powerless except through using power, sees the world about him full of ambitious, unscrupulous, treacherous men—liars, conspirators, demagogues, assassins. He has come to an Egypt plagued with civil war through a squabble over a throne; he has only just defeated Pompey in a struggle over the world. His, at bottom, is a philosophy of Right Needs Might, a policy of conquer or perish. It is a policy not without truth, and certainly not without danger. It is the argument by which all tyrants and dictators justify their tactics; and because many more tyrants and dictators are bad men than good, it is a policy always to be dis-

trusted and usually to be opposed. But with Shaw's Caesar—I
would not say with history's—we have one of the exceptions:
Caesarism, with him, is not owing to a weakness in the man,
but to a condition in the world. "Murder shall breed murder,"
Shaw's Caesar cries, "until the gods are tired of blood and
create a race that can understand." He means that; he is not
hypocritical, but helpless. Were he hypocritical, there would
only be a cheap and obvious irony about the final curtain—the
most tremendous curtain, it seems to me, in the modern theater.
There is instead a tragic irony about it: as Caesar embarks for
Rome and his soldiers, their swords upraised, shout with one
voice, "Hail, Caesar!" it is not his moment of triumph, but his
moment of defeat. And the irony deepens through our knowledge
that the upraised swords and the *"Ave, Caesar"* must culminate
in a stealthy dagger and an *"Et tu, Brute?"*

I seem to have got to the end of the play without so much as a
glance at the beginning; but the method is not quite so haphazard as it appears. For Caesar is the central thing about *Caesar
and Cleopatra.* He is even the central thing about Cleopatra,
for she plays here the role of pupil; she is not allowed to play
the role of seductress. To be sure, by the end she has rather
outdone herself as a pupil; the petulant charm of the kitten has
developed into the strong-willed cruelty of the cat. But by with-
standing her lure, by withholding his heart, Caesar has escaped
her claws. Yet there, too, he seems less winner than loser,
having saved himself from heartbreak at the cost of all delight.
He embarks, ruefully promising to send Cleopatra Marc Antony, to join youth to youth. And there's the rub. Caesar is
middle aged. He is bald. He wears a laurel wreath as a toupee.
And being bald, what does it avail him to be Caesar? The first
words Cleopatra addresses to him from between the paws of the
Sphinx—her very first words in the play—are the deadly words,
"Old gentleman." No subsequent homage can blot out the
blighting realism of that phrase. He is the Roman eagle, but,
like the eagle, bald. He is a great man and an old gentleman.
Up to a point, the play offers the usual rueful comedy of middle
age beguiled by youth, of youth half-bored, half-fascinated by

middle age. But as Caesar is not just any man, so Cleopatra is not just any girl: she can be cruel and false, as she one day will be passionate; she is proud, violent, a little insecurely regal. It is not Cleopatra whom love with an older man may hurt, it is the older man; and from concern, not for her but for himself, Caesar declines the gambit and goes away.

But how dry-of-mouth is it to be wise—or rather, merely prudent! And how melancholy is wisdom, because how power-less and unavailing. Caesar can teach his pupil how to act the queen but not, certainly, how to govern well. She takes to con-spiracy like a duck to water, she revels in violence, she craves revenge; and yet hers being the more desperate and instinctive wisdom, she is not altogether mistaken. Meanwhile, it needs all that is authoritarian about Rome to save stealthy barbarian Egypt from lawless carnage. The air in *Caesar and Cleopatra* is very chill at times, for all the tawny Mediterranean sunlight. And all the more because so much of it is comic and even farcical, there persists a sense of the tragic about the play—doubtless augmented by the historic fact of tragedy to come. But Caesar's assassins and Cleopatra's asp are not the pre-eminent reason. It is rather this recognition of how hard it is to be wise, and withal how futile; of how terrible is power, yet how impossible is peace without it; it is rather the knowledge that not one man will die for an arrived-at principle where a hundred will die shouting hoarsely, *"Ave, Caesar!" Caesar and Cleopatra* is not least a political play.

Like so much Shaw, it is too long. The prologue were better omitted; Shaw indulged himself in places, handled some of his minor characters with more flippancy than success. Britannus could be more fun, and Ftatateeta should verge less on the farcical. No doubt all these characters, beyond anything they are in themselves, are ways of relaxing the intellectual tension, for were Caesar to bestride the play more than he does, we should have too much of a mere character study. This kind of play needs a surface bustle, glitter, pageantry, for even a Shavian Caesar must remain more Caesar than Shaw, and even a very young Cleopatra must run through the play like quicksilver,

must already frisk as she shall some day crouch and spring. The
play has this outer color; it has also the color of Shaw's mind:
it is mature. It is some measure of its maturity that we are not
forced to compare *Caesar and Cleopatra* with *Antony and Cleopatra*, that we are always driven, rather, to contrast them. They
are as distinct as prose and poetry; moreover, the one—being
Shavian—brilliantly remolds history closer to the mind's desire;
the other—being Shakespearean—invests history with something more inscrutable than even Time can confer upon it.

Man and Superman is, of course, one of Shaw's major plays,
though it perhaps achieves that rank from being, not one play,
but two. Certainly without the long third-act dialogue in Hell,
Man and Superman—for all that it dramatizes the best known
of Shaw's theories—would diminish into one of his more tracta-
ble and traditional comedies. With the Hell scene, it expands
into one of the most brilliant and Shavian of them.

Yet to speak of *Man and Superman* as two plays is not quite
happy, either. The whole thing is more like a pleasant three-
course comedy dinner, with an interruption—between meat
course and dessert—in the form of a long dazzling dialectical
floor show. The scene in Hell tremendously sharpens and com-
plicates and enriches the rest of the story, but it is a dialogue
merely, far more akin to several of Shaw's own prefaces than to
any man's third act, and most akin of all to something like
Diderot's equally brilliant dialogue, *Rameau's Nephew*. So that
one is not merely metaphorical in treating Act III of *Man and
Superman* as interpolated fireworks and Acts I, II and IV as
ordinary comedy fare. The two things are related without
being, really, interdependent: it is no offense against art to
offer the play without the Hell scene, and it is all in all in the
interests of art to offer the Hell scene without the play.

In any case Shaw deals here, in one of the most famous of his
comedies, with one of the most famous of all theater courtships
—a courtship that owes its fame to the fact that the woman is
shown to do the courting. This has quite as much value as sheer
entertainment as it could ever have as sexual biology; and the
spectacle of demure Ann Whitefield plotting with all her

strength to nab hardheaded, unconventional John Tanner is amusing enough, and has possibilities enough, simply as farce. She professes to be the most daughterly of girls, to want only to do what would please her dead father, were he alive. Actually she has seen to it that her father's will should have designated John Tanner one of her guardians—as the most practicable way of eventually making him her husband. Beyond that she tells the most barefaced lies, she goes in for the most flagrant hypocrisies—with her mother, with her guardian, with the man she *doesn't* want quite as much as with the man she does. And John recognizes the lies, and upbraids her. And sees through the hypocrisies, and denounces her. And, thanks to his chauffeur, perceives that she is pursuing him—and runs away from her. But she overtakes him in his flight, and he is once again face to face with her. And her sexual lure overwhelms not only him, but even all that he knows about her, and he marries her.

That is the story—which is to say, that is how any ordinarily competent light-comedy ironist would have viewed the situation, positing that no man is smart or strong-willed enough to escape a really determined woman whom he happens to find sexually attractive. And though Shaw has much to say on other subjects in *Man and Superman*, on *this* subject he hasn't, in the end, much more to say than the ordinary competent writer of light comedy. Shaw, to be sure, brings in the Life Force; and Shaw ultimately identifies the Life Force with humanity's upward striving rather than its intersexual strife. But in *Man and Superman* (the three-act play) Shaw's Life Force seems little more than what the old poets would have termed Nature, or at most the desire to carry on and improve the race. The Life Force is here, at least, something that can swamp the reason and defeat the will, something that can even rattle Shaw, and convert so great a champion of rationality to a kind of mysticism.

Philosophically, we may allow that Shaw's Life Force—if only because it *is* so instinctive a force, or metaphysical a process— might, for argument's sake, exist. But theatrically, in the case of *Man and Superman*, Shaw's Life Force, rather more than it is Bergson's *élan vital* or Shakespeare's plain nature or your mat-

ing instinct or my desire to carry on and improve the race—
theatrically, Shaw's Life Force here seems more than half our
old friend, the god from the machine. It requires the Life Force
at its most compelling to get Tanner to marry Ann. For the
facts simply don't permit us to regard Tanner as the mere male
who is no match for the scheming female. The whole basis of
that theory is that the male isn't on to the female, or at least to
all of her, that he interprets her aggressiveness as solicitude,
that he supposes the ideas she plants in him to have grown there
of themselves. Or he knows the worst about women, but finds his
own woman an exception; or he is portrayed as an idealist, or
an idiot, or ripe for plucking, or catchable on the rebound. Tanner, however, is not only in the general sense a very emanci-
pated and extremely unsentimental man; he also knows exactly
what Ann is up to: how deviously she conspires, how ruthlessly
she pursues. He has every reason to dislike and distrust her, and
Shaw—to make his point—has to make Ann somebody we dislike and distrust as well. Nor is Tanner presented as head over
heels in love with the girl and powerless to resist her. For argument's sake, one may concede that she attracts him more than
he will allow. But that is still not enough of an argument: the
Life Force simply overpowers Tanner so that Shaw can make his
point and have his joke, as some god from the machine appears
in a more usual kind of play so that the author can round off his
plot. The psychology behind Tanner would be more convincing
if we treated him as ruefully resigned to marrying the determined Ann rather than unable to resist her; if he, quite as much
as the audience, relished the irony of his situation; if, tied up
with this transcendental mating instinct there were just a touch
of a martyr complex.

Fortunately the Ann-Tanner relationship is not the only one
that counts in *Man and Superman*. There are, in terms of subplot, Violet's marriage to Malone, and in terms of byplay, Tanner's relations with Straker. The matter of Violet Robinson,
who we are led to believe is quite brazenly about to become a
mother without having become a wife, is in Shaw's best prankish manner; for after milking the situation for all it is worth,

and having all kinds of people react in all kinds of ways, Shaw lets Violet indignantly reveal that, of course, she's married. As for Tanner's relationship with Straker, though it seems more traditional than the joke about Violet seems pat, actually it has a good deal about it that is—or that once was—new. And what is new about the relationship is what is new about Straker, who is not just the resourceful, impertinent servant found in comedy of every age and nation, but the servant who has become educated and intellectually enlightened. A chauffeur or mechanic today, Straker will be an engineer or inventor tomorrow. In caste terms, he is of course still a cockney, and in cultural terms, which is more significant, he is still an outsider—fo reducation does not quite mean culture, any more than birth means breeding. But that is by the way: the point is that Straker can not only, like a dozen Figaros, tell his master that Ann is set to have him; like no Figaro, when Tanner ascribes a quotation to Voltaire, he can say, oh no, it's from Beaumarchais. Intellectually Straker can talk Tanner's language, even though he still lacks his enunciation.

All this is good enough Shavian philosophy and Shavian fooling, but it operates at a different level, and for that matter in a literally quite different world, from the third-act scene in Hell. The Hell scene is only technically a part of the play. Indeed, it can only very doubtfully be regarded as playwriting; but that is of no importance, for nowhere in English during the twentieth century has there been a more dazzlingly sustained discussion of ideas in dialogue form. The Hell scene is a great blaze of fireworks and something more than fireworks, even if of something less than clear intellectual light. The scene, which is a dream scene, contains four characters: Don Juan Tenorio, not only Mozart's and Molière's and Shadwell's and history's and legend's libertine, but John Tanner's ancestor; Doña Ana, whose descendant or double is Ann Whitefield; Doña Ana's father, the Commendatore whom Don Juan slew; and the Devil. None of these people is at all as we last met him elsewhere, nor is Hell or Heaven at all like what others have painted them. The Devil is not much of a surprise: as in his earthly appearances he is extremely eager to tempt, so in his own country he is exceedingly eager to please. He is rather like the owner of a resort hotel trying to dangle before the better type of guest the very best type of entertainment. He is much helped by the fact that, though Heaven has all the prestige of a Newport, it displays all the dullness of Old Point Comfort. Hell is indeed a home for the escapists, the pleasure-seekers, the reality-shunners, for those whose lives, conceived in frivolousness, have on earth gone unfulfilled. It is an ideal place for living an animal existence on a non-physical basis: where, that is to say, one can always be as young and look as young and act as young as one chooses, unmenaced by the ravages of Time. Shaw's Hell is a sort of vulgar idea of Heaven. There has been a great deal of switching over from the real Heaven; Ana's statue father, the Commendatore, a military man of worldly tastes and conservative values, has just come down from Heaven, leaving a forwarding address in Hell.

Ana, perhaps the most famous of the ladies whom Juan betrayed, has recently died and is incensed to find that she has been relegated to Hell. She is incensed even more to find that her father has turned his back on Heaven; indeed she is appalled in a great number of ways—as a wronged woman sent to the afterworld for wrongdoers; as a religious woman abandoned to the Devil; as a wifely and motherly woman thrust into a pit of courtesans and strumpets. She insists that Heaven be her reward, whether or not it turn out rewarding. Better to yawn in Heaven than whoop things up in Hell: though Doña Ana is quite sure that Heaven must be very agreeable.

It is Shaw's Don Juan who is most purely, most drastically Shavian. First of all, his reputation as a heartless rake and libertine is an ill-founded one: he kept running away from women because he found them getting possessive, not because, having possessed them, he found them getting dull. He ran away out of fear and in self-defense, exactly as John Tanner ran away from Ann Whitefield. He accordingly renounced the flesh, and he means now to reject the Devil. He believes in the brain, which alone distinguishes man from the brute, and by means of which man may, in time, evolve the superman. The Devil attempts to answer him:

> *And is Man any the less destroying himself for all this boasted brain of his? Have you walked up and down upon the earth lately? I have; and I have examined Man's wonderful inventions. And I tell you that in the arts of life Man invents nothing; but in the arts of death he outdoes Nature herself, and produces by chemistry and machinery all the slaughter of plague, pestilence, and famine. The peasant I tempt today eats and drinks what was eaten and drunk by the peasants of ten thousand years ago. . . . But when he goes out to slay, he carries a marvel of mechanism that lets loose at the touch of his finger all the hidden molecular energies, and leaves the javelin, the arrow, the blowpipe of his fathers far behind. In the arts of peace Man is a bungler . . . I know his clumsy typewriters and bungling locomotives and tedious bicycles: they are toys compared to the Maxim gun, the submarine torpedo boat . . . Man measures his strength by his destructiveness.*

Don Juan has his answer for this:

> *Your weak side, my diabolic friend, is that you have always been a gull: you take Man at his own valuation. Nothing would flatter him more than your opinion of him. He loves to think of himself as bold and bad . . . Call him tyrant, murderer, pirate, bully; and he will adore you . . . Call him liar and thief; and he will only take an action against you for libel. But call him coward; and he will go mad with rage: he will face death to outface that stinging truth.*

Don Juan is going to Heaven—the Exchange Plan works both ways—precisely because it is not for those who are forever seeking happiness, but because it is for those who will work and strive, who will face and become the masters of reality. Shaw's Heaven is a Puritan's Heaven where the Life Force can operate with benign efficiency (and in the Hell scene the Life Force approximates a kind of spiral movement upward, during which man sheds everything physical except his wings). It guides the one kind of man who, Don Juan says, "has ever been happy, has ever been universally respected"—the philosophic man. For Woman, Juan confesses, there was much to be said: through her he obtained not only amorous but much esthetic pleasure. What spoiled it all was that whenever he took happy leave of women, they murmured "When will you come again?" Since that meant falling into their clutches, it constituted the signal for running away, and he was asked the question so often, and ran away so often, that he became famous for running away— or, as Doña Ana puts it, infamous. The wrangling between Juan and Ana has its share of good things, as when Juan says to her: "I say nothing against your chastity, Señora, since it took the form of a husband and twelve children. What more could you have done had you been the most abandoned of women?"—and she answers, "I could have had twelve husbands and no children."

There is a good deal of point to the revision of ideas and reversal of values that go not only with Shaw's conception of Don Juan, but equally with Don Juan's conception of Hell and Heaven. Juan's Heaven is rather the headquarters of progress than the seat of perfection; a celestial workshop and meeting hall rather than a final abode of the blest. And the demonstration—or at any rate the dialectics—is brilliant. If Juan himself is more than a little windy, the general effect—as language, as wit, as paradox, as repartee, as intellectual gymnastics—is extraordinary. If there is a weakness, it is that Juan and Juan's Heaven and Hell can only be startlingly unorthodox as the cost of being uncommonly improbable. In turning accepted ideas inside out, the problem is always to provide something that seems challenging without seeming false. Sir Osbert Sitwell has recently told the story of Cinderella, in which Cinderella comes off a prig with a martyr fixation, whose stepsisters talk themselves blue in the face trying to get her to come out of the scullery. That idea is both amusing and conceivable, and so is Shaw's that Don Juan did not abandon women from boredom, but ran away from them out of fear. But even the fact that he ran away from so many of them does not acquit him of first approaching them out of sexual desire: he may not have been the profligate of legend, but even less does he seem a Puritan like Shaw. Almost the reverse psychology would be sounder, I think: had Juan really been a libertine leading an altogether self-indulgent life of the flesh, he might so much have had his fill of sex on earth as to seek something almost immoderately spiritual in Heaven. And if the answer is that in that case he would have been a sinner and ineligible for Heaven, the counter-reply is that anyone is eligible for Shaw's Heaven—the point being that almost no one is eager for it. In strict logic, Heaven for Juan would be—among other things, at least—a place where beautiful and obliging ladies merely said *"Au revoir"* instead of "When will you come again?"

As for Heaven and Hell, though they need not be conventional abodes of bliss and suffering, it is hard to accept them on the terms offered by Shaw. I mean this less as a matter of morality than as a matter of taste. Shaw's Hell, though a place of pleasure rather than pain, remains morally sound because its inhabitants are shown to be second-rate—shoddy, spineless, pleasure-seeking. All the same, one is not much tempted by the spectacle of Shaw's Heaven, and for that matter, one is not much convinced. One could easily accept it as high-thinking and plain-living viewed as an end in itself—for the severity of that idea possesses real moral grandeur. But Juan's Heaven has a real odor of up-lift and the social worker about it, a sense, in fact, of preparation for a still higher life to come. There aren't many things to insist on as basic requirements for Heaven, but surely one of them is that it should be more than a mere way station, a mere rung on a ladder. And the real reason for its not being is that Shaw's Life Force remains valid only as long as it remains evolution-ary, as it continues to strive and progress; once it achieves its goal, not only has it no further reason to exist, but the Super-man it has brought into existence would seem peculiarly lacking in personal—or even identifiable—qualities. Shaw's Superman would be at most a vibration in a void.

The brilliance of the Hell scene is thus a trifle self-defeating: the whole thing is a kind of triumph of Shaw over sense, and *any* triumph over sense must smack partly of failure. On a serious plane, Shaw is at once too doctrinaire about the Life Force and too vague about what it culminates in, just as when he isn't making sport of Heaven he is rather too solemn about it. But perhaps the main trouble with his brilliance here is that it is progressively at the expense of each of his characters and of all of their ideas: they kill one another off, they cancel one another out—which makes for very good comedy, but quite doubtful "constructive" thinking. One can only end as one began, by saying that the Hell scene is a very grand-scale and long-drawn-out display of fireworks. This whole dazzling side is, indeed, its magnificent merit; its doctrinaire side is its rather considerable weakness. Don Juan is jockeyed into being a mouthpiece for Shaw just as John Tanner is jockeyed into being a mate for Ann; they have no choice; the Life Force has about it more than a touch of *force majeure;* the superman, at several removes from Nietzsche's *Übermensch*, bears the stamp of Shaw himself. But the scene's defects of logic, its perversities of argument, can at worst only shrivel it to a mere triumph of wit.

John Bull's Other Island to my mind isn't a very good play: but being a play about Ireland, and about the English in Ireland, it is one that Shaw clearly had to write. And whatever its faults, it remains extremely much worth reading—for to piquancy of subject-matter must be added great pith of observation. No longer speculative about Life Forces or Supermen, or contrasting an odd kind of Heaven with a startling sort of Hell, Shaw is using his eyes and his memory—no less than his imagination and his wit—to contrast Ireland with England, O'Leary with John Bull; and as a matter of fact is dividing O'Leary in two. He writes here of something real to himself as well as to the world, and with all the more seriousness because the popular ideas of what he writes about are so frequently false.

It is all real enough to him, indeed, to prevent his writing the sort of high-farcical satire, at the expense of both of John Bull's islands, that he must have had a natural inclination to do. It isn't difficult to imagine a high-spirited play of Shaw's in which every time one island held the trump card it turned suddenly into the joker—a sort of comedy of the lion and the leprechaun. But this time Shaw had not quite the specific ability or desire. The subject did not rouse the comic imp in him; it stirred the natural Irishman—not so much to spring to the defense of his country as to make plain its defenselessness, the habit of its sons to do one of two things—either run away from Ireland or run away from reality. Thus Father Keegan is a kind of hero in the play, but a hero who won't fight, and an Irishman whose country is in any case but part of the Kingdom of God; while Larry Doyle is a kind of small potentate who won't help, and for whom Ireland is in any case but a province in the empire of business. The two men may stand morally at opposite poles, and the one be as visionary as the other is money-minded; but so far as they stand in relation to Ireland, they little differ, for they fail it equally.

Shaw's Englishman, Tom Broadbent, certainly comes off no better at Shaw's hands; he, indeed, is the real joke of the occasion, only the joke in the end is not at Broadbent's expense but at Ireland's. Broadbent stands forth nakedly enough, a subject for Shaw's own easy contempt, for the audience's frequent amusement, for the Irishman's consistent laughter. He is appallingly English in his monstrous innocence, his racial arrogance, his self-seeking idealism, his unblushing opportunism. So far as gaucherie, insensitiveness, and a gift for shattering certain social and moral decencies go, Tom Broadbent in Ireland seems like John Bull in a china shop. He makes a fool of himself when he encounters a girl; he makes a fool of himself when he encounters a pig. His manner is no better than his mission, which seems all the more to serve Mammon for claiming to serve Ireland. Broadbent, of course, is ultimately the more comic and contemptible for being in his own British way rational and intelligent, for following a policy that can be shown to help others while helping oneself, and for having no personal conscience to wrestle with, it having been absorbed by his political and social philosophy. Broadbent is not personally a hypocrite, only—as it were—nationally so. Neither is he himself any kind of empire-builder; he is simply doing business in Ireland because developing Britain's possessions is part of the national tradition. Nor even out of abstract principle, perhaps, is he a Liberal: he belongs to a particular party because all Englishmen belong to a party of some kind. We must not be misled into thinking that because we find him funny, he is a fool, or that because we find him clumsy, he is a duffer. He enjoys the immense advantages of his limitations. Being of undivided mind, he is always on the march and never at the cross-roads; being of undistinguished mind, he is never foxed by his own cleverness; being, finally, of untroubled mind, he will pay no moral tax on his material gains, will wear no hair shirt, bestow no conscience money. He goes into Ireland with the aims of a conqueror but the air of a liberator. And on to his every move though Ireland may be, it is by no means up to them. It was once said that the British lose all the battles but the last one; similarly all the laughs but the last are at Broadbent's expense.

Shaw, of course, knows this—that is the point of the play—and that almost certainly explains why the play is not just a high-spirited farce, or an Irish-English wrestling match in which both contestants are thrown and sadly bruised, but neither is much hurt. It wouldn't be so dispiriting or one-sided if Broadbent's—and Britain's—victory were simply a material one; but it is hard to claim a moral victory for Ireland. There is much to admire in Keegan, and his final preachment constitutes a magnificent sermon, but that only returns us to the root of the matter, to an Ireland with a far greater gift for words than for deeds, for preaching than for practice, for fiery denunciations and haunting laments, for a nation to whom so many things are fighting words, but in whom the fighting spirit, when most needed, may be lacking. There is the light of God and Eternity in Keegan's eyes, set as they are in his unflinching head; yet the unflinching head is set upon faintly shrugging shoulders. Keegan, who has not fared well of Ireland, has taken mundane refuge in irony; and so he dissolves in irony, as Larry Doyle escapes in cynicism. Larry Doyle left Ireland to make his fortune, knowing he could not make it at home; and he has made it, not by believing—like Broadbent—that the English way is the right way, but by accepting it as the sure one. Broadbent is a humbug to us, but not to himself; fun to watch, but expensive to play against. Larry Doyle is realistically, unrepentantly out to win, and only the more coldblooded for knowing that he is Irish and not naturally so. The spectacle of an impotent Ireland has been partly the spur to his own hardheaded career.

In Broadbent, Keegan, and Doyle, Shaw has concentrated his serious feelings about the conflict between the two countries and the complexion of their countrymen. It is with minor characters and passing incidents that he manages to have his fun. He can spoof the traditional appeal—for foreigners—of the Irish voice, by having Larry say:

> *When I first went to London I very nearly proposed to walk out with a waitress in an Aerated Bread Shop because her Whitechapel accent was so distinguished, so quaintly touching, so pretty . . .*

And of course Shaw has his go at the stage Irishman that outsiders accept as the genuine article. And there are outright gags, such as the reason why Broadbent's English valet is for Home Rule: "I want a little attention paid to my own country, and that'll never be so long as your chaps keep hollering at Westminster as if nobody else mattered." But *John Bull's Other Island* is not, for Shaw, a very high-spirited play.

Nor is it a very good one. It has little story value; it moves rather heavily through long bouts of talk; too much of it is directly concerned with politics and local matters; and though the proud touchy Nora is not a bad heroine, hers is not—except for her first encounter with Broadbent—a very interesting romance. Perhaps one is merely falling into the kind of foolishness about Ireland that Shaw is so severe about, but somehow his reasoned, realistic approach to the subject deprives it of something it needs for the stage. It remains—however cogent a one —a demonstration rather than a drama. Yet its three key characters are sharply defined; and the voice of Keegan at his best is worth a good deal of the usual lyric outpourings in the Irish theater.

Major Barbara is one of Shaw's key plays, even though what it carries, in a sense, is the key to Bluebeard's closet. At any rate, though there is a sad sincerity about its reasoning, and a hard core of truth to its conclusions, Shaw here can only amend the weakness of the world's position toward his theme by making clear the weakness in his own. He can only explode Barbara's attitude by exalting Undershaft's; he can only show that poverty is the greatest of crimes by suggesting that certain other things aren't crimes at all. He can only insist that the saving of souls is a matter of the nourishing of bodies by making bodies and souls, sustenance and salvation, more or less indistinguishable. God, in Shaw's demonstration, is totally dependent on Mammon, and to clean up the slums, Shaw would let his munition-makers blow up the universe.

That Shaw fully perceived the irony, the tragic irony, in all this, that he understood in how literal a sense millions of people keep alive by making things that will blow others to bits, goes without saying. We haven't far to look for factual confirmation; we could hardly find a better analogue for Andrew Undershaft than Alfred Nobel. Nevertheless, it is hard to feel that Shaw, here, was writing in a very successful or a quite unambiguous ironical vein. It is hard to feel that—whether approving of Undershaft's arguments or not—Shaw was in any way up to answering them. It is hard to feel that Barbara's capitulation is not in some degree a conversion as well. She may still abhor, or at any rate deprecate, her father's profession and her father's philosophy. But she has certainly come to admire, or at any rate respect, her father's force of character. Mrs. Warren's daughter, when she learns that Mrs. Warren has gone on running brothels not to keep alive but to grow rich, breaks with her mother. Andrew Undershaft's daughter, when she feels that Undershaft makes armaments less to grow rich than to keep other people alive, is reconciled to her father. The difference seems to me much less important in terms of daughters and parents than in terms of Shaw. Mrs. Warren's brothels gave people employment no less than Undershaft's munition works, and there had only to be enough of them for Mrs. Warren's benefactions to rival Undershaft's. Yet for Mrs. Warren Shaw has no respect, while for Undershaft it seems to me he has all too much.

Undershaft is, of course, one of the great Shaw types, the protagonist of a number of Shaw plays. We have seen him, more or less, as Caesar and, more or less, as Broadbent. But both times we have seen him more ambivalently. Shaw's Caesar, with what I have termed his Right-Needs-Might philosophy, makes out a good enough case for himself, but we are fully aware that he sets a most dangerous example. Shaw's Broadbent, with his philosophy of ruling-class liberalism, his faith in the world getting ahead slowly and himself getting ahead fast, is a perfectly understandable kind of practical idealist. But though Broadbent is not consciously a hypocrite, unconsciously he is so much one as to be all but a figure of satire. If Shaw backs him, so to speak, against the Irish it is from feeling that he at least acts on his beliefs, where Larry Doyle acts cynically and Keegan does not act at all. Shaw is backing the English *character* against the Irish character, and not in terms of right or wrong, but only of success or failure.

With Undershaft, however, Shaw in effect is backing the English capitalist against all comers, or rather, against only such comers as it is advisable for Undershaft to take on. The case against Undershaft would seem peculiarly strong: he is not only a world-powerful industrialist, but his is the most destructive of industries. Yet the case for Undershaft is made, on both personal and philosophic terms, as persuasive as possible. The man himself is intelligent, magnetic, attractive, good-humored, alive— the sort of man that even people who disapproved of him would like. And not only is what he represents and believes argued with the greatest vigor; it is opposed with no vigor at all. The very set-up—in comic, not to say Shavian, terms—is all in Undershaft's favor: he is painted black before he appears; he looms at the outset an ideological villain, a merchant of death, a prince of darkness, an enemy of the people. Even in melodrama, he could hardly get worse, and in comedy he has every incentive to come off appreciably better. He has a role to play in pure opposition to his Salvationist daughter, and the gauge is thrown down at once, the contest at once proclaimed between the saver of souls and the destroyer of bodies:

UNDERSHAFT: *May I ask have you ever saved a maker of cannons?*
BARBARA: *No. Will you let me try?*
UNDERSHAFT: *Well, I will make a bargain with you. If I go to see you tomorrow in your Salvation shelter, will you come the day after to see me in my cannon works?*
BARBARA: *Take care. It may end in your giving up the cannons for the sake of the Salvation Army.*
UNDERSHAFT: *Are you sure it will not end in your giving up the Salvation Army for the sake of the cannons?*

It follows naturally that Barbara must learn that it is the destroyers of bodies who, in modern society, finance the saving of souls, the industrialists who keep the Salvation Armies on the march. That—whether as realism or irony—is crucial, and with that, there must be driven home the whole impossibility of absolute positions, the whole jostling of good with evil, the whole idea of the illegitimate birth of our most moral attitudes and actions. There is plainly a case of a kind for Undershaft— if only that with his money he provides large benefactions, and that with his factories he offers vast employment. Nor is there the slightest reason why he, personally, shouldn't be a most intelligent benefactor and a model boss, why he shouldn't make the thousands who work for him healthy and content, and the thousands who visit his libraries or art museums or soup kitchens that much the happier.

But Shaw, before he is finished, goes a great deal farther than that. His Undershaft is not simply the very best kind of international capitalist. The Fabian, the Socialist Bernard Shaw comes close to saying that international capitalism is the very best form of society—and on a rather odd basis, to boot. For it is the Salvation Army, not the Socialist or any Liberal party; it is religious idealism, not a different social program, that is pitted against Undershaft. Odder, even, than the way the Fabian Society has been stood in the corner, is the way the Life Force has been tossed into the street. Don Juan in Hell could only lament man's genius for being destructive, could only describe material progress in terms of new gadgets for killing, new devices of death. And here, in *Major Barbara*, the most colossal of all human instruments of destructiveness—the very symbol of the Death Force—enjoys, if not to be sure an absolute victory, yet certainly a relative one.

Much of all this is very brightly and amusingly done; and doubtless some of it is done tongue-in-cheek. And of course Undershaft makes clear to Barbara something profoundly true and relevant when he talks of money as what might be called the root of all good.

> UNDERSHAFT: *Cleanliness and respectability do not need justification, Barbara: they justify themselves. I see no darkness here, no dreadfulness. In your Salvation shelter I saw poverty, misery, cold and hunger. You gave them bread and treacle and dreams of heaven. I give from thirty shillings a week to twelve thousand a year. They find their own dreams; but I look after the drainage.*
>
> BARBARA: *And their souls?*
>
> UNDERSHAFT: *I save their souls just as I saved yours.*
>
> BARBARA: [revolted] *You saved my soul! What do you mean?*
>
> UNDERSHAFT: *I fed you and clothed you and housed you. I took care that you should have money enough to live handsomely—more than enough; so that you could be wasteful, careless, generous. That saved your soul from the seven deadly sins.*
>
> BARBARA: [bewildered] *The seven deadly sins!*
>
> UNDERSHAFT: *Yes, the deadly seven.* [Counting on his fingers] *Food, clothing, firing, rent, taxes, respectability and children. Nothing can lift those seven millstones from Man's neck but money; and the spirit cannot soar until the millstones are lifted. I lifted them from your spirit. I enabled Barbara to become Major Barbara; and I saved her from the crime of poverty.*

CUSINS: *Do you call poverty a crime?*

UNDERSHAFT: *The worst of crimes. All the other crimes are virtues beside it: all the other dishonors are chivalry itself by comparison. Poverty blights whole cities; spreads horrible pestilences; strikes dead the very souls of all who come within sight, sound, or smell of it. What you call crime is nothing: a murder here and a theft there, a blow now and a curse then: what do they matter? they are only the accidents and illnesses of life: there are not fifty genuine professional criminals in London. But there are millions of poor people, abject people, dirty people, ill fed, ill clothed people. They poison us morally and physically: they kill the happiness of society: they force us to do away with our own liberties and to organize unnatural cruelties for fear they should rise against us and drag us down into their abyss. Only fools fear crime: we all fear poverty. Pah!*

This is the real wisdom of the play: it is what an Undershaft —or one aspect of a Shaw—has to teach, and what Barbara— and large numbers of the human race—have to learn. But because poverty causes so many crimes hardly means that munitions-making is the one way to prevent them or that munitions-making doesn't beget crimes equally grave.

The truth, the trouble, here—straight on to the end, where all Undershaft's family fall equally in love with him and his ideas—is that Shaw did not grasp to what lengths he had gone. Shaw's love for the strong, practical man of the world, whom he endows with his own supple thinking, and superlative gifts of speech, is—I strongly suspect—the great love of his life. It is the guilty secret, the Bluebeard's closet, of his mind. It is what made him exalt Caesar, admire Stalin and Mussolini, and even put in a few good words for Hitler. Obviously the type fascinates him, obviously he tends to identify himself with it. A trifle less obviously, for certain vices in these strong men he substitutes certain virtues of his own. Shaw's sense of mischief is magnificent, but his sense of real evil—individual evil—is far from acute. Just because Shaw knows that bad social and

(255)

economic systems cause so much wrongdoing and crime, he perhaps minimizes the villainy of individuals. In any event, his most ambitious and power-haunted and presumably ruthless characters have a decidedly good-natured or philosophical or idealistic side. Shaw, as a result, not only swallows Undershaft; he half seems to swallow the arguments he puts into Undershaft's mouth. He wanted, quite wisely, to make the evil-sounding Undershaft into a thoroughly engaging human being; he wanted, perhaps no less wisely, to show that he too had a case. But what happened was that Undershaft came very close to being a hero, and his case to being a veritable cause.

Simply as a play, *Major Barbara* has much merit of one kind or another—good wit, good scene-writing, some extremely good characters. The first act is bright and enjoyable throughout, with all the ease and verve of drawing-room comedy, all the accumulating stage interest brought out in the family relationships, all the formulation of the issues to be fought out in the acts to come. The second act—though, in the reading, one roundly curses Shaw for his pages and pages of phonetic cockney—has its genuine merits too—all the more for being in such brilliant contrast to the first. Lady Bridomart is a good character of a kind, and Adolphus Cusins a good one too, though as Undershaft's foundling successor in the armaments dynasty, he doesn't strike me—as he does the people in the play—as so certain of success. Presumably he will give munitions a certain cachet based on his love of culture and knowledge of Greek, and his love of culture and knowledge of Greek will presumably make him the greatest Undershaft of them all. But the point about Cusins, assuming it is not just a joke, seems almost as obscure as the point about Undershaft seems excessive. Still, the final point about the play is a quite valuable one, for it is very likely the final point about Shaw. Very simply, Shaw is a better wit or artist or playwright than he is a propagandist or philosopher or political moralizer.

Getting Married is not one of Shaw's better-known or better-liked plays, though I think it needs only to be better known to be better thought of. Its most outlandish vindication is Chesterton's, who said *Getting Married* was all the more worth considering as a play because it was *not* one. What Chesterton was presumably implying was that anything so entertaining didn't need to be a play. In any ordinary sense, I suppose *Getting Married* isn't a play, though the reason is scarcely that it lacks the usual ingredients. It has situations galore, and even the basis of a plot; it has characters whose lives have been full of conflict and have even come to a crisis. It offers possibilities for all varieties of action, from the wildest farce to the purplest melodrama. If *Getting Married* is not, in any ordinary sense, a play it is because Shaw refuses to *mix* his ingredients—to make his soup boil or his bread rise—in the usual manner. He doesn't resolve his situations, his conflicts, his crises by action; he resolves them by argument. What things do happen, what action does occur, has as deliberately undramatic and offbeat an air as possible. For despite Shaw's title—which is both concrete and dynamic— Shaw's concern here is *not* with one's getting married: it is somewhat more with getting unmarried, and far more with marriage itself. This is not a play of action for the simple reason that Shaw is not concerned with marriage as an activity. He is concerned with it as an institution.

Hence we have everything that should go into a play, and everything that should come out of one—the required ingredients, the desired solutions. What we haven't is any of the usual treatment. We have not action, but talk—and talk, moreover, that suggests the debating society rather than the drawing room; so that one might call *Getting Married* a dialogue rather than a play, though I would call it a static play rather than a dynamic one. But whatever it is, it justifies its form in at least two ways. It justifies it, first and most important and most unanswerably of all, by being stimulating and entertaining. And it justifies it again by managing to include many more points of view, to explore and challenge many more avenues of opinion, than it could as a "dynamic" play. As Chesterton said also, it entertains all views on marriage that are held by anybody, and even some views on marriage that are held by nobody.

The scene is an English bishop's palace; the occasion the marriage of his daughter. There arrives on the scene the Bishop's one brother, a General who for years has been proposing in vain to the sister of the Bishop's wife: she keeps refusing him because, though she adores the idea of children, she detests the idea of a husband. Next arrives the Bishop's other brother, Reginald; then, quite separately, the young wife Reginald has just divorced; separately also, Hotchkiss—the reason for the divorcing. Just about there, it becomes known that Edith, the bride of the day, refuses to dress for her wedding till she has finished a pamphlet on marriage which will determine whether she shall marry at all, and while this communiqué is agitating the family, the young bridegroom Cecil Sykes turns up, himself of two minds about marrying.

Thus a large number of people are involved in the business of getting married or getting unmarried, while others—Mr. Collins, the greengrocer in charge of the wedding arrangements, and Soames, the Bishop's chaplain—are equally involved in debating the pros and cons. The entire symposium, or symphony, is conducted in a typically Shavian manner—both as regards the voicing of all kinds of views and as regards having certain views voiced by the last people that any one would expect. Marriage is discussed as an institution: marriage is equally discussed as an experience. To the Bishop's wife it simply came natural; to the stuffy, correct General, monogamous marriage is the only conceivable thing; when he suggests that his former sister-in-law has ideas that smack of polygamy, the broadminded Bishop reproves him:

> *Well, the great majority of our fellow-subjects are polygamists. I cant as a British Bishop insult them by speaking disrespectfully of polygamy. It's a very interesting question. Many very interesting men have been polygamists; Solomon, Mahomet, and our friend the Duke of — of — hm! I never can remember his name.*

For most of these people, the crux of the whole matter is the actual terms of marriage under British law; the difficulties of divorce; the fact that a husband is responsible for certain actions, such as libel, brought against his wife. The bride-to-be, a modern young woman who speaks her mind and whose mind when spoken is libelous, sees no reason why she need marry for better for worse: "What sort of servants, friends, prime ministers should we have," she demands, "if we took them for better for worse all their lives? We should simply encourage them in every sort of wickedness!" The alternative to the rigors of marriage, for many of these people, would seem to be a simple legal agreement between the parties concerned. Only, somehow, no agreement turns out to be simple, and agreements, furthermore, would bring rigors of their own. Thus two people who have never been married, but are bound together by a legal paper, can never be divorced.

There is talk all around the subject; and the Gordian knot is finally cut—or rather the marriage knot is tied—by sending for the greengrocer's sagacious sister-in-law, the Lady Mayoress. This extremely formidable female is a pythoness or oracle or seer of sorts, given to speaking in trances. She fails to set straight the marriage of the hour because, while every one is debating it, the young people steal quietly off and get married. Young Sykes's fears that Edith's frankness may ruin him financially are despatched through taking out a large insurance policy to cover possible costs. The Reginald-Leo-Hotchkiss triangle is set straight by having the virulently snobbish Hotchkiss find his fate, his destiny, his *femme fatale*, in the lower-middle-class Lady Mayoress, though since she is already married and averse to dalliance, Hotchkiss is boxed all around. I must confess that the Lady Mayoress far from lives up to the advance reports we get of her, and is the great fraud, the great fiasco, of the play. One expects a sort of wise woman and merely gets a sort of wild woman; one looks for Shaw at his most dazzling and gets Gilbert & Sullivan at their most farcical. But a truly glamorous, even a truly appealing, even a truly feminine woman, is what Shaw never can create.

Nor does *Getting Married* yield up any final wisdom on the subject of marriage which isn't also largely familiar. Shaw favors marriage as more sensible and convenient than any alternative arrangement, and he is clearly suggesting that what it needs —or needed in the England of 1908—is to be put on a more sensible and workable basis. Not marriage, but British rules and regulations concerning it, are in fault; and not abolition is what's needed, but reform. Any pamphleteering value, however, that the play may once have had is by now certainly gone. And any philosophical value, of a special Shavian sort, has vanished also, if it was ever there. The real merit of *Getting Married* is that it remains a fountain that has multiple jets of bright and clever, and contentious and contradictory, and stimulating and amusing, ideas and suggestions. If drama has been well defined as character in action, *Getting Married* might be summed up as ideas in action, or as talk raised to the level of action. It is a kind of paper-chase of ideas, a whirling, slightly whimsical triple fugue of opinions. Only the last part, involving the Lady Mayoress, fails: only there does *Getting Married* grow boring and out-of-hand alike. Otherwise Shaw's determination to include "all views on marriage that are held by anybody" is matched by his ability to invent clever ways of voicing them; otherwise this spate of talk exhibits a sufficient measure of wit, and keeps glittering and burbling as it flows.

Androcles and the Lion embraces a very large subject: the subject of the Christian martyrs, and so in a sense of Christianity and martyrdom; but on a scale that is modest if not small, and in a spirit that can only be called sunny. It is one of the gayest and most truly farcical things Shaw ever wrote, deriving its right to be fantastic from the traditional fable of Androcles, and to be gay from the high-hearted faith of the true martyr. Still, there is a kind of wild jocular energy, a sort of incorrigible, impenitent verve about it that can hardly be linked up with its subject, that can only be traced back to Shaw. To a certain extent, the subject has been thrown to the lions quite as much as the hero. To a certain extent, the old fable of Androcles seems a model of realism compared to this new farce. Properly staged, this very short, highly extravagant, thoroughly entertaining play can be the very best kind of fun.

How much "serious value" it has, I don't know: at the outset we should have to decide what we mean by serious. As writing, it is serious enough: it fulfills the proper conditions, it creates the right effects of farce or of fantasy. As a play about Christian martyrs, and hence in some sense about Christianity and martyrdom, it may seem rather lacking in stature. This is not only a matter of treatment; it is equally a matter of plot. For Shaw will not permit his martyrs martyrdom; there is a happy ending that, with a theme like this, can only smack a bit of anticlimax. Yet the sense of faith in Shaw's Christians, their aspiration toward martyrdom and sainthood, does stand out with some purity, does override, not only the happy ending, but all the jokes and *opéra-bouffe* throughout, all the playboy-emperors and waltzing lions of the piece. Shaw's Androcles, Shaw's Lavinia, Shaw's Ferrovius have, personally, all the more stature for being so frivolously presented. Not to feel this is to admit that we cannot identify a hero unless he is placed on a pedestal, or a saint unless she is equipped with a halo. To most of us, with our own incapacity for martyrdom, a martyr is never easy for a writer to make convincing; but Shaw, at the very least, has made his plausible.

Edmund Wilson has said that one of the chief patterns in Shaw is that of opposition between practical worldling and saint —between Broadbent and Father Keegan, between Undershaft and Barbara. In *Caesar and Cleopatra* it is the practical man who is glorified, in *Androcles* it is the saint. We shall have a greater saint and heroine, of course, in *Saint Joan*, but rather a lesser glorification, for in *Joan* Shaw makes sainthood more controversial, so to speak, and gives the case for Joan's persecutors. Here the only one of the Christians' opponents who comes off very well is the lion, and the lion is no opponent.

It is true that, for the most part, the opponents are not at all villainous—are no sadistic persecutors, no brutal totalitarians— and that the alternative to persecution is paying mere lip-service to the State religion, is the mere dropping of a pinch of incense on an altar. The Emperor himself is scarcely worse than effete and irresponsible, and Shaw, in his after-remarks, makes clear that Christian martyrs weren't thrown to the lions because they were Christians, but because they were cranks. There is no real religious issue. To people who themselves do not believe in Jupiter, it is of no importance to disbelieve in Jesus. But ultimately the skepticism of infidels has nothing to do with the martyrdom of saints: it doesn't matter *why* they are persecuted; it only matters that they are—for without persecution there cannot be martyrdom. Shaw has characterized his martyrs pretty clearly:

> *All my articulate Christians, the reader will notice, have different enthusiasms, which they accept as the same religion only because it involves them in a common opposition to the official religion and consequently in a common doom. Androcles is a humanitarian naturalist, whose views surprise everybody. Lavinia, a clever and fearless freethinker, shocks the Pauline Ferrovius, who is comparatively stupid and conscience ridden. Spintho, the blackguardly debauchee, is presented as one of the typical Christians of that period on the authority of St. Augustine, who seems to have come to the conclusion at one period of his development that most Christians were what we call wrong uns. No doubt he was to some extent right: I have had occasion often to point out that revolutionary movements attract those who are not good enough for established institutions as well as those who are too good for them.*

Of these four, only Spintho proves inadequate. Ferrovius has simply missed his vocation—he is too physically strong for a martyr, as Spintho is too morally weak. Androcles has the quiet faith that, if it does not move mountains, always stands its own ground, and Lavinia is a woman of notable character, forged to resist good and evil, love and glory alike.

The upshot, as I said, is an anticlimax: the martyrs are deprived of martyrdom. But in Roman eyes they achieve a no less Christian feat—deprived of martyrdom, they yet accomplish miracles. Ferrovius slays six men, and the Emperor elects to have none but Christian fighters. Androcles has a fine sentimental reunion with the lion, and they waltz round the amphitheater together to the consternation of the spectators. Ferrovius's ability to kill men, Androcles's ability to tame beasts, Lavinia's ability to resist handsome soldiers may add up to a kind of joke, but the joke is not at their expense. They who would happily have been martyrs end up victors instead; and their story, for all that it smacks of vaudeville, has yet something resonant and splendid about it. If it is comedy, it is heroic comedy. Some one has said that Milton's most important poem is *Paradise Lost*, but that his best poem is *Lycidas*. *Androcles* is far from being Shaw's most important play; but it is not so very far from being his best.

Pygmalion is one of Shaw's pleasantest plays: it is also, in spite of appearances, one of his most human. Nothing would seem less human, or more peculiarly Shavian, than a play that turned on the science of phonetics; no one would seem a worse hero—or *is* a worse hero in the romantic sense—than Shaw's phonetics professor. As fascinating as Professor Higgins' experiment is, the matter of making a duchess out of a flower girl by teaching her to speak like one, is scientific rather than human, a question of vowels and consonants rather than flesh and blood. Moreover, Shaw refuses to humanize his story by making what begins as something between teacher and pupil wind up as a matter of husband and wife. Pygmalion never marries Galatea.

Shaw actually humanizes his story by *not* having Pygmalion marry Galatea, by not letting a phonetical experiment end up a mere mechanical romance. It is Shaw who brings Galatea to life by realizing that that is precisely what Pygmalion has not done; for to Pygmalion—whom let us from here on call Higgins, and the lady Liza—all this was purely an experiment, was transforming a flower girl into a duchess with no sense that she was also a woman. Shaw is very generally the champion of life, reality, humanity; Shaw is very generally on the side of the non-angels. But he doesn't always make us feel that his people are quite flesh and blood—just to begin with, they are never at a loss for the right word or the wrong opinion. But in Higgins, Shaw offers some one so wholeheartedly scientific and inhuman, so much more enraptured by vowel sounds than the Life Force, that Shaw can emerge not only as one who champions humanity, but even, for the nonce, as one who breathes it.

As a story, this is one of Shaw's prettiest ones—a pure scientific fairy tale. The plot is so immemorial and indestructible as to make us wonder whether Shaw's own contribution isn't, theatrically speaking, immaterial. The public will always watch —whatever the method—drudges being turned into duchesses; nevertheless, Shaw has freshened the story and made it fit for cultivated audiences. His particular merit is his treating a fairy-tale in scientific terms, his creating a duchess by scientific means, and his sense not only of what the undertaking involves but of what the upshot involves—for when one has at last become a lady, life does not end but begins.

Much of the outright fun of the play consists in watching Liza on the way to duchessdom; and the midway scene at Mrs. Higgins' At Home—where Liza has learned to pronounce but not yet to converse, and where her lapses into billingsgate are palmed off as samples of the latest fashionable slang—is usually, in the theater, the show-piece of the evening. But if the fun of the play has to do with Liza's becoming a lady, the point of the play involves her becoming a woman. Always a person of strong feelings, she is now equally a person of sensitive ones. And what was sport for Higgins is a matter of life-and-death for her: having been raised to a world of culture and breeding, shall she now be tossed back into the gutter? Having been brought into her teacher's own house, having lived in the closest contact with him, shall she now be—without even a "thank you"—dismissed? She has, beyond question, the right on her side. Although Higgins' experiment may be finished, Liza's new life has only just begun, and Higgins owes her something. The fact is, however, that Liza's rights have got tangled up with her resentments, that her claim on Higgins for what might be termed social security is mixed up with her demanding of Higgins a great deal of personal attention. Her vanity is everywhere wounded—not just for being a mere experiment in Higgins' life, but equally for *not* being an experience. Thus, so far as

Liza resents Higgins as heartless, we must condemn him, but not where she resents him as heartfree.

Hence, it is not just the audience that assumes Higgins must marry Liza: it is almost equally Liza herself. For him not to marry her, for the fairy prince not to claim Cinderella, for Pygmalion not to grant his statue her statutory rights, is to do more than insult the lady: it is to sin against romance. Still, in the moment of her rage Liza isn't in a fury because Higgins hasn't fallen in love with her and suggested marriage—that much she hasn't consciously yet come to expect: she is in a rage because she really doesn't mean anything to him at all. And in a sense she doesn't, which is why he can stand up to her and fight back with solid, reasonable arguments—if his emotions were involved, the arguments might occur to him less promptly. As it is Higgins can suggest that there is no way for him to be properly protective of Liza since she, given any chance, will at once become boldly possessive of him. Higgins is shrewd enough to grasp that with Liza there can be no middle ground; she must constitute for him either an experiment or an experience.

Higgins' fate might for all that have been ultimately John Tanner's—he might have been sealed of Liza Doolittle through passion or propinquity or the Life Force—had it not been for his mother-fixation. Liberated by phonetics, Liza was done in by Freud. The lady Pygmalion brought to life from a statue had no chance against the lady he had set up on a pedestal. Hence we have here not simply a play whose ending is unromantic; we have a hero who from the outset is incapacitated for romance. Pygmalion isn't Pygmalion at all, he is Oedipus.

So Liza—as we are told in Shaw's epilogue—marries Freddy and with help from Higgins and the Colonel makes a fair go of things running a flower shop. In the end, she doesn't become a duchess, after all. But if she doesn't become a duchess, at least she doesn't remain Higgins' mere doll; and if snubbed by romance, she is at any rate not sacrificed to irony or crude realism, not flung back into the gutter.

Mother fixation or not, Higgins is a very good teacher, for

the incidental no less than the intended things he has Liza learn. By his manner toward her—even though it was very much his manner toward everyone—she learned that big fact that "the difference between a lady and a flower girl is not how she behaves, but how she is treated." One may question how much she profited from his insisting that

> *The great secret, Eliza, is not having bad manners or good manners or any other particular sort of manners, but in having the same manner for all human souls—the question is not whether I treat you rudely, Liza, but whether you ever heard me treat any one else better.*

Her answer is at least as good as his defense because it is much more germane to their relationship: "I don't care how you treat me; I don't mind a black eye; but I won't be passed over."

Pygmalion is, I repeat, one of Shaw's most human plays, one where we are more concerned with the psychology of the characters than with their ideas, and with their relationship one to another than to the world at large. It is human, too, in being the most concrete sort of social comedy—a comedy of accents, one might call it; and in England a comedy of accents is in itself a comedy of manners. The play's humanity extends also to Liza's father, Alfred Doolittle, who strikes a very human note, however difficult he may be to swallow as a human being. He is, in fact, a brazen piece of Shavian ingenuity, but a successful and a likable one. His frankness about being a member of the *un*deserving poor is, of course, part of his game, exactly as artful creations like Alfred Doolittle are part of Shaw's. Just who, one must sometimes wonder, *is* the underdog, in a world where things are looked at upside down?

Heartbreak House is plainly one of Shaw's major plays, but it is not one of his major successes. There hangs over it, as over *Man and Superman* and *Back to Methuselah*, the sense of something greatly intended, of something meant to be writ large. That Shaw (as he said) wrote it as it came, without formal scheme or planning, in no way disproves the essentially ambitious nature of the undertaking. Here, also, was a subject that must long have engaged, must long have fascinated, Shaw's mind. *Heartbreak House*, as Shaw said right off in his preface to it, "is not merely the name of the play which follows . . . it is cultured, leisured Europe before the war." It is also, as is equally well-known, a kind of Shavian—or would-be Shavian—version of Chekhov, a kind of Sussex *Cherry Orchard*.

It is thus an overtly symbolic or at least symptomatic play, in which Shaw, with all England for his stage, depicts the states of mind, styles of living, social and political programs, or want of them, that preceded, and no doubt helped to produce, the first World War. Shaw in a sense is concerned, as Chekhov more narrowly was in *The Cherry Orchard*, with the outward life of a people and the inward death of a society. He sets his play in a rambling Sussex house that its owner, an ancient retired sea captain, inhabits as though it were a ship. It is personally a symbol of Captain Shotover's own need of a more masculine, more adventurous and highsouled world than the fiberless England all about him; it might also be regarded as a sort of Noah's Ark into which each species has come before the deluge: here every kind of animal can at any rate be observed, whether or not it can be saved.

Fortunately, for both Shaw and ourselves, we cannot put exact labels on most of these exhibits. Still, some of them are good symbols enough: one of the Captain's daughters, Lady Utterword, has the ruling-class outlook, the belief that when the right people aren't running an empire they are riding a horse. The Captain's other daughter, Hesione Hushabye, is an attractive, formidable female, who perhaps represents Woman in a society where women are held down to being ladies. Her husband, Hector, is a man of dash and courage, too shy and English to admit to the heroic things he really does, yet so romantically English he must boast of heroisms quite imaginary. Hector's bachelor brother is simply the footless, dabbling, philandering, cultivated leisure-class Englishman; Mangan is simply capitalist big business. Ellie Dunn, who stands at the opposite pole to Captain Shotover, is young enough for her whole life to lie before her, as the Captain's lies behind; young enough to act decisively and be decisively acted on. She is the future in the process of becoming the present, she is romantic youth meeting, head-on, the realities of life. It is she who, in the course of the play, can learn the most, change the most, suffer the most, as Shotover can learn and change and suffer least. They are the play's two extremes, but equally the play's twin centers.

The characters are all these things on a kind of schematic basis rather than any true-to-life one, for *Heartbreak House* is so loosely cross-sectional a picture, and in form so unremitting a conversation piece, that nobody acquires the precise emphasis derived from a sharp, significant design, and nobody gathers the dramatic importance derived from the development of a plot. There is a certain amount of incident, but no causation or complication. Mangan is hypnotized; a burglar is caught out; at the end there is a bombing, and Mangan and the burglar are killed. Equally, the characters are involved in all sorts of ways with one another, are enlightened in all sorts of ways about one another: Ellie, for instance, learns the truth about Hector Hushabye, about Mangan, about her father—and so, if not the truth about life, then the falsity of her previous conception of life. But for the most part the play drifts because the people in it do; it is one of talk rather than action because so Shaw regarded cultured, leisured Europe before the war. They are not so much dead people as they are dead-ended, products of a world incapable of changing itself; culture with them has no element of creativeness, and leisure provides no opportunity to do what they want—only to do what they think they want or, worse yet, do nothing.

At the end, German bombs rain down from the skies, as axes, at the end of *The Cherry Orchard*, hack into the cherry trees. But it is interesting to note that the very class that in Chekhov is dispossessed is the one that Shaw permits a certain chance of salvation. It is the bourgeois parvenu, the rising big-business Lopahkin, who conquers in Chekhov. In Shaw, an advanced example of the same type is killed—Mangan, the symbol of predatory capitalism, and with him the burglar, the outright thief. Where Chekhov has shown sentence of death being carried out on Russia's leisure class, Shaw has granted a reprieve to England's. Or if not salvation itself, then an illusion of salvation, or a natural and lingering rather than accelerated and violent death. It is those whom Shaw regards as the real enemies of society—rather than as just their own enemies—that he kills off at the end, in the traditions of the old morality play or even the old melodrama.

It is hard to imagine on what realistic or prophetic grounds Shaw could be doing this. To be sure, Mangan and the burglar are killed because they alone seek safety during the bombing; they alone are prudent and, if you will, cowardly; they, outward symbols of the ruthless and the lawless, are inwardly the worst weaklings. And on ironic, and again on moral, grounds all this has point enough, but surely not on the terms set, surely not inside the framework of cultured leisured Europe. Surely it wasn't the thieves and the tycoons whom the upheavals of the era finished off. Wasn't Shaw—in the sense of *being* Shaw—letting his audiences down in the same sense that he was cheering them up, to put so "right" an ending to so hard-to-come-right a story?

If the outcome is not Chekhovian, neither is the general effect. Where Chekhov seems perhaps the most sharply selective of all modern playwrights, Shaw is the one most given to dialectics and discursiveness—and nowhere more than in *Heartbreak House*, or at any rate nowhere more noticeably. *Getting Married* is a more outright conversation piece, but on just that ground it is a more allowable one; moreover, there is plot enough in *Getting Married* for its thesis to seem "dramatized." Here, except for two lives that are terminated, none seems resolved. And Chekhov's are not only more fragrant symbols, but more breathing people. The characters in *Heartbreak House* are mere types sharpened into "humors": collectively they may add up to England because individually each represents something palpably English. But Chekhov's characters add up to more without adding up to so much: whatever they "stand for," they ultimately stand for themselves; they *reveal* what they represent.

Hence as symbolism *Heartbreak House* seems impaired by its

conclusion; lacks appeal as a story, if only because it never is one; and is full of people who seem more like puppets. This, of course, is saying nothing very scathing about Shaw, many of whose plays tend to lack plot, most of whose characters are mere talking machines or points of view. But what elsewhere merely describes Shaw must here, I think, a little discredit him. On its own set terms, the play essentially fails. For the terms are large; plainly the whole thing is meant for a full-dress performance. And it has, indeed, a decided appearance of size. But it also creates a certain impression of sprawl—and, a little, of windiness.

It comes off as brilliant improvisation. We can believe that Shaw, in writing it, did not know where it was taking him, for it conveys little more sense of direction than of destination. Shaw himself, here, is a kind of brilliant drifter, because his theme is not really a theme: it is only a framework. In *The Cherry Orchard* we watch a class committing suicide before our very eyes: suicide is a very positive and dramatic act, and entails a sense of loss and might-have-been. The characters in *Heartbreak House* are all so busy explaining to one another what they suffer from that we get the most forcible sense of diagnosis, but only the feeblest awareness of disease. Nor does the sense of portent in the air—or even the air-raids themselves—quite convey the feeling of human fate or social change. Where *The Cherry Orchard* is like a decisive chapter of history, *Heartbreak House* is more a rambling chapter of social memoirs. In the one we are shown how one kind of people died, in the other how all sorts of people lived. Shaw shows at most what his people are; Chekhov both what they are and what they become. As a result, though Chekhov can be dull on other grounds, his plays never have what I agree with Stark Young that *Heartbreak House* has—a kind of inner monotony.

Shaw's subject is too big for Shaw's method, too big to be so dependent on Shaw's wit; and if it was to be denied the sturdy scaffolding of a plot, it needed the spaciousness of a panorama. Or, Shaw being Shaw, perhaps his real chance lay in devising a wild and whirling extravaganza: in finding for his mythical ship and eccentric Captain, a more wayward and picturesque crew, a more adventurous and perilous voyage. The way Shaw's subjects are introduced, the way *Heartbreak House* is orchestrated and "opened up," it promises either large-scaled symphonic or large-scaled operatic development; it emerges a protracted, flatulent tone poem, with massed brass effects and general fireworks near the end.

The play is full, to be sure, of striking things, and is plainly the work of Shaw's maturity. The Captain, even if there is more of boom and rumble than of flesh and blood about him, is strangely unforgetable. The whole last scene, in the moonlit garden, with the relaxed charm of the immemorial English countryside suddenly charged with the tensions of the approaching air-raid—a scene where people seem sleeping till they talk —has, as nothing else in *Heartbreak House*, that sense of something sweetly leisured about to come to an end, about to come to grief. Here, indeed, as voices speak and answer, as figures come and go, as all are pulled apart by their private perturbations and desires, as all are swept together by the danger in the skies, we catch that gift of harmonious orchestration that Shaw got from his knowledge of musical form. And if the magnitude one once ascribed to *Heartbreak House* now seems wanting, the peculiar magic of the last act does still persist. But it is precisely heartbreak that one fails to believe in here. Shaw himself seems to have no understanding of heartbreak; he can no more be a tragedian than Dr. Johnson's old school friend could be a philosopher; somehow cheerfulness—or worse yet, mockery—is always breaking in.

Such episodes as that of the burglar, and of Mangan being hypnotized, are mere Shavian didoes, too facile and familiar to impress us or seem right; but all the noisy comings and goings, the meeting and mingling of the characters gives an *appearance* of life, despite the inner monotony of the piece. And even regarded as symbols or talking machines, how good are Hector Hushabye and the ineffably snotty Lady Utterwood and some of the others! With Shotover's famous speech toward the end, I am less impressed than I once was:

> *The captain is in his bunk, drinking bottled ditch-water; and the crew is gambling in the forecastle. She will strike and sink and split. Do you think the laws of God will be suspended in favor of England because you were born in it?*

I am less impressed, not because it isn't vibrant writing, but because it suggests what the play should have been rather than sums up what it is. Without the true force of the play behind it, it smacks of rhetoric and seems even tinged with melodrama. Despite much that is brilliant here, and a certain masterfulness of manner, *Heartbreak House* seems partly to shatter itself in talk, partly to flatten itself in sprawl; it seems to have largely acquired the very vice it meant to expose, to have found in a drifting pre-war Europe the occasion for a drifting post-war play.

We cannot take leave of Shaw without speaking of *Saint Joan* —for though not in itself a comedy, it is widely regarded as the outstanding work of the outstanding comedy writer of our time. Yet even here—and very noticeably in the epilogue—we feel the presence, the point of view, the style of attack of the assured comic writer. What is more, we feel the sense of the tragic imbedded in the comic: the hard realistic tragedy of things as they are rather than the high romantic tragedy of things as they might have been.

Saint Joan is one of many plays (*Caesar and Cleopatra*, *The Man of Destiny*, *Man and Superman*, *Androcles and the Lion*, *Great Catharine*, *Good King Charles*) in which Shaw deals with figures of history or legend; and *Joan*, in a sense, is the one in which Shaw least seems to use history as a mere point of departure. He seems concerned with Joan as she was; he seems also concerned with making her real rather than illustrative or fascinating. Perhaps that is the peculiar problem of treating Joan: in all that we know about her, she could scarcely seem more fascinating—and could scarcely seem less real. Whether inspired by genius or God, inspired she clearly was; whether or not her voices were real, they were real to her, and the problem, consequently, is to make them real to us. And all the more because Shaw intended to give the case *against* Joan in his play, he must—as cogently as possible—put the case for her, which means communicating her physical presence as well as her spiritual force. There must be vibrations as well as visions; unless Joan has magnetism, a genius for leadership, a capacity to transmit to men what she received from God, she will only be the girl of legend, a painted figure on the scroll of time.

Knowing this, Shaw struggled to make Joan seem real. He failed, I think: he was for once a little too conscientious, as he was also, and not for the first time, too canny. After the fashion of much inferior writers, he tried to make Joan real by making her realistic. He had her talk patois, he had her talk slang, he had her call the Dauphin Charlie. All this is the merest routine of the comedy writer, whose purpose is to deflate, to make the heroic seem life-sized. But it somehow only makes it harder for us to believe in the greatness, to credit the heroism: by having Joan call the Dauphin Charlie, Shaw makes her more mysterious, not less. In the early scenes of the play, Joan is little more than a stage character, and if she sometimes rather stirs or thrills us, it is not from what she does, but from what she is said to do. This, to be sure, does not ruin her as a stage character; it merely reduces her to one.

It is thus not in victory, when she is acting for herself, but only in defeat, when she is speaking for herself, that Joan becomes in any sense real. And what makes her real then is not what makes her like every one else but what makes her different from every one else. In the grip of inspiration, she cannot merely be intelligent; in the frenzy of faith, she cannot simply be reasonable; she cannot ever explain herself, she can only insist upon herself. It is her faith that makes her obstinate and her obstinacy that makes her human. Her reality as a character doesn't rest on whether we are made to feel that she heard voices, only on whether we are made to feel that *she* heard them. The question is not whether she is right but whether she is Joan, and at the trial we do sometimes feel that she is Joan.

And dialectically and dramatically it is important that we

should, for Joan, in the trial scene, is brought up against not only all the power of the Church, but all the power of the Church's arguments. She is not beaten down by clever arguments or deceived by disingenuous arguments or bullied into spluttering or cowed into speechlessness. As a true Catholic she is bound to obey the Church, and hence by disobeying it truly becomes a heretic. There is no question that she is in the wrong, except that for Joan herself there is no question that she is in the right. In the certainty of her vision, in the incontestable divinity of her voices, she—like Luther—*kann nicht anders*. Only —as Shaw makes plain—in demanding the right to private judgment, she has ceased to be a Catholic and become a Protestant. She is one of the great heretics of history quite as much as she is one of its great heroines.

As her essential Protestantism is a menace to the priests, so her essential nationalism, her France for the French, is a menace to the peers—which is why Warwick buys her from the Burgundians and insists that she must burn. That is part of the plot of Shaw's play as it is part of the plot of history, and to the extent that Joan stands for historical change, she sums up the conflict between the revolutionary personality or movement on the one side and the status quo on the other. But the real, the more profound and insistent issue here, is that between Joan and her judges, between inner light and outer law, between the supremacy of self and the supremacy of authority. The case against heresy, and hence against Joan as heretic, is put with finality by the inquisitors. Against it, Joan can only put herself, which is to say her deepest and most unshakeable instincts. The grandeur of the trial does not rest, in the end, on how brilliant it is, or even how solemn and impressive, but on how basic. It is indeed the basic and eternal clash in religion, in politics, in society, in art: the clash between church and chapel, classicism and romanticism, liberal and Tory, bourgeois and bohemian, between those to whom it is the institution that comes first, and those to whom it is the individual.

One of the massive virtues of *Saint Joan* is that, as Eric Bentley has said, Shaw appears in all this as "not on neither

side, but on both." Here for once Shaw is not twice the prose-
cutor but twice the pleader, and his instinct is twice right. As a
dramatist, by taking the positive view—in terms of Joan and her
judges alike—Shaw gives to the conflict far more dignity and
power than he could give by seeming merely impartial (for he
must then have seemed a little indifferent). Had he found them
both wrong—well, two wrongs simply don't make a drama.
Shaw could not but be on both sides: to have been on one side
would have involved writing a kind of propaganda play, and to
have been on neither side, in this most fundamental of all
clashes, would have seemed cynical and shallow.

The play thus becomes a defense of Joan, not as a heroic
figure but as a mystical one, not in the sense that she did right
but in the sense that she could not do otherwise. And it becomes
a defense of the Church not so much on ethical as on institutional
grounds, in the sense that, like the State, its interest outweighs
the individual's and constitutes a sort of spiritual right of emi-
nent domain. If the conflict is too basic to be resolved, so that
dialectically it may seem to end in a draw, actually it does no
such thing—because dramatically it ends in a death. Our minds
may be pulled two ways, but our emotions are of course with
Joan, who is successively five very sympathetic things—a young
girl, a dazzling conqueror, a heroine, a victim, and a martyr.

But though dramatically it ends in a death, that death is not
quite the end of the play. There remains the epilogue, that
scene that takes place twenty-five years after Joan was burned,
when to her family's satisfaction she was vindicated in the Courts
—and to the King's satisfaction, too, since now he need not feel
that he had been crowned "by a witch and a heretic." In this
scene where all those concerned—some dead and some still
living—crowd into the King's bedchamber, Joan's vindication
is made complete. Her very judges acknowledge, now, her moral
and spiritual courage and greatness, and when some one appears
out of the far-distant twentieth century to announce that Joan
has been canonized, there is general rejoicing. But her glory,
she discovers, rests on her being gone from earth, and when she
inquires whether she shall rise from the dead and come back a

living woman, those about her are affrighted and appalled. The scene, enforcing the great gulf between practicality and piety, between the real and the ideal, makes its point in comic terms, but the point itself is tragic—and harsh tragedy, not high— realistic, not heroic. Between the real and the ideal there is not a clash, but a gulf. So long as Joan and the Church represent two fundamental points of view, their differences do both of them honor, but to the extent that their eyes are not equally fixed on Heaven, and that the Church must mix worldly wisdom with spiritual truth and use worldly methods for temporal power, Joan must be a tragic victim, not of spiritual, but of realistic forces.

When we try to close with *Saint Joan*, virtues and shortcomings somehow crowd together. It is a great story, but we may wonder whether other writers have not made it seem a far greater *story* than Shaw did. As a piece of dramatic creation, Joan herself is in large part a failure. As a dramatic work, *Saint Joan* quite lacks organic strength. The earlier scenes are of a piece with those in a chronicle play; it is not till Joan's career as warrior is done that Shaw's play in any vibrant sense begins. What counts is the great blaze of argument that characterizes the trial, and the great dash of cold water that characterizes the epilogue. If many people would single out the trial scene as Shaw's most impressive writing for the stage, it is not for one but for several reasons. There is to begin with, the brilliant vigor of the writing itself, which here—thanks to the weight of the subject—lacks the sense of mere pyrotechnics of *Don Juan in Hell*. Together with the weight of Shaw's material goes the special force of Shaw's manner; for here, by being on both sides, Shaw brings an affirmativeness of feeling to the trial scene in excess of anything like it in his other major work. He has, as it were, given his themes the right resounding orchestration, has resisted those playful little passages for oboe and flute, those sour or sarcastic entrances of tuba and trombone, those gaudy crashings of the cymbals, those giddy flourishes for the trumpet, that are just as likely to be disastrous as triumphant. Along with something peculiarly affirmative, there is something—for Shaw

—almost uniquely austere. Finally, of course, Shaw possesses in Joan and her judges the two great types that have most fascinated him, the two hemispheres of his admiration. Here, opposed to each other, are saint and worldling, moral passion and practical force; here we have this aspect of Shaw *in excelsis* —in the confrontation of one of the greatest individuals in history with one of the greatest institutions of all time.

The Epilogue, if not so immediately impressive as the trial scene, has its own true and tragic meaning, and is one of the highest vindications of Shaw's comic method in driving home realistic or tragic truth. If it takes off from the intensity of the play, it strengthens Shaw's interpretation; indeed it constitutes Shaw's interpretation, his insistence that men glorify the Joans as much because they are dead as because they are great.

Saint Joan is very far from being Shaw's most perfect play; and if it is possibly his greatest one, we may doubt, even so, whether it is great. Shaw is not a playwright of single great plays. His work is rife with repetition, unevenness, self-indulgence, frivolity, exhibitionism. In places it is dull, in spots it is foolish. Moreover, as thinking, as philosophy, as point of view, it is likely to puzzle as well as dazzle, to seem contradictory and a trifle conscienceless. Shaw had a little of Dr. Johnson's way of taking one side of an argument as quickly as the other, from the feeling that he could handle both sides equally well. And Shaw, rather more than Dr. Johnson, had a real ability to *see* both sides of any argument, and a real compulsion to criticize the one by the other. But there is a sense, even so, in which he seems a little unprincipled. He is a Socialist who admires industrialists and dictators; a Puritan who in moments of crisis will turn intellectual playboy; his Life Force, however glowing a process, becomes meaningless as soon as fulfilled. The puritan in him will flay the bohemian, only to let the bohemian smite the bourgeois; he will equally defend or denounce any number of human institutions; he is drawn equally to the idealist and the master of reality. He wrote on virtually every social, political, economic, religious, scientific, artistic, and moral question, and he became, as a result, the supreme commentator of his age. Nevertheless, the very scope and exhaustiveness of his subject-matter suggests how badly he overstretched his intellectual activities; how superficial, how wrongheaded, how rash and irresponsible he could prove to be. It is becoming fashionable in certain quarters to assert that Shaw *was* a thinker after all; but far from being a great thinker, Shaw is not everywhere a trustworthy popularizer, and it is a pity that many people, through going to Shaw less from a love of literature than from an interest in eugenics or economics or reform, should have misplaced the emphasis and insisted that Shaw was above all else "deep"—when he was actually, above all others in his generation, dazzling.

He is brilliant—in his wit, his mischievousness, at times his irreverence, brilliant in his ability to make ideas dance and leap, to make opinions butt and thump, brilliant in releasing the comic sense of life as an electric current that runs through the social organism of his times. Whether or not he has disproved the accepted ideas that he went to work on, he has made it harder for other people to accept them blindly, and whatever we may think of his paradoxes, they have constituted an assault on a vast array of complacent platitudes. Intellectually, it is enough that Shaw should have made people grow thoughtful or skeptical or militant, for only people themselves can make themselves grow wise.

What should be said last is simply that here is one of the great masters of dialogue, one of the ablest writers of prose, in the whole range of English writing, whether drama or literature. Whatever he might have to say—whether it was true or false, wise or silly, grave or frivolous, respectable or shocking, said hand on heart or tongue in cheek—he had not the slightest difficulty saying it. A man so superlatively articulate who is also imbued with comic genius must remain, after all deductions have been made, extraordinarily alive and entertaining, and though Shaw wrote no play that I cannot imagine being considerably strengthened and improved, he wrote a dozen that will go on being read and enjoyed for longer than you or I need think about.

CHAPTER XVI

Synge

BETWEEN Shaw and Synge the contrast is perhaps as odd as it is glaring. Both men, after all, were Irish, indeed upper-middle-class-Protestant Irish, and both left Ireland in their youth, Shaw for England, Synge for the Continent. But of course the great biographical difference—which helps explain the glaring artistic contrast—is that Synge went home again. He went back; he went first to the Aran Isles, after Yeats recommended that he live among Irish peasants and hear their speech and know their ways. It was good advice; it served Synge well and has served the theater well. But it took more, of course, than a trip to the Aran Isles to nurture Synge's talents. The trip merely released them. And the contrast between the expatriated Irish-Protestant Shaw and the re-patriated Irish-Protestant Synge is at bottom not racial but personal, a matter of particular tastes and temperament. Their common heritage of Ireland means much less, in the end, than their clashing theories of art. Synge is poetic where Shaw is not, but it would be rash to insist that he is on that account, at least in any literary sense, the more Irish of the two. Certainly it is Shaw who has much in common with the outstanding Irish writers of the past—with Congreve or Sheridan or Swift. But it was Synge who not simply returned to Ireland but became part of its Renaissance—who with Yeats

and Lady Gregory and the others was part of the Abbey Theatre
and the prime cause of the rioting it begot.

Theirs was a literary Renaissance that sought to bring about a
literary Reformation, and the contrast between Shaw and Synge
is even more an esthetic matter than a personal one. Shaw is
very definitely an artist of the middle classes—and all the more,
really, for being an antagonist of the middle classes. His chief
subject is bourgeois life and thought; his main object is to dis-
sect and expose it. Ibsen could be his father, assuming that
Ibsen had married a woman with a great sense of humor. The
point is that Shaw simply took a comic, even a cockeyed, view
of Ibsen's world. But Shaw's is yet the same world, endowed
with the same problems, subject to the same troubles; and
Shaw's plays, like Ibsen's, are problem plays, are plays "about"
something, usually something that threatens or distracts modern society. To be sure, by tempering realism with comedy,
Shaw converted purpose into what has been termed purposeful
fun. Egon Fridell, in his *Kulturgeschichte* says that Shaw, being
a sly one, always coated the pills he made up for the public
with chocolate. But, says Fridell, the public was even slyer—
it licked off the chocolate without swallowing the pills. The remark is more than witty; it equally exposes the slick tactics of a
bourgeois artist and the incorrigible shallowness of a bourgeois
audience.

Synge himself—to scramble chronology—takes up the metaphor precisely where Fridell leaves off. "We should not go to
the theater," wrote Synge in the preface to *The Tinker's Wedding*, "as we go to a chemist's or a dram-shop, but as we go to
a dinner where the food we need is taken with pleasure and excitement. This was nearly always so in Spain and England and
France when the drama was at its richest . . . but in these days
the playhouse is too often stocked with the drugs of many seedy
problems." We thus have in Synge one of the most clearly and
musically dissenting voices to the whole theater of Ibsen and
Shaw, to the whole tradition of the realistic or satiric problem
play, to the whole theory of art as having an immediate purpose
or ulterior motive. And as art, with Synge, must be pure, so

must it be joyous—something that stimulates the appetite rather than aids the digestion. This—if it is *any* gospel—is the gospel of art for pleasure's sake, on the educative principle of "The days that make us happy make us wise"; and we are not so much brought back to earth with Synge as lifted above it. What he offers, essentially, is not art as escapism but art as enlargement. The choice need not be a strict alternative between the black coffee of straight naturalism and the opium pipe of sheer escape. Art—at least minor art—can offer just the degree of exhilaration and heightened living provided by a cocktail, and can offer it in the same spirit, the spirit not of deception but of festivity.

As a writer of comedy, Synge avoided not simply naturalistic methods but the more realistic sort of plot. In turning to the peasants for language, he couldn't help being caught up in their lore. Obviously, their kind of story-telling involved their kind of story; or, to put it another way, their kind of language reflected their kind of fancy. The language was rich and pungent partly because the fancy was wild and strange. Neither the language nor the fantasy was merely pretty; the folk imagination was wild, not genteelly whimsical; wild, with something hard and coarse, even jeering and savage, about it. What is good generally about folk imagination is that it is at once so unfettered and yet downright. It displays what a child displays, an impatience with reality, but no feeling whatever of idealism. The folk mind soars on wings, but the wings of birds, not angels.

Synge, in turning to folk life, did not merely exploit what was picturesque about it, or stop at its humor or verbal charm; he equally accepted its genuine disrespectability, its smell of stale whiskey as well as peat, its ability, even its tendency to be cruel, callous, bedeviling. A romantic he may have been, but he was not a sentimentalist: he neither endowed the peasantry with more virtue than it possessed, nor insisted that anything peasant-like was, *ipso facto*, picturesquely innocent or gay. We have only to read a dozen pages of Synge to realize what is so monstrously counterfeit about a dozen plays of Saroyan, for even were we to find, in both, the sense of how good it is to be alive, that is far from saying that life itself is good, even when cruelly beset by suffering and want. And Saroyan is so busy creating angels that he often hasn't time to give them wings. They are thus forced to sojourn on earth without being people, and nothing could be duller for either them or us.

It is different with Synge. There is something a little savage or brutal about his comedy because there is something a little savage or brutal about so many of his characters. Whether or not they are true peasants, they are never products of the squeamish bourgeois mind, the opportunistic bourgeois morality. And as Synge will let nothing puritanical mar or soften their peasantlikeness, so in a pinch he will let nothing poetic mar it either. Their jokes, their pranks, their revenges are primitive and even gross, and childlike not in their innocence but in their malevolence. Where justice is concerned, the folk mind and the comic spirit see much alike—believe, that is to say, in a sort of *poetic* justice, in paying people back in their own coin, in making the punishment fit the crime, rather than in furthering moral or social ends.

Synge goes at this squarely. In his very first play, *The Shadow of the Glen*, a man tricks his unfaithful wife by pretending to be dead, and eventually, after she has brought home her lover, springs out of bed and orders the woman from the house. The lover stays behind: now that she lacks the dead man's money his passion has cooled, and indeed, after she goes, husband and lover calmly sit down and drink together. Pervaded by folk feeling, the story achieves a strangely mixed effect. Married to a much older man, living meagerly in an out-of-the-way place, the woman led a desolate, lonely life, so that in her fate there is a touch of the tragic. But with the folk spirit dominant, an attitude enters in, an atmosphere spreads around, that includes something quite ghoulish, quite cynical, and—though largely unspoken—quite definitely humorous. For one thing, the husband's trick is so clumsy, inefficient, uncivilized—like many a similar child's trick, it is humorous in the very degree that it is inhuman. And of course it is humorous through justifying itself in the very act of being perpetrated: the lover is brought in before the husband would have had time to grow cold. And the ending, with the two men drinking together, has a brutal humor, as great an absence of chivalry as of sentiment, which only people who pay not even lip-service to appearances could achieve. Only those who never heard of respectability or are in embattled revolt against it could enact such a story: hence only a Synge, seeking out the primitive, or a Maupassant, spying out the cynical, could evolve such a plot.

In *The Tinker's Wedding*, the humor is far more explicit and pervasive. It is also quite low. The play concerns a tinker who has agreed to marry the woman whom for years he has consorted with. Neither he nor his hard-drinking rip of a mother really wants the marriage, but the woman has become insistent and finally gets the village priest to agree to marry them at bargain rates. But the mother steals part of the priest's fee to buy whiskey with; the priest, finding himself bilked, angrily refuses to perform the marriage; and mother, son, and fiancée band together, bundle the priest into a sack and sling it into a ditch.

It is not, as even this conservative résumé will indicate, an edifying story. Morally, it thumbs its nose at virtually everything but murder and treason. It shows no respect for the cloth, for matrimony, for honesty, for sobriety, for the standard conception of motherhood; it takes a purely carnal view of love; it snaps its fingers at the law; and though it might allow that cleanliness is next to godliness, it cares no more about the one than about the other.

Its excuse must be the gusto with which it is set down, the pungency of the language, the exhilaration of the humor. The virtues of *The Tinker's Wedding* are real and even rich in their way, though limited. Frank Connor, an Irishman to be heard with respect, speaks very slightingly of the play, calling it the worst thing Synge ever wrote, and saying it was as though Synge had decided that it was enough to write of tinkers to write well. And though I think that is to brush aside the play's merits, one knows what he means. *The Tinker's Wedding* is the sheerest genre stuff, and to an Irishman (who would take the pungent speech for granted) it would doubtless seem a mere gamy slice of life, with a streak of oh-what-a-bad-boy-am-I running through it. Artistically it rather lacks dignity, not because the characters are disreputable, but because their disreputableness is played up for its own sake. Yet the play has the merit of portraying a world as raffish and rowdy, as stripped of social pretences and moral hypocrisies, as we find in Villon, or the Elizabethan picaresque writers, or the Burns of *The Jolly Beggars*. What *The Tinker's Wedding* lacks is their overtones, their sense of light and shade, not to mention Villon's aching, anarchic melancholy. Even as comedy, Synge's play has no vibrations, stirs no depths; it simply exists for its own sake.

Yet it seems to me well worth having for its own sake, for its prose, its humor, its vivid drunk-and-disorderliness. It has the wrong kind of bravado, but the right kind of audacity; there is raw whiskey, but equally fresh air.

The Playboy of the Western World—which, despite not meaning what it seems to, is yet one of the most magnificent of all titles—is the great comedy of the Irish renascence. During its first Dublin run it threatened, of course, to be the great tragedy of the Irish renascence, being hissed and booed and the cause of almost bloody commotion. Even in the knowledge that *The Playboy* is sharp satire and that the Irish are a touchy fighting race, it is hard to grasp what should have set off so much excitement—especially as we know what did: a reference to underclothing in the form of the word *shift*.

But that was long ago, and for *The Playboy* today one may perhaps call out such reviewers'-cliché words as robust and exuberant. For here is a great wild yarn told in language that does it justice, a yarn, indeed, that seems saturated with the very fancifulness it laughs at. Never did romanticism, while being so soundly thrashed, so gloriously hold its own. If *The Playboy* is not otherwise heroic, it is at least a kind of heroic joke, a tale of a worm that turned, that turned indeed into a lion. It is a tale that sorts out the strange ingredients to be found in hero-worship; that chronicles the behavior of those who suddenly have heroism thrust upon them; that shows, once again, the romantic effect of distance, the matter-of-fact appearance of one's own backyard.

I scarcely need re-tell the story. Enough that into a pub on the remote wild Mayo coast, crawls a scared dirty youth frightened of the police, who confesses he has been walking for days after killing his father, in a brawl, with a loy. To the villagers this tired, shaky boy seems suddenly a great romantic outlaw, a heroic criminal to regard with awe, to shield from the police, and to save from punishment, for would any one, as they say, "kill his father if he was able to help it?" They quickly transform Christy Mahon's rather grisly act into a high Homeric feat. To their teeming imagination, Christy ceases to have done anything so crude as bash in a father's skull. Distance lends enchantment to the blow, and the crowd's admiration soon lends courage and a fine new cocksureness to the parricide. Informed that he is a hero, Christy comes to believe he is a hero, to behave as a hero. In a trice the scared lout becomes a swaggering Irishman who says quite gravely and solemnly, "Wasn't I the foolish fellow not to kill my father in the years gone by?"

Only he hasn't killed his father. Soon enough, while all the girls in the neighborhood fight over him and he wins all the events at an athletic meet, his father—heavily bandaged but otherwise none the worse for wear—turns up at the pub. And when he confronts his son, and seeks to bully him as of old, Christy—all eyes upon him, the townsfolk's applause still ringing in his ears—goes at his father and lays him low again. But this time, it seems no deed of legend or balladry: as Pegeen says, it's only a squabble in your own backyard, and there's a great gap between a gallous story and a dirty deed. Christy's stature diminishes, not only from his having at his father in his own backyard, but from not having killed him with his great faraway blow. And of course after this second whack, old Mahon is still alive. But if Christy has not learned how to put an end to his father, he has learned very well how to put an end to his father's domination of him.

(285)

CHRISTY: [scrambling on his knees face to face with old *Mahon*]. *Are you coming to be killed a third time, or what ails you now?*

MAHON: *For what is it they have you tied?*

CHRISTY: *They're taking me to the peelers to have me hanged for slaying you.*

MICHAEL: [apologetically]. *It is the will of God that all should guard their little cabins from the treachery of law, and what would my daughter be doing if I was ruined or was hanged itself?*

MAHON: [grimly, loosening *Christy*]. *It's little I care if you put a bag on her back, and went picking cockles till the hour of death; but my son and myself will be going our own way, and we'll have great times from this out telling stories of the villainy of Mayo, and the fools is here.* [To *Christy*, who is freed.] *Come on now.*

CHRISTY: *Go with you, is it? I will then, like a gallant captain with his heathen slave. Go on now and I'll see you from this day stewing my oatmeal and washing my spuds, for I'm master of all fights from now.* [Pushing *Mahon*.] *Go on, I'm saying.*

MAHON: *Is it me?*

CHRISTY: *Not a word out of you. Go on from this.*

MAHON: [walking out and looking back at *Christy* over his shoulder.] *Glory be to God!* [With a broad smile.] *I am crazy again.* [Goes.]

CHRISTY: *Ten thousand blessings upon all that's here, for you've turned me a likely gaffer in the end of all, the way I'll go romancing through a romping lifetime from this hour to the dawning of the judgment day.* [He goes out.]

MICHAEL: *By the will of God, we'll have peace now for our drinks. Will you draw the porter, Pegeen?*

SHAWN: [going up to her]. *It's a miracle Father Reilly can wed us in the end of all, and we'll have none to trouble us when his vicious bite is healed.*

PEGEEN: [hitting him a box on the ear]. *Quit my sight.* [Putting her shawl over her head and breaking out into

wild lamentations.] *Oh, my grief, I've lost him surely.*
I've lost the only Playboy of the Western World.

The Playboy remains one of the most viable and spirited of
satires because it pricks the bubble of so many assorted, if related, illusions. That the shoe seems particularly to fit the Irish
foot, that the bluster and brag have so very Irish an air, that
the fine language is so Irish a virtue, and the love of fine
language so Irish a fault, only serves to emphasize Synge's wise
use of the near-at-hand to convey what is far more general.
He has given his satire a local—a very local—habitation and a
name. From this picture of admiring villagers making a hero
of a nobody, *The Playboy* works outward, to indicate how often
reality is no match for romance, how much faster lies will snow-
ball than the truth, how if you tell a goose it is a swan, it may
act as though it were one.

But if the point, here, is how easily and happily we swallow
engaging lies, the final point is that the lies *must* be engaging.
The final point—to start on the surface—isn't the Irishman's
ability to believe a fine yarn, but his ability, rather to invent one.
The Irish appear here in the role of artist and audience alike.
Similarly, what applies in Christy's case also applies in Synge's:
as Christy's village audience is befuddled and beguiled by fine
talk of high deeds, so in a sense must Synge's audience, must
we ourselves, be. What we are concerned with here is the
power of words—with their capacity to ignite the imagination,
to make magic of anything, even murder; with language as a
joy and an exhilaration, with language as a snare and a delusion. In this fable of Christy Mahon and County Mayo, Synge
—as Ronald Peacock suggests—is really writing of art and
artists. In the end, diction—even more than distance—lends
enchantment to the view. And Synge is laughing a little ruefully
at the very lyricism, the very beauty of language, that he is
exploiting, and so is laughing finally at himself.

Which helps explain why his achievement in *The Playboy* is
so rich and satisfying. He can show what a charlatan "art"
can be in the very act of exhibiting it as a true magician. He

can find—in terms of romantic susceptibility—so many targets to shoot at and hit, beginning with the Mayo villagers and ending almost with the human race. He can impart glamour while setting out to expose it; he can fuse fun and poetry into a single unit, and give to the stage at once a truly lyrical comedy and a penetrating satire. Aldous Huxley has somewhere remarked that sixteenth- and seventeenth-century English writers had the ability to be funny and charming, comic and beautiful at the same time. Synge (and Synge perhaps alone) had much the same gift; and here, though his aim is unerring and he brings down his targets, they fall, not like dead pigeons, but like bright shooting stars.

CHAPTER XVII

Maugham

MAUGHAM returns us to the fixed tradition, the main avenue, of the Comedy of Manners. So long as comedy, and manners, and theaters remain, this tradition will never die; and in an impure form—manners plus water, or plus syrup, or plus rum —it will always flourish. So long as there are old families or new millionaires, debutantes or dowagers, transatlantic liners and international marriages, boarding-house parlors and summer hotels—so long as there are social contrasts and social crises—the comedy of manners is sure to survive. Yet the kind that is worthiest of the name, and that deserves remembrance or revival fifty years after it was written, has grown quite rare in the English-speaking theater. The descendants of Etherege and Congreve have any number of other ancestors as well. Romantic grandmothers, sentimental great-grandfathers, farceurs, fantasists, even preachers and propagandists, all mix their blood with Etherege's, their standards with Congreve's. Sheridan, in *The School for Scandal*, still knew what the comedy of manners meant; Oscar Wilde, the next great holder of the title, did not. He had a greater wit, an equal ability to write chatter, a certain knowledge of the world; but three of his plays are essentially society melodramas, and the fourth, though a masterpiece, is also half a farce. Although Shaw from time to time, in

You Never Can Tell or *Pygmalion*, wrote something akin to the comedy of manners, he was too much absorbed by ideas, moralities, beliefs, the design rather than the décor of civilization, to do anything very vital with the form. *Pygmalion*, in one sense a strict comedy of manners, suffers also from being a kind of laboratory experiment: the accent, the atmosphere (except for the At-Home scene) suggests, much more forcibly, the comedy of ideas.

But Maugham brings us back to the truest kind of comedy of manners—the Restoration kind. This is not altogether because he has the Restoration talent, though he largely does: it is also because he has the Restoration temperament. He sees life, with insistent dispassionateness, for what it is, and what he sees he records quite as he sees it, expurgating nothing, extenuating nothing. This is by no means to accuse him of indifference. A quite cold but also quite pervasive moral disapproval is easy to detect in *Our Betters*. At moments the moralist almost seems to get the upper hand of the worldling. But the moralist makes himself so conspicuous only because the realist proves so uncompromising: the story preaches its own sermon. What is technically an exhibit is actually an exposé.

In a sense, no playwright since Vanbrugh turned architect had drawn so harsh and unredeemed a picture of London society as Maugham did in *Our Betters*. It is true that before making his assault upon the London social scene, Maugham took one precaution: he made his targets American. He did not fire into his own ranks; while giving his audience a moral shiver, he raised no patriotic blush. English audiences might take offense at hearing the word "slut" used on the stage, but they must have found some consolation in knowing it was used of one American by another. And what Americans had Maugham assembled in his play! If all good Americans go to Paris when they die, *Our Betters* would suggest that all bad Americans go to London when they marry.

From the days of Henry James straight on to the 1930's, the subject of the "social" American in London is rather a painful one for the American in America to contemplate. The American stooped in every conceivable way to conquer, though the one effective way was through his bank account. Nor would unlimited gold turn the trick alone: quite as necessary was unlimited brass. It is one of the more obviously paradoxical manifestations of society life that climbing can only be achieved through stooping, and that the best way to get through the door is to take up residence in front of it, as a doormat.

Our Betters is one of the best testimonials to American push ever written. Here social-climbing is converted, if not into an art, into an onslaught, and here at the same time is a gallery of Americans apparently as remote from the center of English life as they are bewitched by the surfaces. But then, they are remote from anything rooted and responsible; they are not simply Americans, they are even by American standards upstarts. It is part of their tactics to make copy of their own background—to make laughingstocks of their own families; wherever they cannot buy their way, they proceed to burlesque it. The women have acquired a variety of British titles, but always the same kind of British husband—one who married them for their money—so that actually they have no husbands: those who are not dead or divorced just don't bother to come home. Having married for name only, the women have found their pleasure, and even their profit, elsewhere. Pearl Lady Grayston has a millionaire American lover whom she doesn't love, but whose vast means are needed (she herself has but a scant million dollars) to maintain her as the formidable hostess she has become. Lady Grayston is still on the young and attractive side; the Duchesse de Surennes, formerly Minnie Somebody-or-Other, is sadly rouged and middle-aged, and she is struggling to hold the latest of the good-looking good-for-nothings she has bought herself. These, and one or two other Americans, are Maugham's chief targets.

In very Jamesian fashion, as well as to satisfy the most elementary demands of stage romance, Maugham has plumped down in the middle of all this a young sister of Lady Grayston's who has just arrived from America—as well as the young man she broke her engagement with just before coming away. The young man—who still loves the girl but wisely refrains from bothering her while she has thoughts of marrying a title—is proud to be an American from the outset, and prouder as he prolongs his visit and sees how the Anglo-Americans behave. The girl, Bessie, is on the other hand tempted and even torn: her sister has dazzled her with parties and balls, and young Lord Bleane, who is suitably blueblooded and broke, seeks her in marriage. Though she doesn't love him in the least, he makes things harder by being nice, and they at length become engaged. But Bessie's discovery of her sister in a summerhouse with the Duchess's young man, plus Bessie's awareness of her sister's liaison with the millionaire, plus her sister's whole way of life and circle of friends, so disgust the girl that she goes back to America by the first boat.

Bessie's role is conventional enough: she is the ingénue whose eyes are to be opened before her mind is quite made up. We need not linger over her, nor over her suitor from back home, who is an offset to the others, and a mouthpiece through whom Maugham can dress the others down. These two are less drawn into the action than would their counterparts in Restoration times have been; nobody attempts seducing him or debauching her. But though the young people are spared in *Our Betters*, the older ones are handled quite implacably, in terms of manners and morals alike. It is because Maugham goes well beyond making fun of them as coronet-crazed Americans, beyond satirizing their methods of getting on, beyond pointing up the differences between America and England, that he is a direct descendant of Restoration comedy. His characters are not mere hummingbirds and peacocks, but foxes and even birds of prey. Theirs is not a half-romantic aspiration, but a realistic assault. When they are not socially on the make, they are sexually on the prowl; and while buying their way among others, they cheat and bribe and blackmail among themselves. The relations between Lady Grayston and her millionaire American lover are too broadly treated to achieve the right effect: Maugham, here, is at great disadvantage in writing of Americans, whose coarseness of soul is not to be conveyed by mere crudities of speech;

and the lover, who would (and should) possess a mixture of qualities, is far too much simplified. But Lady Grayston herself is perhaps no great exaggeration of the American-born London hostess of her day; she is, at least, no harder to accept than the corresponding woman of ambition in Restoration times. The play is truly comedy-of-manners in the way it exhibits Lady Grayston at work, the way it makes plain her methods and manoeuvres in detail, whether in so simple a matter as ordering books by one of her dinner guests that will go back to the book-shop next morning or—much more dramatically—in seeing to it that her summerhouse indiscretion cannot be turned into a scandal. Indeed, in the last act, when Lady Grayston is oc-cupied with extricating herself, her methods count for more as clever entertainment than as convincing exposé: we are too much absorbed by the methods to be much shocked by what they reveal, and there is a certain drop in pressure. By then, to be sure, we welcome the comedy; we have had enough of the criticism; we know what the people are like, and are happy to see them perform. Their performance perhaps ought to be more finished; they would at least have a little more veneer than Maugham allows them, and he goes wrong in places with their speech. On the other hand, Maugham, in assigning part of the blame to England, is perhaps a little too charitable. England may be bringing out the worst in them, but they are people in whom the worst clamors to come out. In America, Pearl and Fenwick and Thornton Clay might be on safer ground, but they would not be any nicer people. Moreover, Pearl is a type that no America could contain: like Mrs. Wharton's Undine Spragg her ambitions are vast, her methods utterly unscrupulous. Maugham happens to be writing of a specific social group, and his play is the more pointed for so restricting itself, but as types, his people rise above personality and above any particular age. Pearl reveals herself, frankness and all, in a way that has little to do with her being an American around the year 1920, while much of the small talk could come straight out of Wilde.

Maugham has found his own angle here, but *Our Betters* falls smoothly into place as part of a tradition. Very probably it ought somewhere to rise above it, or a little alter or enrich it. We look in vain for the distinctive fizz of an Etherege, the unmistakable polish of a Sheridan. We find varnish rather than polish, and something merely craftsmanlike rather than creative. But in the hard certainty of its approach, the unbroken worldliness of its knowledge, *Our Betters*, like Restoration comedy, invokes reality through artifice.

Maugham's *The Circle* seems to me one of the very few creditable high comedies written in English in the twentieth century. This is not to rank it as a masterpiece or to heap the wrong kind of praise on Maugham; it is rather to make clear how rare an event a properly satisfying high comedy is. I would distinguish here between "comedy of manners" and "high comedy" not at all out of pedantry, and not without an awareness that the two may easily blend and overlap, but because I think there is a fundamental difference even between plays with as much in common as *Our Betters* and *The Circle*. Both—to use yet a third term—are drawing-room comedies, and in both we are repeatedly concerned with how people will behave in certain ticklish or complicated or embarrassing situations. But in *Our Betters* the play would cease to exist without the drawing-room; in *Our Betters*, Lady Grayston's drawing-room has been the aim, and has now become the achievement, of her life, while those who fill her drawing-room are much like herself, people who married for position and were taken in marriage for their money. The young American girl and her beau can go on an inspection tour of English society, can sip and sample it, and then—appalled and disapproving—reject it and sail for home. Their tastes are involved, their susceptibilities to what is glittering and glamorous. But Bessie, by noting that an American girl has only to marry a lord to cease to be a lady, can find the price comes too high—or, in any case, that the purchase would make no sense. She can reject an English drawing-room because she winds up unimpressed. But—more crucially—she can do so because she winds up uninvolved.

The choice in other words, is not one that concerns her innermost desires, that cuts across circumstances to character. It is true that her sister, Lady Grayston's passion to be a great London hostess constitutes something truly "innermost"; but it is something so utterly worldly as to make the intensity of the wish seem wildly disproportionate to the emptiness of the attainment. Intensity, more than any other one thing, can make things seem tragic: but it can also, more than any other one thing, make them seem comic. The whole tragedy of character rests on a right intensity of feeling; the whole comedy of humors rests on a wrong one. What Antony feels about Cleopatra, Sir Fopling Flutter feels about handkerchiefs. To care too much about some things is equally as shallow as to care too little about others. Any one who ruins her life trying to get into fashionable society must, in the deepest sense, be comic. On the other hand, some one who ruins her daughter's life from the same ambition sets much deeper currents in motion.

The drawing room, in any case, is the hero—or, rather, the villain—of *Our Betters*. Remove it, and the point of the story, if not the actual story itself, disappears. But though the drawing room plays a large and special role in *The Circle*, it is not indispensable to what *The Circle* has to say. Indeed, the point of *The Circle* is that the drawing room, however desirable as an outer circumstance, is no match for a true innermost desire. *The Circle* represents a real clash between worldly advantage and personal emotion. In *Our Betters*, people sacrifice all they are to ambition; in *The Circle*, they sacrifice all they have, for love. Lord Porteous, who gave up being Prime Minister to run off with Lady Kitty, has little in common with the people of *Our Betters*, is infinitely closer, in fact, to Marc Antony, to "All for love and the world well lost."

The basis here is not what one stands to gain, but what one is prepared to sacrifice: the drawing room, in *The Circle*, becomes a symbol of social security rather than of social position. The situation in *The Circle*—even to the way it is repeated—could take place equally well in a middle-class living room or a lower middle-class parlor. Marc Antony, who could rule the world; Lord Porteous, who could be Prime Minister of Britain; some one else, who in time could own a brewery; some one else who in time could own a pub—the situation is for each man identical: the stakes, in terms of each man's future, are the same. The choice, in each case, is between love and career.

In all high comedy—as distinguished from drawing-room comedy or the comedy of manners—we must cut across circumstances to character, to something rooted and decisive, to something akin to the tragic. But though this is the fundamental condition, the prime donnée, it yet seems true that high comedy flourishes best in a kind of high-society setting. This is partly true because only at such a level will the worldly advantages seem a formidable enough offset to the personal desires. If a woman who is president of the East Montclair Bridge Club runs off with a man who might some day own a brewery, though the bridge and the brewery may constitute for them an unimaginable sacrifice, it will hardly seem one to us; the whole thing will smack far more of suburban drama. High comedy, again—and precisely so as not to become suburban drama, or sordid naturalism—requires a certain sense of polish, starching, form, as equally it involves a constant spraying with wit and irony, and keeping a strong hold on the wrong sort of emotion. High comedy is something that reaches us through the mind; it is a distillation; and if it affects a touch of elegance, it is from not being permitted to wear its heart on its sleeve.

I have preceded Maugham's modest coach of a play with rather a host of richly dressed outriders, but no coach more splendid exists, in the modern English theater, for our purposes. And in its own way *The Circle* could hardly be bettered. It is immensely skilful playwriting; it has a neat story that it exploits to the full; it has a clear thesis that it sets forth almost cracklingly; and the tone throughout is dry, worldly, wellbred, a little brittle, a little mocking—and yet never merely frivolous. And (at least on its own terms) *The Circle* is too serious a play ever to be a sentimental one.

The play tells how—some thirty years before the curtain rises—Lady Kitty Champion-Cheney, leaving a note on her pincushion, had run off with Porteous, her husband's best friend. She has never seen her husband or son since, but now, when the son is thirty-five and married, she and Porteous have been asked (largely at the insistence of her son's wife) for a visit. They arrive. Lady Kitty, once one of the great beauties of England, now rouges her cheeks and dyes her hair and goes in for little airs and affectations, while Lord Porteous, his love grown cold, is snappish and pompous and choleric—rather to the amusement of the deserted husband, Champion-Cheney, who tactlessly intrudes himself upon the gathering, and blandly plays off his former wife and her lover against each other. He, who has been most wronged, emerges after thirty years least hurt. The other two could endure, while still madly in love, the snubs of the respectable, but as love oozed away and fear crept in, and they were thrown on the society of people like themselves and worse than themselves, and their looks went, and their world grew a little shabby, they might begin, indeed, to wonder.

But with this object lesson staring her in the face, Lady Kitty's daughter-in-law Elizabeth, having fallen madly in love with Teddy Luton, prepares like Lady Kitty to leave her husband and brave the slings and arrows of social ostracism. Nothing Lady Kitty can say will dissuade her; nothing she sees in Lady Kitty (she feels sure) need ever befall herself. And so she too runs off.

In itself the whole thing is obviously a little too neat; the whole demonstration a little too patly Euclidean, with its proof of how two triangles are equal in all respects. But though, in his novels and short stories, Maugham is generally harmed by making everything fit too well, by often being distastefully slick, in a stage-piece like this, where a certain artifice is a virtue and a degree of simplification an advantage, the neatness is really part of the effect. (The theater, with what it stands to gain from possessing form, is entitled to be aphoristic about substance.)

But there is more to *The Circle* than the geometry of the two triangles. There is the gloomy arithmetic of advancing years; there is the sense of how little, really—far from learning through other people's experience—one is willing to learn from one's own, and there is all the comedy of character which has something so much more wry and malicious about it than the irony of fate. Tristan dies, and Isolde after him, to the strains of the *Liebestod*. But Lord Porteous lives, and Lady Kitty with him, and after thirty years they play bridge together, and snap and snarl at each other. And after thirty years the wronged husband is revenged without having had to fire off a revolver or even contrive a denunciation. There is a sad kind of fun, a rueful kind of amusement about it all. If Time heals all wounds, it equally mars all loveliness. What could be more consoling than that nothing matters after a time—and what more dispiriting and tragic? By its very neatness, *The Circle* is able to show how similar, how almost interchangeable, high comedy and tragedy can be, and yet how unlike they are in their effect. For high comedy is tragedy stripped of all that is heroic and exalted and affirmative. There is indeed—it is the merest cliché—something joyous about tragedy, because something exultant. There is a rising tide about it, and at the end a high whelming tide in which to drown. Cleopatra puts on her crown, Othello falls on his sword, the Duchess is Duchess of Malfy still. But high comedy must watch the tide go out, and see all the driftwood and wreckage left upon the beach. It is concerned with something infinitely sadder than the death of people: with the death of their dreams, the débris of their aspirations, the pressed leaves of their high impassioned vows. Tragedy carves out in granite the fact that Character is Fate; but high comedy knows that everything is writ in water, that the real enemy, the real betrayer and barbarian, is Time.

Index

I.

Index of Persons

(i)

Index

(ii)

II.

Index of Plays, Books, Operas

(v)

Index

A NOTE ON THE TYPE
IN WHICH THIS BOOK IS SET

This book is set in Monotype BELL, *a copy of the English Monotype face of the same name. The Englishman John Bell (1745–1831) was responsible for the original cutting of this design. The vocations of Bell were many — among a few might be mentioned bookseller, printer, publisher, type-founder, and journalist. His types were considerably influenced by the delicacy and beauty of the French copperplate engravers. Monotype* BELL *might also be classified as a delicate and refined rendering of Scotch Roman.*

Composed, printed, and bound by

THE PLIMPTON PRESS, NORWOOD, MASS.